PURSUING THE KNOWLEDGE ECONOMY

Building Progressive Alternatives

Series Editors: David Coates†, Ben Rosamond and Matthew Watson

Bringing together economists, political economists and other social scientists, this series offers pathways to a coherent, credible and progressive economic growth strategy which, when accompanied by an associated set of wider public policies, can inspire and underpin the revival of a successful centre-left politics in advanced capitalist societies.

Published

Corbynism in Perspective: The Labour Party under Jeremy Corbyn
Edited by Andrew S. Roe-Crines

The European Social Question: Tackling Key Controversies
Amandine Crespy

Flawed Capitalism: The Anglo-American Condition and its Resolution
David Coates

The Political Economy of Industrial Strategy in the UK: From Productivity Problems to Development Dilemmas
Edited by Craig Berry, Julie Froud and Tom Barker

Pursuing the Knowledge Economy: A Sympathetic History of High-Skill High-Wage Hubris
Nick O'Donovan

Race and the Undeserving Poor: From Abolition to Brexit
Robbie Shilliam

Reflections on the Future of the Left
Edited by David Coates

PURSUING THE KNOWLEDGE ECONOMY

A SYMPATHETIC HISTORY OF HIGH-SKILL HIGH-WAGE HUBRIS

NICK O'DONOVAN

For Theo and Arthur, with love

First published in 2022 by Agenda Publishing

Agenda Publishing Limited
The Core
Bath Lane
Newcastle Helix
Newcastle upon Tyne
NE4 5TF
www.agendapub.com

ISBN 978-1-78821-514-5 (hardcover)
ISBN 978-1-78821-515-2 (paperback)

British Library Cataloguing-in-Publication Data
A catalogue record for this book is available from the British Library

Typeset by JS Typesetting Ltd, Porthcawl, Mid Glamorgan
Printed and bound in the UK by CPI Group (UK) Ltd, Croydon, CR0 4YY

CONTENTS

Acknowledgements   vii

Introduction   1

Part I The rise of the knowledge economy

1. The invention of the "knowledge economy"   15
2. "Knowledge 2000"   38
3. Taming the market   52
4. Continuity and change   73

Part II The knowledge economy in crisis

5. The crisis of growth   87
6. The crisis of work   100
7. The crisis of inclusion   118
8. The new world order   129

Part III Beyond the knowledge economy

9. Political backlash   145
10. Paradigm shift   166

Notes   191
Index   220

ACKNOWLEDGEMENTS

First and foremost, I would like to thank my social worker mum and my computer geek dad for inspiring a lifelong interest in public policy, politics and technology. Without their love and support, I would not be in a position to write anything; without their particular idiosyncrasies, I would not have written this book.

I am also hugely indebted to the teachers who encouraged and inspired me throughout two-and-a-half decades of formal education: from the first day of infant school through to the end of high school, from the start of my undergraduate studies through to the completion of my PhD. I am particularly grateful to Peter Hall and Nancy Rosenblum: not only did I learn a great deal from them over the course of graduate school, but they both continued to advocate for me long after I had finished my studies. Without them (and the reams of recommendation letters that they wrote on my behalf), I would not have been able to return to academia almost a decade later.

I have benefited from many people's advice and suggestions while writing this book. Peter Hall provided invaluable feedback on an early sketch of these ideas, as did Colin Hay and two anonymous reviewers for *New Political Economy*. Members of the Future Economies Research Centre at Manchester Metropolitan University have been a vital source of ideas and support, sharing their own insights and guiding me towards literature and data that I would never have discovered otherwise. Particular thanks are due to Dan Bailey, David Beel, Craig Berry, Will Cook, Matthew Gobey, Tim Jackson, Sabaa Jahangir, Sophia Kuehnlenz, Donna Lee, Claire Levison, Sean McDaniel, Jonny Rae, Rory Shand, Kathryn Simpson, Christian Spence and Richard Whittle. I am also indebted to Uta Kohl and Jacob Eisler, who helped me to refine the book's analysis of the digital sector during a workshop at the University of Southampton and the development of an essay for their edited volume, *Data-Driven Personalisation in Markets, Politics and Law*. Thanks also to Sir Derek Morris, for permission to quote his "joke poem" about post-neoclassical endogenous growth theory, which provides a better explanation of debates in academic economics in the space of 314 words than I manage in 3,140.

During the pandemic, I was extremely lucky to take part in a series of illuminating conversations about the future of economic policy: many thanks to Arun Advani, Emma Chamberlain and Andy Summers for inviting me to contribute to the UK Wealth Tax Commission, to Sayantan Ghosal and Adrian Pabst for involving me in a National Institute of Economic and Social Research workshop on populism and to Robert Palmer of Tax Justice UK. David Hope and Julian Limberg pointed me in the direction of excellent recent research on the knowledge economy. Although geography and life mean that we do not speak as often as we used to, this book owes much to exchanges and conversations with old friends from graduate school, including Ed Baring, Daniela Cammack, Sam Goldman, David Grewal and Yascha Mounk. Thanks are also due to friends outside the world of academia who discussed ideas, read drafts and advised on how to make this book more intelligible, in particular Adam Barnard, Aidan Miller and John Wrathmell. I am hugely grateful to Craig Berry, Paul Cammack and Sean McDaniel, who not only read the whole thing from start to finish but also provided copious notes that have made this book substantially better than it would otherwise have been. Needless to say, all remaining faults are entirely my responsibility.

It has been a genuine pleasure to work with Agenda Publishing, who have from the first moment onwards made the process of creating this book both straightforward and enjoyable. Thanks to everyone involved, including Steven Gerrard, series editors Ben Rosamond and Mat Watson, and above all Alison Howson, who has been a constant source of advice and encouragement.

At various points over the course of my career, I have had the immense privilege of studying and working with three people who played important roles in the development of New Labour's economic agenda: Ed Balls, Ed Miliband and Chris Wales. All three helped me to appreciate the sincerity of the ideals that informed mainstream progressive politics over the 1990s and 2000s, as well as the extent to which architects of knowledge-driven growth were already aware of – and sought to address – the limitations of this policy approach.

Finally, my biggest debt of all is to Louise Cowen, who has been both unstinting supporter and meticulous critic, not just during the writing of this book but throughout the best part of my adult life. There are no words.

Nick O'Donovan

INTRODUCTION

On 19 October 2015, Bill Clinton took the floor at a fundraiser in Potomac, Maryland. A few months earlier, his wife, Hillary Rodham Clinton, had launched her campaign to become the Democratic Party's candidate for the 2016 US presidential election. At first, the erstwhile senator and secretary of state was the clear favourite in the primary race. Polls showed that she consistently commanded the support of more than 60 per cent of potential voters.[1] The Democratic establishment, including both prominent elected politicians and major donors, overwhelmingly backed her candidacy. And yet by that day in mid-October – somewhat chilly for the time of year – her lead had begun to slip away, eroded by the challenge of Bernie Sanders, a self-described socialist who offered a radical break with the economic consensus of the recent past.

Addressing attendees at that fundraiser in Maryland, the former president was dismissive of Sanders' campaign. Bracketing the veteran Vermont senator with the ex-communists of Greece's Syriza and the hard-left leader of the UK's Labour Party, Clinton described all these political outsiders as "reflective of" the fact that, "when people feel they've been shafted and they don't expect anything to happen anyway, they just want the maddest person in the room to represent them". According to Clinton, Sanders was a symptom of economic discontent, but he was not the solution to America's problems. In place of Sanders' radical agenda, the former president offered his own alternative plan for the people and places that had been bypassed by prosperity:

> If we had universal, affordable broadband, it would do more than an-
> ything else to help growth to return to areas that have been left out
> and left behind … So if all those people in eastern Kentucky and West
> Virginia and southwest Ohio and southwest Pennsylvania had universal
> broadband, you could give people incentives to invest there and they'd
> actually be able to hook on to the global economy and sell what they're
> doing.[2]

This argument was reminiscent of Bill Clinton's own presidential bid more than two decades earlier: a campaign that was built around a similar kind of outward-looking, technology-enabled approach to growth. In a 1992 campaign brochure entitled "Fighting for the Forgotten Middle Class", Clinton vowed to shift America towards a "high-skill, high-wage economy". Through "investment in research and development" and "world-class education", he claimed that the USA would be able "to compete and prosper in the world".[3] Armed with this vision, Clinton wrested the support of electors in Kentucky, Ohio and Pennsylvania away from his Republican rival George H. W. Bush.

Twenty-four years later, Hillary Clinton would go on to win the Democratic primaries, seeing off Sanders' challenge with the support of the Democratic establishment and a policy offer that paralleled her husband's earlier campaign. She pledged to "restore America to the cutting edge of innovation, science, and research by increasing both public and private investments", as well as to "invest ... in our most important asset, our people", without which "our country won't be competitive or fair".[4] Yet on the night of the presidential election itself, all four of the "left-behind" states identified by her husband in that speech in Maryland would vote against her candidacy and throw their support behind Donald Trump. By 2016, the vision of growth that the Democrats had sold so successfully in 1992 no longer appealed to a decisive proportion of the American electorate.

This book charts the rise and fall of that vision: of a high-skill, high-wage economy based on innovation, openness and social investment. It explores both how this policy agenda appealed to a broad coalition of voters within diverse developed democracies and how that coalition has fallen apart as the shortcomings of those policies (and the understanding of the economy that underpinned them) have become increasingly apparent. It explains how these political and economic shifts have created electoral space for radical outsiders touting unconventional (and in some cases unpalatable) policy alternatives.

Three decades of hubris

The Clintons were far from alone in championing this high-tech approach to growth. Since the early 1990s, similar ideas have found favour with policy elites in democracies the world over, leading politicians of diverse nationalities and partisan loyalties to pursue remarkably similar economic strategies. These strategies were characterized by the belief that social investment in education, infrastructure and research will not simply upgrade the productive capacity of the economy but also deliver social justice; that dynamic markets and international openness combine to drive technological progress and global competitiveness; that individual economic security no longer depends on trade unions or formal employment rights but can instead be achieved by investment in skills coupled with expanding demand for knowledge workers. At the same time, policy-makers have insisted that this reform agenda must be pursued within a wider framework of fiscal "prudence", lowering taxes to attract highly mobile knowledge workers and the businesses they work for, controlling public borrowing to avoid crowding out private investment in innovation.

To be sure, different politicians and parties have emphasized different aspects of this agenda, but the basic analysis remains broadly the same. In words that might have been lifted directly from the campaign literature of either Clinton, President Obama argued in a 2010 speech to the America's Promise Alliance that "for America to compete and to win in the twenty-first century, we know that we will need a highly educated workforce that is second to none. And we know that the success of every American will be tied more closely than ever before to the level of education that they achieve. The jobs will go to the people with the knowledge and the skills to do them – it's that simple."[5] Two days later, on the other side of the Atlantic, the European Commission announced its new economic strategy. The foremost priority in its "Europe 2020" agenda was "smart growth: developing an economy based on knowledge and innovation", an objective that was to be achieved by increasing research and development (R&D) spending, improving education systems and accelerating the roll-out of high-speed internet.[6] The Organisation for Economic Co-operation and Development (OECD), in its 2015 report on "The Future of Productivity", argued that economic stagnation could be tackled by encouraging research, removing labour market rigidities, easing regulation of services, increasing cross-border trade and improving the international mobility of skilled workers.[7] The UK's 2017 White Paper on Industrial Strategy emphasized R&D spending and skills investments in order to "put the UK at the forefront of the artificial intelligence and data revolution".[8] That same year, ahead of the French presidential election, Emmanuel Macron's En Marche! party outlined an "economic project" at the centre of which stood a €15 billion investment in skills to "reduce unemployment" by enabling people "to retrain for the jobs of the future and fast-growing industries" while simultaneously liberalizing French employment regulations to allow for a more dynamic allocation of labour to productive businesses.[9] Across the border in Germany, Angela Merkel's Christian Democratic Union was campaigning on a manifesto that pledged to attract new jobs in "digital services, biotechnology, green industries and healthcare" by improving the education of German citizens and reforming immigration to meet rising demand for highly skilled workers.[10]

Proposals such as these are now so commonplace as to constitute conventional wisdom. Less charitable commentators might dismiss them as platitudes. Yet they were not always so self-evident, and, as the declining electoral fortunes of politicians and parties that espouse these ideas suggest, they may no longer be as self-evident as once they were.

New economy, new policies

The origins of this policy agenda can be traced back to debates about the so-called "knowledge economy", the term used by policy-makers in the 1990s and early 2000s to refer to the rapid technological, social, economic and political changes taking place in developed democracies. These debates are easily over-looked, forgotten or mocked: by the mid-2000s, commentators already spoke dismissively of "the heady optimism of the late 1990s about the then trendy knowledge economy".[11] Since the heyday of the "knowledge economy" concept, developed democracies have been wracked by terrorist atrocities, financial crisis, political turmoil and a global pandemic, developments that make the 1990s seem like ancient history. Nevertheless, this book argues that these earlier debates decisively shaped the way in which policy-makers have pursued economic growth ever since, that this approach to economic growth has proved to be remarkably resilient despite the intervening upheavals and that it remains highly influential today. Even though present-day politicians and policy-makers rarely refer to the "knowledge economy", ideas that first rose to political prominence in the 1990s are still visible in contemporary policy debates about productivity growth, the divide between skilled and unskilled workers and the economic importance of high-tech industries.[12] The assumptions that this earlier generation of policy-makers made continue to inform efforts to "build back better", to "level up" economically marginalized regions and to create a "high-wage, high-skill economy".[13]

What was the knowledge economy? According to its proponents, the knowledge economy marked a new phase of economic growth, in which workers would increasingly produce ideas rather than tangible goods and services. These ideas might take the form of code for a new computer programme, the formula for a new medicine, the recipe for a new burger or the script for a new movie. The concept of the knowledge economy encompassed industries ranging from software development to film production, from financial services to pharma-ceuticals research: anywhere highly skilled workers were needed in order to produce new knowledge, to capture and analyse new data, to design new products embodying ever more sophisticated ideas or to create new instructions for people and machines to execute. Indeed, the rise of the knowledge economy ultimately extended to all kinds of organizations, in so far as they deployed new technologies (and staff with the expertise to use them) in functions ranging from supply chain management to marketing, from finance to HR.

The knowledge economy concept rose to prominence against a backdrop of innovation-inspired economic optimism. In the 1990s, policy-makers argued that the explosive growth of knowledge-intensive industries such as information technology (IT), life sciences and advanced manufacturing heralded a paradigm shift, which could help to overcome the economic anxieties of the preceding years: years in which economic policy had been dominated by a fundamentalist view of the benefits of free markets, years that saw skilled blue-collar jobs decline, unemployment spike, inequality between regions widen and levels of social exclusion rise. Capitalizing on the rapid adoption of advanced computing and telecommunications technologies over the 1980s and early 1990s, and a boom in demand for highly skilled knowledge workers capable of using these new technologies, a policy programme predicated on knowledge-based growth appeared to offer an alternative to the market-focused economic agenda of the 1980s. In this brave new paradigm, private enterprise, technological progress and global economic integration could all be harnessed for progressive purposes, and progressive policies could be justified in terms of their positive effects on prosperity, productivity and competitiveness in the global marketplace.

Proponents of the knowledge economy argued that traditional forms of capital, such as plant and machinery, would become increasingly irrelevant in this era of knowledge-based growth: you do not need a factory in order to produce ideas and manipulate data. Instead, the new economy would empower human capital and the workers who possessed it, offering them both prosperity and security. High-speed internet connections would enable knowledge workers to telecommute to the virtual offices of cutting-edge companies, with public investment in skills, research and digital infrastructure sufficing to spread wealth to previously marginalized people and places.

Evangelists of knowledge-based growth claimed that the rise of the knowledge economy was an inevitable consequence of technological progress. At an advanced stage of economic development, they argued, more and more workers would find employment in knowledge-intensive roles. This shift to knowledge work would occur whether governments liked it or not; indeed, it was already under way. The only question was how countries would respond to this development. Would they cultivate the well-educated employees and citizens needed to carry out knowledge work, or would they fall behind because of their unwillingness to invest? Would they open their economies and societies to new ideas from outside, or would they instead opt for stagnant isolation?

Politicians constructed detailed policy platforms on the back of the knowledge economy concept, claiming that their proposals could position their countries at the technological frontier, allowing them and their citizens to reap the lion's share of the rewards. They argued that growth in cognitively demanding, well-paid work was in principle unbounded and could compensate those who had lost out from the preceding wave of deindustrialization and globalization, provided only that these economically marginalized groups were connected up to global markets and equipped with the skills necessary to compete. This new economic agenda was not tainted by association with the discredited policies of previous left-of-centre governments: namely, the postwar consensus in favour of a mixed economy of private enterprise and state-managed growth, which came to be associated with economic stagnation and rampant inflation during the 1970s. Instead, prominent politicians including the US President Bill Clinton, the German Chancellor Gerhard Schröder and the UK Prime Minister Tony Blair, as well as international institutions such as the European Union and the OECD, claimed that knowledge-based growth offered at once a synthesis and a supersession of traditional left- and right-wing policy, a "Third Way" or "New Centre" in which the ideological dogmas of the past would give way to evidence-based pragmatism.

This policy agenda involved four key components. Through *social investment* in skills, infrastructure and research, governments would provide the foundations for knowledge-intensive industries to thrive while simultaneously combating poverty and enabling everyone (regardless of class background or geographic location) to share in the proceeds of growth. By removing obstacles to *market dynamism*, governments could encourage innovation and entrepreneurialism. *Macroeconomic stability* was essential to giving high-tech businesses the confidence necessary to invest in long-term research projects. Finally, *international openness* would enable firms and workers to draw on cutting-edge technologies, expertise and insight from around the world. The precise policy mix required was a matter of debate, sometimes necessitating trade-offs between competing priorities, and different countries adopted different approaches to knowledge-driven growth at different times. Nevertheless, proponents of knowledge-driven growth claimed that some permutation of these four elements would position developed democracies at the forefront of the global knowledge economy and counteract the social fallout caused by deindustrialization and globalization.

From optimism to anxiety

With hindsight, it is easy to dismiss these claims as hubris. Today, technological progress is more likely to be seen as a source of job destruction rather than job creation, with advances in automation and artificial intelligence threatening to render many existing roles redundant. Looking back over the last 30 years, it seems that the emergence of the knowledge economy has not been associated with social inclusion but rather with rising income and wealth inequality, declining social mobility and widening disparities between economically successful regions and their more marginalized counterparts. Even the pace of growth has disappointed. Yet the policy agenda of knowledge-driven growth continues to be seen as a remedy to these problems, albeit with diminished expectations about the degree of economic prosperity and social inclusion that it can achieve.

This book tells the story of how the techno-optimism of the knowledge economy came to be supplanted by the anxieties of the present day. It shows how key assumptions made by policy-makers back in the 1990s proved to be unfounded or misguided, and how these failings meant that the knowledge-based growth agenda has produced unintended consequences, consequences that are only now becoming fully apparent. Far from alleviating the economic dislocations, inequality and insecurity that sprung from the era of market liberalization and globalization, in many respects the emergence of the knowledge economy – and, crucially, the ways in which policy-makers chose to respond to it – has ended up exacerbating those problems. This book explores how the gulf between the promise and the reality of knowledge-based growth has fed popular discontent, destabilizing the political systems of developed democracies, shifting the centre ground and creating opportunities for radicals and racists alike.

At the same time, it documents how knowledge-driven growth remains the default setting for mainstream policy-makers in many advanced capitalist democracies today. To be sure, many of today's policy-makers are highly critical of their forebears, arguing that their plans fell short of the truly transformative level of social investment that the challenges of the knowledge economy era required. Nevertheless, in their pursuit of social justice and economic growth through a strategy of social investment, coupled with policies to encourage private sector enterprise and innovation, contemporary policy-makers are following a template that is already three decades old – one that has played a key role in creating the patterns of economic exclusion and political discontent that characterize developed democracies today.

The Covid-19 pandemic has thrown these issues into even sharper relief. The lockdowns introduced in many developed democracies highlighted the disparity between office-based knowledge workers – who could often continue to work remotely from the relative safety of their own homes – and other members of the workforce, who risked exposure to the virus if they were able to continue working or penury if they were not. The pandemic has revealed how, in developed democracies, knowledge-based growth has bypassed a large number of people: because they have not secured one of the limited number of knowledge jobs available, because they do not live in the places where those jobs are concentrated or because they lack the social networks, education and capital necessary to access those jobs. At the same time, lockdown has prompted more and more people to shift more and more of their social and economic activities online, sending the share price of technology stocks to new highs, despite the wider global slump.

As countries emerge from the emergency, governments face urgent decisions about how to rebuild, what economic strategies and policies they should put in place to facilitate recovery and what kind of society they want to create. Confronted by the comparative resilience of tech businesses and knowledge workers during the crisis, as well as the enhanced reputation of research-intensive parts of the economy (and the healthcare sector in particular), some politicians and policy-makers are already reaching for the rhetoric of knowledge-based growth, following the template provided by the policy consensus of the last three decades. In 2020, for example, the former head of the European Central Bank (and soon-to-be Italian prime minister) Mario Draghi exhorted developed democracies to invest "in human capital, in crucial infrastructure for production, in research", in order to rebuild in the wake of the Covid-19 pandemic.[14] Heralding his government's post-pandemic levelling-up agenda in 2021, the UK Prime Minister Boris Johnson argued "that having the right skills and training is the route to better, well-paid jobs".[15] The idea of a high-skill, high-pay economy – with people highly paid *because* they are highly skilled – is presented both as a solution to inequality and as a shortcut to economic recovery in a post-pandemic world.[16] In making these claims, policy-makers implicitly assume that the political and economic problems of the knowledge economy era to date can be attributed to the inadequate implementation of social investment strategies: that a more wholehearted approach will draw more and more people into secure, well-paid, empowering knowledge work, closing the social, economic and political divisions that have characterized developed democracies over recent years.

There is some merit to such arguments. In retracing the history of the knowledge economy concept, it will become clear that there were moments over the last 30 years where better implementation of knowledge-based growth strategies could have led to better outcomes (as well as countries where better implementation of these strategies *did* lead to better outcomes). Even today, a more robust approach to social investment would still prove beneficial. Furthermore, as we will see, the knowledge economy concept was not monolithic but rather encompassed a range of competing understandings of knowledge-driven growth. Although politicians in most developed democracies ultimately gravitated towards a relatively modest policy agenda, more radical alternatives were available. Perhaps, rather than abandoning the pursuit of the knowledge economy altogether, what developed democracies need is a different approach to knowledge-driven growth.

Yet this book also provides evidence that the reality of knowledge-driven growth over the last three decades has departed from the models dreamed up by early advocates of the knowledge economy, in ways that this previous generation of policy-makers failed to anticipate altogether. Knowledge work is far from abundant, capital has not faded into irrelevance and knowledge-intensive industries are less dynamic than policy-makers once supposed. In other words, the policy agenda of knowledge-driven growth has suffered from flaws that are more fundamental than inadequate implementation, more fundamental even than the implementation of policies predicated on the wrong set of assumptions about the nature of the knowledge economy. These flaws imply that the policy recommendations of the knowledge economy era cannot, *in principle*, deliver the kind of inclusive prosperity that they once promised, however radically they are recalibrated, however diligently they are put into practice. This does not mean that knowledge-driven growth is no longer important, nor that it cannot be made to work better; but it does mean that policy-makers will need to reach beyond this agenda if inclusive prosperity remains their ambition.

The knowledge economy and political crisis

This analysis matters not just to policy but to politics more broadly. As we will see, the shortcomings of the knowledge economy agenda are deeply implicated in the political turbulence experienced by many developed democracies over recent years. Academics, politicians and journalists alike have already devoted countless column inches to analysing the electoral inroads made by political outsiders, often disparagingly (and in some cases unjustly) referred to as "populists": politicians such as Bernie Sanders and Donald Trump in the USA; Jeremy Corbyn, Nigel Farage and Boris Johnson in the UK; or Beppe Grillo and Matteo Salvini in Italy.[17] Some accounts focus on the economic factors underpinning the rise of outsider parties and politicians: blaming the global financial crisis and the austerity policies pursued in its aftermath, or reaching further back to the pro-market revolutions of the 1980s and the pattern of deindustrialization and deregulation that they helped to create.[18] Other accounts identify a cultural backlash against liberal and democratic values: a rejection of immigration, women's liberation and the gay rights movement; hostility to the compromises required to govern complex, diverse and globally interconnected societies; or complacency born from the peace and comfort of the post-Cold War era.[19]

These analyses all illuminate important aspects of present-day politics. Yet they miss a crucial stage in the political and economic trajectory of developed democracies, one that has exerted a decisive influence over both the timing and the complexion of today's political upheavals. Politicians and commentators in the 1990s were acutely aware of widening inequality between people and regions, and they believed knowledge-driven growth offered a solution to the social problems associated with these trends. In order to implement this solution, champions of knowledge-based growth had to construct election-winning coalitions of support within the societies that they served. And this policy agenda appeared to work tolerably well, at least for a sizeable proportion of society, for a time. This book documents how it is only relatively recently that the electoral coalition that once supported knowledge-driven growth has begun to fragment, and it demonstrates how the economic shortcomings of this policy agenda map on to contemporary patterns of political discontent.

What are the implications of seeing our present political predicament in terms of a crisis of knowledge-based growth rather than as a crisis of capitalism or liberal democracy? First, recognizing that knowledge-based growth strategies have already been tried, and found wanting, means that we should be sceptical of claims that the policy agenda of this era – involving strategic public investments in education, infrastructure and research, allied with macroeconomic stability, deference to market forces and unqualified international openness – offers a comprehensive solution to present-day challenges, both economic and political. Second, to the extent that the weakness of the political centre in developed democracies today is attributable to a crisis of knowledge-based growth, contemporary political grievances will not only appear more explicable but also more *tractable* than would otherwise be the case. To the extent that "populist" political insurgents are inexorably opposed to liberal democracy, there is minimal scope for any rapprochement with them without a radical reconstitution of our collective way of life. But to the extent that they are opposed only to the prevailing growth regime of the last three decades, then the outsider challenge poses less of an existential threat. There are alternative ways in which we can pursue economic growth, and while we might have reservations about (and even revulsion for) some of the alternatives championed by political outsiders, we can nevertheless recognize that the search for alternatives is itself a legitimate enterprise.

Outline of the argument

Part I of the book charts the rise of the knowledge economy. Chapter 1 provides a broad historical and theoretical overview of the concept, examining the origins of the term and its defining characteristics. It argues that the era of knowledge-driven growth constitutes a distinctive phase in the development of advanced capitalist democracies, accompanied by a distinctive set of policy tools that political elites use in order to pursue economic prosperity, drawing support from a distinctive coalition of voters. In so doing, it highlights differences between the social investment strategies of the knowledge economy era and more market-driven approaches to growth, sometimes described as "neoliberalism".

Chapters 2 and 3 examine what knowledge-driven growth implied for public policy from the early 1990s through to the first years of the new millennium. Chapter 2 focuses on social investment, detailing how public spending on education and skills was supposed not just to accelerate growth but also to combat poverty and widen opportunity. Chapter 3 explores other aspects of the knowledge-driven growth agenda, such as its embrace of globalization and its support for competitive markets. These chapters also outline the understanding of economic growth that underpinned these policy recommendations, highlighting both the assumptions and blind spots of this account. Chapter 4 traces the influence of these ideas after the knowledge economy concept had fallen out of fashion, demonstrating how they continued to feature prominently in the rhetoric and policy choices of the political establishment from the global financial crisis and its aftermath through to the eve of the pandemic.

Part II explores how the results of the knowledge-driven growth agenda fell short of the outcomes anticipated by a previous generation of policy-makers, and how the realities of growth in the knowledge economy era have contradicted the assumptions on which this agenda was constructed. Chapter 5 calls into question the dynamism of the knowledge economy, showing how levels of competition, growth and investment were already beginning to falter before the global financial crisis hit, and how the decade that followed has been characterized by economic stagnation and market concentration. Chapter 6 critically examines the relationship between the rise of the knowledge economy and the expansion of knowledge work. Although the last three decades have seen many people move into higher-skilled occupations, they have also witnessed a hollowing out of mid-skill, mid-pay jobs and an expansion of insecure lower-paid work. Furthermore, even comparatively highly skilled roles do not appear to be as secure or as lucrative as evangelists of knowledge-driven growth once anticipated. Chapter 7 challenges the inclusivity of the knowledge economy, highlighting how wealth and geography have become increasingly influential determinants of life chances over the last 30 years. Contrary to progressive hopes, investment in skills alone has not resulted in equality of opportunity or widely shared prosperity. Finally, Chapter 8 interrogates the place of developed democracies in today's global order, showing how they face intense competition from emerging economies for knowledge-intensive jobs and investment.

Part III evaluates the implications of these economic shortcomings for politics and policy in developed democracies today. Chapter 9 focuses on the political backlash against the knowledge economy agenda. Although originally conceived as a solution to the widening inequality and growing insecurity that were already apparent in developed democracies by the end of the 1980s, knowledge-driven growth strategies generally did little to arrest the polarization of wealth and opportunity between different regions, occupations, generations and social strata; indeed, they may even have exacerbated these trends. The decline in popular support for centrist parties and politicians associated with these strategies testifies to their dwindling political appeal. Declining levels of support are particularly pronounced among groups with particular reason to be disappointed by this growth agenda, such as young people, the less educated and residents of regions undergoing relative economic decline.

In the final chapter of the book, we examine the future of growth in the post-pandemic era. We begin by looking at how knowledge-based growth might be rebooted in order to address the shortcomings we have identified. From the early days of the knowledge economy onwards, alternative accounts of knowledge-based growth existed alongside the techno-optimism popularized by mainstream politicians and policy-makers. These accounts emphasized the importance of tackling market dominance in the name of market dynamism and the need for a transformative programme of social investment in order to make the knowledge economy genuinely inclusive. This strand of thinking could form the basis for a more effective and egalitarian form of knowledge-driven growth. But, in the age of the algorithm, at a time of increasing automation, it is by no means clear that there is enough knowledge work available to underwrite such a growth strategy politically, nor that doubling down on social investment and market dynamism alone can mitigate the knowledge economy's divisive tendencies. In addition to rebooting the knowledge economy, politicians and policy-makers will thus need to reach beyond it: rediscovering, reprioritizing, revaluing and revitalizing realms of social and economic endeavour far from the technological frontier, and far from the places where knowledge-intensive industries have tended to cluster.

PART I

The rise of the knowledge economy

1
THE INVENTION OF THE "KNOWLEDGE ECONOMY"

> But when, later, wise men asked where all the growth came from
> Then many, even great economists, were struck dumb
> All the statistics that they gathered were quite clear
> The hard toil of people and machinery were small beer
> Only inventions seemed to have any effect
> And from where these arose everyone was quite bereft
> So people then began to get rather weary
> Of the once almighty neoclassical growth theory
> But then new analyses, oh so subtle
> Questioned all this and led to its rebuttal
> A new explanation arrived, over which there was quite a fuss
> Technical progress – innovation, ideas – were "endogenous"
>> Sir Derek Morris, "Ode to Post Neoclassical
>> Endogenous Growth Theory"[1]

This chapter outlines the origins of the knowledge economy concept, as well as its core characteristics. Drawing on recent academic scholarship, it distinguishes knowledge-driven growth strategies from the market-driven approaches to growth with which these strategies are often conflated. It explores how transitions between different "growth regimes" occur, through a combination of intellectual developments, socioeconomic change and political leadership. Finally, it applies this framework to the rise of the knowledge economy, demonstrating how new ideas – such as the "endogenous growth theory" referred to in the poem above – provided politicians in developed democracies with tools both to critique market-driven approaches to growth and to map out an electorally-appealing alternative.

Origins

The concept of the "knowledge economy" can be traced back as far as the 1960s and early 1970s, when the term was first used to contrast "manual workers" (who engage in physical labour to produce conventional goods and services) with "knowledge workers" (who engage in intellectual labour and produce ideas and information).[2] According to these early commentators, technologically advanced economies were experiencing a shift from manual work to knowledge work, which would drive future growth and prosperity for individuals, firms and countries alike. The "knowledge economy" was conceived as the end point of this upheaval, a state of affairs in which knowledge work would become the dominant productive force in society.

The concept was not widely adopted during the 1970s and 1980s (see Figure 1.1). Relative to the broader shift from manufacturing to services in developed democracies over those two decades, the trends associated with the knowledge economy were small in size and significance. Many of the new service sector jobs that emerged during this period were not particularly knowledge-intensive, and productivity performance – the pace at which efficiency was improving, at which the output produced by a fixed quantity of labour and capital was increasing – was not particularly impressive, even in knowledge-intensive sectors.[3] As the economist Robert Solow famously quipped, "you can see the computer age everywhere but in the productivity statistics".[4]

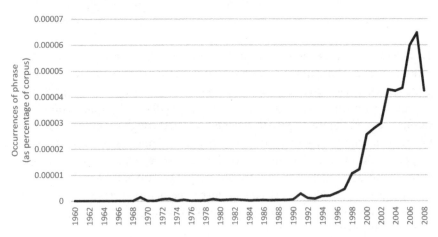

Figure 1.1 Google Books NGram showing relative frequency of the phrase "knowledge economy" in corpus of English-language books, 1960–2008

Source: https://books.google.com/ngrams; Jean-Baptiste Michel *et al.* "Quantitative analysis of culture using millions of digitized books", *Science* 331:6014 (2011), 176–82.

The knowledge economy concept found new resonance in the late 1980s and early 1990s. The exponential growth of IT sector businesses such as Apple, Intel and Microsoft seemed to herald a paradigm shift in the wider economy. New "weightless" business models – whereby a company's assets were conceived primarily in terms of personnel and institutional knowledge rather than plant and machinery – appeared in sectors ranging from marketing through to finance, testifying to the growing significance of knowledge work.[5] After two decades of unspectacular productivity growth, the US economy made rapid gains in the final years of the last millennium, driven in large part by the success of knowledge-intensive industries, including computing, biotechnology, advanced manufacturing, media and telecommunications.[6] The inflation of the dot-com stock market bubble undoubtedly also enhanced the credentials of the knowledge economy, although as Figure 1.1 indicates, its collapse in 2000 by no means heralded the demise of the concept.[7]

This economic revolution attracted the interest of academics and policy-makers alike. Management scholars examined how businesses might take advantage of knowledge-driven growth.[8] Economists debated whether the knowledge economy might require changes to fundamental axioms of economic theory, such as the law of diminishing returns.[9] However, it was the interest of politicians – in particular, the US Democratic Party under Bill Clinton and the UK Labour Party under Tony Blair – that brought discussion of the knowledge economy out of academia and consultancy and into the heart of public debate. Throughout the 1990s and into the first decade of the new millennium, the knowledge economy attracted the attention of prominent think tanks, journalists, public intellectuals and policy-makers, who sought to understand how countries might best position themselves in this new economic paradigm.

What, then, were the key features of the knowledge economy, as it was understood in its 1990s heyday? First and foremost, the term "knowledge economy" indicates that knowledge workers, who produce ideas and new technologies, are in the ascendant. This means that they constitute the dominant force in the economy; if not necessarily numerically or even in terms of total output created, then at least in terms of productivity growth. In the knowledge economy, knowledge-intensive industries such as advanced manufacturing, biochemical engineering and IT become essential to prosperity.[10]

A corollary of the increased importance of knowledge workers is that businesses that rely on traditional as opposed to human capital (such as large-scale manufacturing) contribute less to growth in relative terms than their more knowledge-intensive counterparts. The same is also true of businesses that are reliant on cheap but unskilled labour (for example, low-cost service industries such as cleaning and caring). To quote the British sociologist Anthony Giddens, a prominent champion of the new paradigm, output "in the advanced economies, unlike in earlier stages of capitalist development, is no longer so dependent upon the adding of capital or labour to the production process".[11] This development has implications for the bargaining power of knowledge workers vis-à-vis other members of the workforce. It can thus exacerbate inequality and prove socially divisive.[12] However, it also has implications for the bargaining power of knowledge workers vis-à-vis their employers, which can mitigate the social divisions associated with the unequal distribution of wealth. The old management trope that "our people are our greatest asset" becomes increasingly true: in knowledge-intensive businesses, more value is created by skilled employees than by investment in traditional capital goods such as plant and machinery. This means that wealthy investors should no longer see such high returns on their wealth, as their wealth contributes less to the production process in the knowledge economy than it did in the industrial era. When economies are dynamic, when innovation levels are high and productivity growth is rapid, capital takes a smaller share of national income than at other times.[13]

Indeed, in the knowledge economy, owning assets can be actively disadvantageous. Investment in physical assets can reduce the agility of businesses, committing them to processes and technologies that are at constant risk of obsolescence. Agility matters because the knowledge economy is highly dynamic, with a high rate of business creation and a concomitantly high rate of business failure.[14] Entrepreneurs are constantly innovating to identify new markets, new products and new ideas, and they must continue to do so because the knowledge economy is highly competitive – not least because barriers to entry in knowledge-intensive industries are extremely low, because would-be competitors require little more than an education in order to compete.

The rise of the knowledge economy has implications for competition between countries as well as between businesses. Assuming a reasonably strong international intellectual property regime, if a country specializes in the production of knowledge (for instance, the design for a new microchip), the physical embodiment of that knowledge (the microchip itself) can be manufactured elsewhere.[15] The most knowledge-intensive economies will dominate the highest echelons of these international value chains, guaranteeing for their workers and for the wider societies in which they operate a substantial share of global growth, both in terms of output and in terms of high-skill, high-pay knowledge jobs.

The knowledge created by knowledge workers can be replicated countless times at extremely low cost. Indeed, the emergence of the knowledge economy coincided with a dramatic lowering in the costs of reproducing and storing knowledge (the cost of the printed page, the floppy disk, the CD-ROM, the transmission of data down a phone line), a process that was itself driven by technological advances. As the British commentator Charles Leadbeater noted, "[i]t

costs Bill Gates many hundreds of millions of dollars to develop a new generation of his Microsoft Windows software for personal computers. But once the
software is perfected it costs him virtually nothing to reproduce it endlessly for
a mass market."[16] Knowledge is weightless, and so knowledge producers do not
face the traditional logistical obstacles that arise when trying to serve customers
in far-flung locations. Provided adequate telecommunications infrastructure is
in place, even the smallest knowledge producer can access a global marketplace.
Moreover, the same piece of knowledge, once created, can be used simultaneously by countless individuals and organizations. As a consequence, knowledge
producers benefit from near-infinite economies of scale, with each additional
customer increasing the potential for profit.[17]

So understood, the rise of the knowledge economy has particular consequences for public policy. If governments are to capitalize on knowledge-driven
growth, they need to invest in R&D, as well as in education, and to encourage
such investments on the part of private individuals and companies. They must
persuade the most talented knowledge workers and the most innovative businesses to set up shop within their jurisdiction. And they must harness the creative destruction of the market in order to ensure that good ideas, inventions and
business models are given the resources needed to grow.

The knowledge economy and neoliberalism

Is the knowledge economy, so construed, really a distinctive phase in the development of today's advanced democracies? Are the policies that politicians
have advocated in its name so radically different from those that have gone before? From the knowledge economy's rise to prominence in the 1990s onwards,
critics (particularly critics on the left) have claimed that its novelty has been
oversold, and that the knowledge economy agenda amounts to little more than
a rebranding of what might be termed "neoliberalism", the pro-market political programme championed by the likes of Reagan and Thatcher in the 1980s.
Indeed, to many scholars of political economy today, the knowledge economy
does not warrant consideration as an approach to economic growth in its own
right, instead representing continuity with the neoliberal era that preceded it.[18]

Neoliberalism is a slippery term, but broadly speaking, it denotes a desire
to roll back the state to make (more) room for market forces: deregulating the
economy, privatizing state-owned enterprises and public services, increasing
the flexibility of labour markets, reducing public spending, cutting taxes and
removing barriers to international flows of goods, services, labour and capital.[19]
Alternatively, it can be understood as a transformation of the state rather than
a withdrawal, reforming government to reflect market principles and undergird

market operations rather than reducing its reach outright: for instance, by shifting public spending from social protection to policing and the penal system to facilitate stricter enforcement of market rules, or by paying the private sector to deliver public services. As many commentators have noted, most developed democracies that underwent neoliberal reforms nevertheless maintained a high level of public spending as a proportion of gross domestic product (GDP), lending weight to the latter account.[20] In any event, on both these accounts of neoliberalism, the private sector is seen as the primary source of growth and prosperity, and therefore the task of policy-makers is to ensure its smooth and profitable operation. This might require weakening trade unions, slashing unemployment benefits or lowering minimum wage levels, all of which prevent labour from finding its "natural" price; privatizing state-backed enterprises and service providers, which "distort" the market in sectors as diverse as energy, transport, education and healthcare; or cutting high levels of taxation, particularly on successful corporations and entrepreneurs, which act as a drag on the inherent dynamism of the private sector.

There is a significant degree of overlap between the policy programme that was constructed around the knowledge economy and the policy programme of neoliberalism. As we will see in more detail in Chapter 3, the knowledge-based growth agenda did involve a celebration of the dynamism and creative destruction of markets, with competition ensuring that only the most efficient and creative companies would succeed and grow, with laggards forced either to innovate or fold. It also implied a broad acceptance of market outcomes and inequalities, both at the level of firms and industries as well as at the level of individuals. Indeed, to the extent that the knowledge-driven growth agenda does contemplate government intervention, its purpose appears to be to make markets work better rather than to block or moderate the consequences of capitalist production, aligning it more closely with the neoliberal project than traditional social democratic values.[21]

However, it is also true that the proponents of knowledge-based growth saw themselves as reacting against (what they understood as) neoliberalism and its negative consequences. "Neoliberalism" was one of the poles against which the sociologist Anthony Giddens defined his "Third Way", in which knowledge-driven growth played a pivotal role.[22] Gordon Brown, the chief architect of British economic policy during the heyday of the knowledge economy concept, described his time in office as an attempt "to swim against the neoliberal tide".[23] Whereas neoliberalism created a stark divide between winners and losers – between individuals, families, communities and regions who thrived and those who faced near-permanent exclusion from market-driven growth – the knowledge economy appeared to offer a way in which prosperity could be extended to people and places who had been marginalized by the disintegrative processes of deindustrialization and globalization. Proponents of the knowledge economy believed that investing in skills and digital infrastructure would allow left-behind individuals and communities to latch on to global markets and sell high-value, knowledge-intensive outputs. Whereas neoliberalism preached the marketization of almost everything and the rolling back of the state, advocates of knowledge-based growth insisted on an active role for government, in providing education, in encouraging R&D, and in creating, maintaining and developing the infrastructure on which the new knowledge-based economy would depend.

To be sure, neoliberalism might be defined so broadly that it encompasses both the market-driven growth strategies of the 1980s and the knowledge-driven growth strategies of the 1990s. However, in so doing, it is far from clear whether we gain an insight or lose a distinction. Indeed, if we ignore the era of knowledge-based growth entirely, it becomes difficult to explain why developed democracies confront a crisis of neoliberalism today, so long after its shortcomings originally became apparent.

Some of the knowledge economy's advocates would concede that their efforts to combat neoliberalism did not go far enough. For example, Robert Reich – a prominent early champion of knowledge-based growth, who would go on to serve as the US secretary of labor under President Clinton – argued that the Clinton administration never managed to mobilize the resources necessary to implement the policy agenda that the knowledge economy implied. Torn between the desire to prove its fiscal responsibility by eliminating the deficit without substantially raising taxes and spending the money necessary to achieve inclusive knowledge-based growth, according to Reich the administration ultimately opted for the former.[24] Similar implementation issues arose in other countries too. For all the rhetoric around lifelong learning and research excellence, changes in public spending during this period were often incremental rather than transformative. Without the promised public investments in education, training and infrastructure, the distinction between neoliberalism and the era of knowledge-based growth diminishes substantially.[25]

There is a great deal of merit to the charge that the policy agenda of knowledge-based growth was only ever imperfectly implemented. However, in downplaying the knowledge-driven growth agenda, and depicting recent decades as a continuation of the neoliberal trajectory of the late 1970s and the 1980s, this line of argument risks implying that knowledge-based growth constitutes a viable *alternative* to the economic strategies that developed democracies have tried (and found wanting) over recent years. It is undoubtedly true that this policy agenda was imperfectly implemented, and that it may well be beneficial – from the perspective of inclusive prosperity – for governments to address these imperfections. Nevertheless, this book demonstrates how some of the key assumptions on which this policy agenda was predicated were flawed, meaning that this agenda could not have delivered on its promises even if it had been implemented perfectly. This also helps to explain why, to the extent that the knowledge-driven growth agenda *was* implemented, it produced underwhelming results.

The knowledge economy as a "growth regime"

If the knowledge-driven growth agenda was more than just a fig leaf covering the workings of neoliberal capitalism, how then should we understand its emergence? To a policy expert, it is tempting to see changes in how governments approach growth as a response to changes in the nature of the economy (due, for example, to technological innovations or shifting patterns of international economic integration) as well as advances in state-of-the-art economic expertise. Over time, as the economy develops and changes (both at the global and the national level), new data points are accumulated, new theories are invented and tested, rejected or accepted, and expert economists update their understanding of the factors that drive growth accordingly.[26] Governments, if they are sensible, will seek to implement policies based on the cutting-edge technical insights of the economics profession. Admittedly, economists anticipate that governments will often fall short of this ideal, as the pursuit of optimal policy is frequently frustrated by politicians' attempts to secure benefits for particular constituencies and/or for themselves.[27] Nevertheless, assuming politics is not too dysfunctional, over the long term economic policy will track expert economic insight, thereby delivering higher rates of growth (and higher average rates of material prosperity) to citizens.

On this account, the introduction of an economic policy agenda premised on knowledge-based growth is a relatively straightforward matter of intellectual advances within the economics profession, which filter through to elected politicians, professional bureaucrats and political advisers, who then put these new ideas into practice. Shifts in public policy can thus be understood as a form of learning process, through which policy elites "puzzle out" how best to achieve broad-based economic growth.[28]

These intellectual advances play an important role in the account of the rise and fall of the knowledge economy agenda advanced in this book. However, there are two major problems with the attempt to interpret policy change as a straightforward learning process. First, this account overestimates the extent to which economic policy experts agree: the extent to which there is, at any given moment in time, a relatively uncontroversial dominant understanding of the factors that drive economic growth, which is sufficiently specific to dictate the choice of one combination of policies over another. Because a range of similarly rigorous readings of existing data (and accounts of what the relevant data are) are available at any one time, because experimental or quasi-experimental data are limited to certain areas of research (and moments in space and time), "reality" is a less rigorous arbiter of truth in economics and the social sciences than in many other domains of scientific inquiry.[29] This indeterminacy is particularly acute when assessing the long-term impacts of policy interventions on aggregate-level growth, because of the vast range of potential intervening variables and confounding factors. Second, the "social learning" account tends to assume a relatively uncontroversial view of the social *interest* that policy-makers are pursuing. It thus neglects the different conceptions of the common good that they (and their supporters) might possess and the different coalitions that policy-makers might seek to mobilize behind their differing visions of growth.

These points are related: the underdetermined nature of economic expertise creates both scope for reasonable disagreement and the need for political decision. At the same time, however, this process is not a complete free-for-all. A particular understanding (or set of broadly compatible understandings) of the economy can become embedded in influential parts of civil society (academia, the media, the think tank community, the education system and so forth) and in the professional civil service, and can even hold sway across partisan political divides. Such a viewpoint can then exert considerable influence over policy-making for a period of years or even decades.

Consequently, in contrast to viewing policy change as a straightforward learning process, political scientists have sought to develop a more nuanced account: one that recognizes the underdetermined nature of economic expertise and the pivotal role that political competition can play in policy formation, which nevertheless allows for the emergence of a dominant view of economic policy-making capable of persisting over a number of electoral cycles and changes in government. One promising way of handling these issues is through the analytical framework of "growth regimes", outlined by the political economist Peter Hall.[30] According to Hall, a "growth regime" refers to the set of economic ideas and policy tools upheld by policy elites, as well as to the broad-based coalition of support in wider society that underwrites those ideas politically. This coalition generally extends beyond the supporters of any particular government or party to encompass a broad cross-section of society, accounting for the persistence of high-level approaches to economic growth despite changes in political leadership, and for similarities in the economic policy agendas of rival mainstream parties at any given point in time. Growth regimes even extend beyond the boundaries of individual countries: as Hall notes, there are interesting similarities in the growth strategies adopted by the governments of diverse developed democracies at any given point in time, as well as in the way in which these high-level strategies have changed over time.

While recognizing important variations between countries, Hall suggests that the economic policies pursued by developed democracies in the postwar period can be crudely divided into three distinct eras: the era of the mixed economy from the 1950s to the mid-1970s; the era of market liberalization from the mid-1970s to the early 1990s; and the era of knowledge-based growth from the early 1990s up to the present.[31] Each of these periods was characterized by a distinctive account of the key drivers of economic growth and of how the kind of growth they promoted would benefit wider society. For example, the Keynesian ideas of the mixed economy era emphasized how full employment and rising worker wages would benefit businesses by bolstering demand for their products, encouraging investment; the neoliberal ideas of the market liberalization era emphasized how private enterprise, unfettered by government intervention, would generate wealth that would trickle down to poorer parts of the population; the knowledge-driven growth agenda of recent years emphasized how favouring the most innovative sectors of the economy would provide all firms and households with the productivity-enhancing benefits of new technologies. Each of these eras rested on a distinctive coalition of political support, the nature and strength of which changed over time in response to changing perceptions of the performance of the growth regime and changes in the composition of society itself.

How, then, can we account for the shift from one growth regime to another? According to Hall, transitions between growth regimes involve "obvious failures of policy" which "set in motion a search for alternatives". Building on his earlier work on policy paradigms, Hall offers the example of the stagflation crisis of the 1970s as motivating a move from the active political management of the economy typical of the postwar period to the pro-market policies of the 1980s.[32]

It is important to note that, on this account, not all unforeseen economic shocks indicate that policy has *obviously* failed, at least not immediately. There is often a lag between changes in economic context and changes in the conceptualization of that context. Unanticipated economic events or disappointing economic performance might initially be viewed by influential stakeholders as anomalies. As the CEO of a major investment bank remarked to the Congressional Financial Crisis Inquiry Commission in 2010, "my daughter asked me when she came home from school 'what's the financial crisis', and I said, 'Well it's something that happens every five to seven years'".[33] Here, the economic shock is presented as a normal, natural occurrence, rather than a more profound challenge to prevailing assumptions. For economic developments to prompt a transition from one growth regime to another, those developments must be *interpreted* as a challenge to prevailing economic wisdom. Persistent shortcomings in models used to predict economic growth, and persistent failures of the conventional policy tools that are supposed to promote growth, can over time trigger a search for alternatives, as can sudden and severe economic crises. Nevertheless, individual shortcomings do not in and of themselves *disprove* a growth regime, as they can almost always be explained away as freak results. An economic policy paradigm is never simply abandoned; it is abandoned *in favour of an alternative.*[34] However, as anomalies build up and economic performance disappoints, a paradigm may become hollowed out, subject to widespread criticism and unable to command popular support. This leaves it vulnerable to challenges from weakly supported outsiders: a point that we return to in Chapter 9.

Moreover, as any set of economic ideas also has different consequences for different social and political interests, favouring some groups over others, questions of which alternative is objectively best are further compounded by questions of which alternative is objectively best *for whom.* Even aggregate-level GDP growth is a controversial objective: as a heckler at a 2016 debate on the merits of the UK's membership of the European Union informed one of the expert panellists, "that's your bloody GDP, not ours".[35] This means that transitions between growth regimes are not (and cannot be) solely the result of the technical superiority of the ideas contained in the new growth regime. Given that, in democratic countries, any new growth regime must be championed by election-winning politicians, political considerations also loom large in the selection of policy paradigms. In addition to the technical merits of a particular set of economic ideas, politicians will also consider the extent to which those ideas align with the existing policy preferences, economic interests, rhetoric and ideology of their party, as well as of the voters to whom they wish to appeal. They will also consider whether these ideas can be weaponized against the positions of political opponents.[36] To take a much-studied historical example, the transition from Keynesian to monetarist macroeconomic management in the UK under Thatcher not only promised to address the technical shortcomings of its predecessor paradigm but also offered new arguments for longstanding Conservative Party policy aims, such as the reduction of public spending and of state involvement in the economy. It also enabled the Conservatives to capitalize on growing public hostility towards trade unions.[37]

The electoral triumph of political actors promising an alternative vision of growth offers an opportunity for the final stage of the transition between growth regimes: the institutionalization of this vision. This is most obvious in the reframing of the objectives of the state bureaucracy and in the transformation of the theoretical apparatus that public officials use to devise and evaluate potential policy interventions. Institutionalization also involves a shift in the parameters of broader public debate, as observed and policed by elected politicians, media commentators, businesses and business organizations, experts in academia (and beyond) and other influential civil society groups. However, as debate in the public sphere at large is generally more wide-ranging and amorphous than the focused problem-solving activities of professional policy-makers, it is usually easier to identify the institutionalization of new economic thinking in the procedures, practices and policy choices of the state and public officialdom than in wider public discourse. Even after a growth regime has been discredited and electorally defeated, its proponents will continue to find outlets for their views – they are just unlikely to secure a particularly wide audience during periods when the new status quo appears to be operating tolerably well. And even within government bureaucracies, change may take place incrementally, as individual members of the policy elite switch to the new paradigm at different speeds and out of different motivations (for instance, civic duty or careerist self-interest rather than rational conviction).

Not every new electorally successful vision of growth will necessarily be institutionalized. Professional policy-makers schooled in alternative ways of thinking may resist change, elected politicians might lack the combination of organizational nous and popular mandate needed to bring about change, and the electorate might turn against politicians before institutionalization can be completed. There may well be an interregnum between the decline of one growth regime and the emergence of another.[38]

To summarize, transition between growth regimes should be understood both as an *intellectual* response to the shortcomings of dominant accounts of economic growth (and the policies they implied) and as a *political* response to the unravelling of the electoral coalition that underwrote the former paradigm. How, then, does this framework help us to understand the adoption of knowledge-driven approaches to growth?

The intellectual foundations of knowledge-driven growth

The intellectual foundations for this shift in growth regime can be traced back to late twentieth-century ideas about the impact of technological change on economic and social life, which were themselves inspired by advances in computing, telecommunications, biotechnology and beyond. Commentaries on these revolutionary new technologies were penned by think tanks, journalists, businesspeople, sci-fi writers and many more besides. Policy-makers wishing to make a case for knowledge-driven growth could draw on a wealth of popular literature on social, technological and economic change, as well as on their own observations and experiences of the emerging "knowledge economy".

From a public policy perspective, however, probably the most influential set of ideas emerged from debates in academic economics over the course of the 1980s. This reflected both the prestige and authority of academic economics among policy elites as well as the direct role that many of the economists in question played in shaping public policy over the course of the 1990s (a point we return to in Chapter 2). These new theories of growth highlighted deficiencies in the economic models on which the then dominant market-driven account of growth was based. Moreover, they offered an alternative framework in which government could play a vital role in facilitating technological progress.

Before grappling with these academic theories, however, we first need to understand the conventional account of economic growth to which they were responding. At the most basic level of analysis, mainstream economics identifies three factors that drive growth: labour, capital and productivity.[39] If more people are working more hours, more output will be produced. If there is more capital investment – more and better machines for people to work with – then more output will be produced. Finally, if labour and capital are used more efficiently, if technological advances mean that workers have cheaper, faster, more sophisticated machines at their disposal, and if they are able to deploy more advanced techniques as they use them, then more output will be produced.

Economists have long been aware that, of these three components, advances in productivity are by far the most important for delivering long-term improvements in living standards. This makes intuitive sense. Consider the early days of the textile industry, when cotton fibres were formed into yarn by individual labourers working at a spinning wheel. Adding more spinning wheels and more spinners to this process would increase output incrementally, although the gains from adding any one element would rapidly diminish (spinners could not use more than one machine at a time; any single machine could only be used by two or three spinners, working in shifts). Consequently, while growth in population and in the number of spinning wheels would increase aggregate output, there would be a limited effect on the amount of yarn individuals produced on average. It took the invention of the spinning jenny, a machine which allowed multiple spindles of yarn to be spun simultaneously, and the water frame, which allowed the spinning jenny to be powered by the revolutions of a water wheel, to increase the quantity and quality of yarn produced per worker dramatically, thereby laying the foundations for the industrial revolution. As the economist Paul Krugman observed, "[p]roductivity isn't everything, but in the long run it is almost everything. A country's ability to improve its standard of living over time depends almost entirely on its ability to raise its output per worker."[40]

Yet, despite the importance of innovation for growth, the origins of innovation tended to go underexplored in the mainstream theoretical literature on the economics of growth that emerged in the postwar era. In Robert Solow's influential model of long-run growth, published by in 1956, productivity acted as a balancing figure, explaining residual increases in growth that could not be accounted for by changes in capital and labour alone.[41] Solow's model assumed that this figure would increase steadily over time. Productivity-enhancing knowledge, on this account, was independent of the inner workings of the economy: technological progress was not an output of economic activity but rather "exogenous" to it. Knowledge was easily and infinitely replicable. Once created, it would rapidly spread through any given society and across the world – it was a "public good" that anyone could enjoy.[42] Such knowledge diffusion should make it relatively easy for economically underperforming businesses, regions and countries to catch up with their more advanced peers, simply by copying their innovations.[43]

It rapidly became apparent that advances in productivity – the "Solow residual" – did a lot of the heavy lifting in Solow's model. In a follow-up paper published in 1957, based on US economic data from 1909 to 1949, Solow concluded that technological progress (as opposed to increases in the capital stock) accounted for 87.5 per cent of the gains in the output of labour made over those four decades. This prompted a flurry of interest among economists, who sought to bring technological change back into the model, to "endogenize" it.[44] However, these efforts ultimately proved unsuccessful, and adaptations of Solow's growth model fell out of fashion in theoretical economic circles as the 1960s gave way to the 1970s. The journalist David Warsh suggests that "the youngsters were discouraged by their elders from pursuing their ambitions. The concerns might be interesting, but the models were not easily managed or controlled or even understood ... [They] moved on to other topics with great success."[45]

Endogenous growth theory

Solow's exogeneity assumption became even more unsatisfactory against the backdrop of the IT revolution. In the later decades of the twentieth century, it was becoming clear that the economic catch-up that Solow's model predicted was not occurring; if anything, technologically advanced companies, regions and countries appeared to be pulling further away from their peers. Cutting-edge corporations placed increasing emphasis on R&D investment in order to gain and maintain a competitive advantage over their rivals. In this context, a growing number of academic economists returned to the growth theory framework, seeking to prise open the black box of innovation bequeathed to them by their predecessors. Among the most influential of these theorists was Paul Romer. Reflecting on real-world economic trends as well as economic theory, Romer's work described how private investments in knowledge yield new "designs" or "instructions for mixing together raw materials", which – once they have been devised – can be deployed over and over again at minimal cost by diverse individuals and firms.

Yet there is a paradox here. If these new designs improve the productivity of society as a whole, why do private sector businesses invest in innovation? If profit-motivated businesses are to be agents of technological progress, then there must be some financial incentive for them to play this role: they must be able to monopolize sales of the new good or service they have designed, or else they will find themselves undercut by competitors who replicate their inventions without incurring the associated R&D costs. However, if knowledge is monopolized by particular firms, then how does this activity contribute to productivity growth in the wider economy? Romer squared this circle by describing new innovations as "partially excludable": comprising both benefits that are monopolized by their inventors (benefits from which other parties are excluded) but also benefits that spill over into productivity gains for wider society (non-excludable benefits). Inventions generate abnormally high returns for the companies that own them, assuming a robust system of intellectual property rights exists to preclude direct imitation. Nevertheless, they also have positive productivity implications for the wider economy, as rival firms are free to study the innovative product, drawing insights that can then inform their own rival inventions.

The expansion of public knowledge that results from these private investments has a cumulative effect. Whereas conventional capital investments exhibit diminishing returns – there comes a point where additional spinning wheels do not help our fixed population of spinners to produce significantly more yarn – investments in the stock of knowledge will continue to increase the productive capacity of society over time.[46] For Romer, knowledge-driven growth in humanity's productive powers was potentially unbounded: "Whether opportunities in research are actually petering out, or will eventually do so, is an empirical question that this kind of theory cannot resolve. The specification here, in which unbounded growth at a constant rate is feasible, was chosen because there is no evidence from recent history to support the belief that opportunities for research are diminishing."[47]

Viewed from the perspective of policy and politics, what are the implications of Romer's theory of endogenous technological change? A number of points stand out. On Romer's model, the private sector acts as the primary engine of innovation. But this does not mean that the private sector must be left entirely to its own devices. Whereas a neoliberal approach to growth suggests that the self-interested decisions of private individuals and firms will result in the most efficient aggregate outcomes, Romer's theory implies that purely market-based incentives will lead to an undersupply of innovative activity. A society that relies on the market alone to provide incentives to engage in research, or to invest in human capital (which Romer conceives as the key input involved in the research process), will not achieve an optimal level of output, because private incentives alone fail to reflect the *public* benefits of knowledge production. If a particular research project promises such "positive spillovers" for the economy as a whole but does not generate sufficient returns for the firm that carries it out, then it will not be undertaken. If a particular training programme helps individuals to generate productivity-enhancing knowledge for society as a whole but does not help them to secure higher wages that outweigh the costs of undertaking that training, then people will not invest time and money in it. There is, in short, a market failure: one that might be overcome by state action to promote research and to cultivate a highly educated population.

The state also has an important role to play in ensuring that wider policy settings are conducive to innovation. As we have seen, for businesses to engage in research, and thereby generate the productivity-enhancing benefits of technological change for society as a whole, research must be profitable. The state must thus uphold a robust system of intellectual property rights, which allows any given innovative business to monopolize at least some of the revenues generated by the new designs, techniques and procedures that it produces. Conversely, however, if these rights are too extensive, they might inhibit positive spillovers to the wider economy. Endogenous growth theory also has implications for trade policy. Because new designs are infinitely replicable at near-zero marginal cost, knowledge-producing businesses can reap massive economies of scale: the more customers they can reach, the larger their potential profits. Consequently, the state has an important role to play in increasing market size through international trade liberalization. According to Romer, this will "induce more research and faster growth".[48] Finally, devoting time and resources to research involves foregoing more immediate financial rewards in the expectation of future returns. If governments want to encourage this kind of future-oriented activity, they need to provide a stable economic environment characterized by predictably low interest rates. Only then will long-term investment in innovation be preferred to other investment opportunities that generate positive cash flows within a shorter time frame.

Technology, path dependence and increasing returns

Romer's research explored the role of knowledge in driving growth at the level of the economy as a whole. Complementing this agenda, during the 1980s other economists were exploring the dynamics of growth in high-tech industries and in the geographical regions in which these industries clustered. Behind this theoretical activity stood a tangible real-world case study: the astonishing economic performance of California's Silicon Valley. In the decades following the Second World War, the area around San Jose became home to an ever-changing assortment of high-tech businesses, many of which had close links to nearby Stanford University. Companies based in the region played a pivotal role in the development of early semiconductors and microprocessors, around which an ecosystem of computer manufacturers sprang up, as well as businesses devoted to developing software and hardware for these new machines. By the 1980s, Silicon Valley was an economic powerhouse, home to leading firms such as Hewlett-Packard, Apple and Intel.[49] Despite a downturn in the semiconductor sector (largely caused by competition from Japan), between 1982 and 1987 alone the revenues generated by the region's high-tech manufacturers and software companies grew by 60 per cent.[50] Explanations of this economic miracle proliferated. It was variously attributed to the networks of knowledge exchange arising from the rapid circulation of staff between companies as well as from informal social interactions based around local bars and schools; the industrial strategy of the US government, and in particular the massive levels of research investment made on behalf of the military during the Cold War; the creative destruction of market forces that saw high levels of business formation and collapse; the ecosystem of suppliers, customers and investors, of educational institutions and the highly skilled workers they produced.[51]

For economists, the challenge was to understand this technological, industrial and regional success story, and to explain it in the formal language of the economics profession; to answer the age-old question of economics, "that may work in practice, but does it work in theory?" Key to this challenge was unpacking the dynamics of increasing returns: the tendency of technologies, businesses and regions that get ahead to stay ahead, with market leaders consolidating their advantages over time. Under conventional assumptions about the efficiency of competitive markets, increasing returns should not exist. Any market sector that seems to be generating above average returns should attract new entrants keen to secure a share of the spoils. As the market becomes more crowded, increased competition should push profit margins down, as companies feel obliged to offer their customers better products at lower prices. Yet the meteoric rise of high-tech businesses such as Microsoft appeared to contradict these assumptions, an anomaly that the market model of growth appeared ill-equipped to explain.

How do increasing returns apply to high-tech industries? What mechanisms enable technologies, businesses and places that establish early leads in the innovation race to consolidate those leads over time? The most obvious factor underpinning increasing returns is the straightforward case of economies of scale, highlighted in the work of economists such as Avinash Dixit, Joseph Stiglitz, Paul Krugman and W. Brian Arthur.[52] The information produced by research-intensive businesses might be very expensive to create in the first instance, but after it has been created once, it can be used over and over again without substantial additional expenditure. In other words, high-tech companies often display high fixed costs but low variable costs. The first copy of any software package sold incurs thousands if not millions of dollars in development costs; each subsequent copy costs a negligible amount to replicate and distribute. The same is true of physical products too: a new jet engine might cost a billion dollars to develop, but that design can be replicated at a fraction of that cost (albeit still running to millions of dollars).[53] Knowledge-intensive industries are thus characterized by huge economies of scale: because fixed knowledge production costs comprise a large proportion of a firm's outgoings, each additional unit sold reduces the average cost of the product, meaning that businesses that achieve high volumes can sell their products at increasingly competitive prices. While in theory, assuming perfectly rational financial markets, a superior rival product should be able to harness sufficient investment to achieve comparable scale, in practice such investment will always be a high-risk gamble in what Arthur memorably described as the high-stakes "casino of technology".[54]

Added to this, many technologies enjoy what Arthur described as "coordination effects", more widely known today as "network effects".[55] These effects arise when there is a larger incentive for people to adopt a particular technology, standard or platform, the greater the number of other people who have already adopted the same technology, standard or platform. For example, faced with a choice between communication technologies, the decisive consideration is often not cost or quality but rather how many of the people you want to communicate with can be reached using the technology in question. As a particular computing platform (such as the IBM PC and its various clones) gains market share, software developers will increasingly focus their efforts on that platform, as they can access a larger market for their products by doing so; at the same time, consumers will find that computing platform increasingly attractive, as they can access a wider range of software on it.[56] These coordination effects mean that rivals to a well-established platform or standard may struggle to find an audience, even though customers might have preferred to adopt the rival product had it been launched at the same time as the current market leader.

Coordination effects also exist with regard to place.[57] High-tech businesses tend to congregate in locations where they can draw on a large pool of highly skilled potential employees; highly skilled potential employees are likely to be attracted to places where a large number of high-tech businesses are based. Added to this, firms might also be attracted by the ecosystem of supporting businesses – suppliers, customers, venture capitalists, lawyers, accountants and so forth – who are themselves attracted by the presence of research-intensive businesses. These coordination effects mean that a location that achieves an early lead in a particular sector will go on to extend that lead over time, unless these effects prove somehow bounded (for instance, as rising demand pushes up the price of land in a particular area, there may come a point where the costs of increased agglomeration outweigh the benefits).

Taken together, these characteristics of high-tech industries create dynamics whereby technologies, businesses and regions that get ahead tend to stay ahead:

a dynamic of increasing returns. According to these models, timing matters, and small, arbitrary differences in the early stages of the emergence of new technologies can have a decisive impact on the eventual market structure, a process often described in the literature as "path dependence". A technology or business that achieves a slender advantage over its rivals early in the life cycle of a particular market can go on to dominate, as coordination effects and economies of scale conspire to consolidate and compound that early advantage, even when faced by rivals who, from a standing start, might have delivered a higher-quality and lower-cost alternative.[58]

What are the public policy implications of this analysis? Intriguingly, the tendency for high-tech industries to exhibit increasing returns raises the possibility that governments can play a positive role in facilitating economic growth. This runs contrary to conventional pro-market narratives, in which political intervention inevitably leads to less efficient outcomes. On the pro-market account, households and businesses are better placed to evaluate the relative risks and rewards of different consumption, saving, investment and production decisions than the state. These individual evaluations are reflected in market prices, and government intervention would only serve to distort these price signals, leading to an allocation of time, effort and resources that differs from that which individuals would ideally prefer.[59] By contrast, increasing returns raise the prospect of market-driven *in*efficiency. Due to the tendency of technologies that get ahead to stay ahead, individuals and businesses might gravitate towards a lower-quality, higher-cost solution, simply because it enjoys early leadership in a market characterized by economies of scale and network effects. Consequently, governments might back particularly promising technologies and businesses, to ensure that they realize their full potential, preventing lock-in of an inferior alternative.

Increasing returns also imply that a business that achieves market leadership in a particular segment of the high-tech sector could effectively stifle competition, enabling it to charge monopoly prices (to the detriment of its customers). Governments might thus be justified in intervening in market outcomes, either to regulate anticompetitive practices and abuses of monopoly power or to break apart monopolies and encourage competition.[60] Conversely, however, it might be in the interests of governments to cultivate such monopolists, enabling them to reach the scale necessary to reap the benefits of size, thereby allowing them to seize a significant share of the international market for a particular type of high-value product. This might require public investment in promising high-tech companies or indirect subsidies (such as the award of public procurement contracts); or governments might support these national champions through protectionist trade policies, shielding infant industries and start-up companies until they are sufficiently large to compete for a share of the global market.

(Clearly, the imperative to cultivate market leaders in pursuit of global market share has the potential to conflict with the imperative to maintain competition to promote innovation and consumer well-being at the domestic level; as we will see in Chapter 3, this would prove to be a major fault line among advocates of knowledge-based growth.)

Admittedly, the economists who formulated these theories were wary of pressing home their interventionist implications. Arthur, for example, acknowledged the possibility of "a central authority [underwriting] adoption and exploration along promising but less popular technological paths", yet noted that such an authority would still face challenges determining which technologies to back.[61] His preferred solution was a set of policies to "strengthen the national research base" and to "encourage industries to be aggressive in seeking out product and process improvements", while resisting the temptation to go further in "subsidizing and protecting new industries ... to capture foreign markets".[62] Nevertheless, that such policy alternatives were even on the table marked an important shift from mainstream pro-market economic thought.

The electoral politics of knowledge-driven growth

Despite increasing academic interest in new growth theories and the economics of innovation, there was no necessary reason why this literature should have influenced the thinking of public policy elites. After all, some of these ideas had been around since at least the 1950s, both in professional economics and works of popular commentary outside the academy.[63] Indeed, when scholars such as Romer and Arthur first began to promote their research findings, they were met with a mixture of resistance and indifference from many within the economics profession, let alone the wider policy-making community. During the 1980s, it was market-driven growth – and the policy interventions that it implied – that dominated both the academic and political agenda. When Romer made his first trip to the American Economic Association's hiring hall in 1981, Reaganomics was the big draw, with the conservative American Enterprise Institute described by the press as "the hottest show around".[64] Even politicians and governments of a putatively socialist persuasion, such as the French President François Mitterrand, found themselves implementing policies designed to entrench fiscal discipline and deepen market competition.[65] By the end of the decade, the fall of the Berlin Wall and the steady unravelling of the Soviet bloc seemed to offer further confirmation of the superiority of Western capitalism, which, at this stage in its history, was increasingly organized around (and justified in terms of) market-driven growth. In all but one of the G7 group of advanced democracies, right-of-centre governments held office.

And yet all was not well in developed democracies. Market-driven strategies had delivered growth but at the expense of exacerbating inequality and insecurity. After falling somewhat in the late 1980s, come the early 1990s unemployment was on the rise once again. The pattern of economic decline appeared to correspond to policy changes championed by advocates of market liberalization. Shorn of government support and wilfully exposed to international market forces, many communities built around heavy industries such as coal extraction or steel production found themselves facing a post-industrial era without the linchpins of their local labour markets. Regional levels of industrialization, once strongly correlated with above average income levels, began to be associated with lower GDP per capita performance after the 1970s, as extraction and manufacturing businesses struggled to compete with foreign rivals enjoying lower labour costs and/or more efficient business models. By contrast, regions with a disproportionate share of skilled service sector jobs tended to outperform their industrial counterparts from 1980 onwards. In many developed democracies, these high-performing regions were based around capital cities, reflecting public sector employment concentrated around the seat of government as well as the headquartering decisions of major companies (and the ecosystem of financial and professional support services that such businesses attract). Following a period of regional economic convergence from 1900 to 1980, inequality between regions subsequently trended upwards.[66]

Growing discontent with market-based growth presented political entrepreneurs with an opportunity, but in order to seize it, they had to formulate a persuasive alternative. Despite the political dominance of market-driven growth throughout the 1980s and into the 1990s, many of its policy recommendations failed to command majority support. Cuts to public spending and privatization were frequently unpopular, as was the deregulation of labour markets to make lower-paid part-time and/or temporary work more commonplace.[67] Nevertheless, discontent and resistance failed to coalesce around an alternative. The conflicting interests of organized and unorganized labour in a climate of industrial decline, coupled with the decreasing relevance of social class to people's voting habits, meant opposition to market liberalization remained fragmented.[68] Patterns of partisan support were further blurred by the increasing emphasis that many voters placed on cultural values. On the one hand, the period from the 1970s onwards saw increasing numbers of socially liberal voters committed to causes such as multiculturalism, environmentalism, women's equality and the gay rights movement.[69] On the other hand – and partly in reaction to the "silent revolution" in values that took place over the 1970s, inspired by the counter-cultural movements of the late 1960s – the late 1970s and 1980s saw increasing numbers of voters drawn to political parties that explicitly espoused traditional values and institutions: the (heterosexual) nuclear family; the (monoethnic) nation; and established (Christian) religion, including its prescriptions and pro-hibitions concerning sex and sexuality.[70] Whereas liberal values translated into a diverse range of voting behaviours – including support for long-established liberal parties or newly formed Green parties, as well as for social democratic parties historically associated with organized labour – traditional values voters tended to congregate around the platforms of the conservative and Christian democratic parties that were advocates-in-chief for market-driven growth. True, some traditional values voters were attracted to parties of the radical right, al-though these parties too tended to espouse a pro-market agenda, in many cases offering a stricter version of neoliberalism than their centre-right peers.[71]

The challenge for critics of market-driven growth, then, was to find an alter-native vision of growth that would appeal to a broad-based coalition, in light of the social, economic and ideological changes of the preceding years. As we have seen, theories that emphasized the linkages between knowledge production and economic growth provided one such alternative, suggesting a more active role for the state in cultivating prosperity, showing how public investments in human capital and new technologies could potentially deliver better outcomes than market forces alone. These theories could be presented as an evolution-ary step forward from the mainstream economic models that had justified the policy agenda of market-driven growth, bolstering the credibility of these ideas among policy elites (and members of wider civil society) who had been attracted to the neoliberal analysis. The knowledge-based growth paradigm was compat-ible with accepting that private enterprise was the primary wellspring of public prosperity, and that entrepreneurial activity could be accelerated by allowing en-trepreneurs to commandeer larger profits, as well as with the notion that trade union powers and labour market regulations inhibited job creation by pushing up the costs of employment to would-be employers.

At the same time, however, knowledge-driven growth could be presented as a prophylactic against the excesses of market liberalization, allowing it to ap-peal to constituencies that had become marginalized under the previous growth regime. Market-driven growth appeared to have little answer to problems of geographically and socially concentrated poverty and exclusion, save for accu-sations of indolence and welfare dependence. By contrast, advocates of knowl-edge-based growth could point to policy decisions that had failed to equip these communities for the post-industrial age, by failing to provide them with the skills necessary to compete in growing areas of the labour market or with the physical and digital infrastructure necessary to access good new jobs. From this perspective, persistent social exclusion was not only unjust but also inefficient: a sign of the wasted talents of potential knowledge workers. Moreover, while promising to ameliorate the damage wrought by deindustrialization and globali-zation, knowledge-based growth could simultaneously appeal to economically successful regions and individuals, identifying them as wealth creators and offering them additional support in their entrepreneurial endeavours by guaranteeing them a steady supply of well-trained workers and a supportive regulatory environment. Knowledge-based growth could act as a rallying point for socially liberal values voters too, who were often well represented among these more affluent sectors of the population. With imagination identified as pivotal to success in increasingly prominent and prestigious creative industries – a category that encompassed music, film, television, fashion, design, advertising, computer games, cookery and more – socially liberal values such as diversity, individuality and openness to new ideas could be celebrated as a source of competitive advantage and reactionary traditionalism presented as a threat to the economic well-being of society.

Consequently, by the 1990s, not only were theories of knowledge-driven growth readily available and intellectually credible, but the policies that these theories supported were politically attractive, given the social and economic changes that had taken place in developed democracies over the neoliberal era. In the following chapters, we examine how policy elites drew on these ideas to construct a policy agenda predicated on social investment, dynamic markets and international openness, exploring the assumptions about the nature of knowledge-driven growth that underpinned these policy choices. Moreover, we will see how this policy agenda, and the ideas and assumptions on which it is based, have continued to dominate mainstream economic policy thinking through to the present day.

2
"KNOWLEDGE 2000"

On 7 March 2000 – three days before the tech-heavy NASDAQ Composite stock index hit a peak that it would not reach again for 15 years – almost 400 people crowded into the Connaught Rooms, a conference venue in central London. The event, entitled "Knowledge 2000", had been organized jointly by the UK's Department of Trade and Industry and Department for Education and Employment. It brought together business and labour interests to discuss how to build a successful, knowledge-driven economy fit for the challenges and op-portunities of the twenty-first century. The attendee list testified to the breadth of the coalition backing this agenda. Representatives from the Confederation of British Industry mingled with representatives from the Trades Union Congress. António Guterres – then Portuguese prime minister and president of the European Council, later to be secretary-general of the United Nations – was also present, a symbol both of the strident internationalism of the New Labour government and of the global appeal of knowledge-driven growth. Topping the bill of speakers was Tony Blair, who was exactly 15 months away from a general election that would see him win the second-largest UK parliamentary majority of the postwar era – eclipsed only by the record he himself had set just under three years before. In his keynote address, Blair outlined an economic strategy that would capitalize on the opportunities of the knowledge economy era, gen-erating a truly inclusive form of growth: "Knowledge and skills, creativity and in-novation, adaptability and entrepreneurship are the ways by which the winners will win in the new economy ... That way we can all prosper."[1]

Over the next two chapters, we will map out the economic policy agenda championed by advocates of knowledge-driven growth in the 1990s and early 2000s. Four elements of this agenda stand out. First, policy-makers believed that *social investment* in education, infrastructure and research would act as a mag-net for internationally mobile knowledge jobs and would help knowledge-in-tensive industries to grow. Moreover, these social investments would combat poverty and social exclusion, overcoming differences in opportunity between economically marginalized people and places and their more affluent peers.

Knowledge-driven growth also required *dynamic markets*, aided by the removal of tax and regulatory burdens that might hamper businesses from responding in an agile fashion to their rapidly changing environment. Dynamic markets would bring competitive pressures to bear on firms, forcing them to adopt new technologies and innovate in their own right. Greater levels of innovation could also be encouraged through *international openness* as well as fiscal and monetary policies designed to ensure *macroeconomic stability*.

This chapter focuses on the first of these elements: social investment. It begins by exploring how the economic theories and theorists discussed in Chapter 1 found their way into the corridors of power. It then outlines how social investment – particularly investment in education – would help to accelerate growth while simultaneously combating social exclusion and equalizing opportunity. As we will see, in order for social investment to bring about these outcomes, certain assumptions about the nature of knowledge-driven growth also had to hold true: in particular, that wealth and geography would prove to be increasingly irrelevant to economic success in the knowledge economy era. Our analysis focuses in particular on policy ideas and practices within the USA and the UK, although it also highlights parallel developments in other advanced democracies and in supranational institutions such as the EU.

Channels of influence

As mentioned in Chapter 1, policy-makers in the 1990s could obtain ideas about the new "knowledge economy" from a diverse range of sources. Nevertheless, the analyses of knowledge-driven growth developed within the economics departments of US universities over the 1980s proved to be highly influential in policy circles, particularly in the USA and UK. Many of Clinton's large team of economic advisers were drawn from American academia and were well-versed in the novel theories of growth that were being debated in the economics profession. Perhaps the most obvious example of an individual who bridged the divide between the academic economics of endogenous growth theory and the Clinton administration was Joseph Stiglitz, a member of Clinton's Council of Economic Advisers (CEA) from 1993 until 1997 and its chair from 1995 onwards. Stiglitz was a prominent figure in the increasing returns debates of the 1970s and 1980s. Moreover, he had directly addressed the structure of high-tech sectors of the economy in his own work on technological change, arguing that the high fixed costs and low variable (per-unit) costs of research-intensive businesses created barriers to meaningful competition.[2]

Larry Summers, another Clinton appointee, also played a role in these academic debates, albeit a somewhat more peripheral one: for example, he was a discussant during a 1988 conference at which Romer hammered out the finer details of his revised endogenous growth theory.[3] Over a decade younger than Stiglitz, he would nevertheless prove highly influential in setting the economic policy agenda of the Clinton administration. In a retrospective review of economic policy-making during the Clinton years, senior members of administration staff recall that Summers "exerted more influence early in the Clinton Administration than his official post as Undersecretary for International Finance at the Treasury Department would have suggested. Summers quickly dominated the Treasury Department; a CEA spoof on the Treasury Department's organizational chart had Summers occupying every position under the Secretary (a position he later filled)."[4]

Another individual prominently associated with both the Clinton administration and the wider US knowledge economy debate was the author and academic Robert Reich. In contrast to Summers and Stiglitz, Reich's training was in law rather than theoretical economics (he was a graduate of Yale Law School), and his academic career focused more on practical questions of public policy than on abstruse debates around the Solow residual.[5] Prior to his appointment as secretary of labor in the Clinton administration, Reich worked as a lecturer at Harvard, during which time he wrote *The Work of Nations*, one of the earliest analyses of the new knowledge economy to reach a mass audience.

The UK Labour Party drew inspiration from many of the same theories and theorists that influenced the New Democrats of the Clinton administration. As early as 1994, the then Shadow Chancellor Gordon Brown delivered a speech in which he referenced "post-neoclassical endogenous growth theory", explicitly invoking the ideas of Romer and his interlocutors. The reference itself was the work of Ed Balls, who Brown had appointed as an adviser earlier that year. (It was originally included in jest, as an example of the kind of wonkish verbiage that should never be put out for public consumption, although Brown liked it so much that he insisted on reinstating "the theory".)[6] Balls, who would go on to serve as chief economic adviser to the UK Treasury after Labour's 1997 election victory, had previously spent two years studying at Harvard University under Larry Summers, where he also took a course taught by Robert Reich.

Outside the Treasury team, the Blair government was closely connected to the Clinton administration in a range of other ways. Blair, Brown and Peter Mandelson (another key architect of the New Labour project) all visited Washington in early 1993 to meet with senior Clinton aides.[7] Jonathan Powell, who would go on to serve as Blair's chief of staff, worked as a diplomat in Washington from 1991 through to 1995 and developed strong personal ties with many figures in the Clinton administration. Powell helped to facilitate meetings between Brown, Balls and a range of Clinton's economic advisers in Washington in 1994.[8] After the 1997 election victory, a group of senior Democratic advisers gathered at Chequers (the UK prime minister's official country residence), with economic policy issues again high on the agenda.[9]

Enthusiasm for knowledge-driven growth was not restricted to the Anglosphere. The OECD had long promoted the idea of the "knowledge-based economy", advocating for higher levels of R&D spending as a way of accelerating growth.[10] The mid to late 1990s saw the election of a slew of like-minded centre-left leaders across the EU, all keen to capitalize on the "new economy". Politicians including Gerhard Schröder in Germany, Romano Prodi and Massimo d'Alema in Italy, Wim Kok in the Netherlands and António Guterres in Portugal were all broadly aligned with the economic programme espoused by the Clinton Democrats and Blair's New Labour, described variously as a "Third Way" or "New Middle". Several of these leaders met at the White House in April 1999, in a conference on "progressive governance for the 21st century" – although some of them argued that the newfangled knowledge-driven growth agenda merely imitated the common-sense approach to growth through social investment that they had long advocated and that their countries had long practised.[11]

The centre-left's dominance of European politics in the mid to late 1990s provided an opportunity for embedding the new policy paradigm within EU-level institutions. To be sure, the rise of the information society was already on the radar of European policy-makers in the early 1990s. The European Commission's 1993 white paper, *Growth, Competitiveness, Employment*, identified the emergence of information networks as a major source of social and economic change, enabling companies to "further globalize their activities and strategies".[12] Yet the policy agenda that the rise of the information society implied to EU leaders in the early 1990s still bore many of the hallmarks of market-driven approaches to growth. A 1994 report into information infrastructure in Europe, commissioned by the European Council, "urge[d] the European Union to put its faith in market mechanisms as the motive power to carry us into the information age".[13] By contrast, by the start of the new millennium, under the influence of social democratic leaders such as Blair and Guterres, the EU pivoted towards an explicit strategy of knowledge-driven growth backed by government spending. At a special meeting of the European Council in Lisbon in late March 2000 – a fortnight after the dot-com bubble reached its peak – these leaders agreed a new European-level strategy, committing the EU to becoming "the most competitive and dynamic knowledge-based economy in the world, capable of sustainable economic growth with more and better jobs and greater social cohesion".[14]

Education, social investment and social inclusion

What policies, then, did centre-left leaders propose, in order to capitalize on the rise of the knowledge economy? First and foremost, knowledge-driven growth required knowledge workers. Without knowledge workers, knowledge-inten-sive industries could not expand their operations, and internationally mobile knowledge-intensive businesses would not choose to invest. Bill Clinton's 1992 economic manifesto, *Putting People First*, declared that "the only way America can compete and win in the twenty-first century is to have the best-educated, best-trained workforce in the world".[15]

As skilled workers engaged in knowledge work generate public benefits (in the form of productivity spillovers), over and above the private rewards they cre-ate for themselves and their employers, market incentives alone would generate a suboptimal level of educational investment. Governments had to correct this market failure, through spending public money on education. In the UK, while still in opposition Tony Blair vowed to increase education spending as a propor-tion of national income, declaring "there is only one lasting route to higher living standards, better wages, more secure jobs in today's world – we will win by our brains and our skills or not at all".[16]

These new educational investments, and accompanying educational reforms, were explicitly targeted at the perceived needs of knowledge-intensive indus-tries: in the somewhat clunky words of a 2002 UK Department for Education Green Paper, "we must reap the skills benefits of an education system that matches the needs of the knowledge economy".[17] Parallel ideas could also be found in the EU's Lisbon Strategy, which called for "a substantial increase in per capita investment in human resources", with a particular emphasis on "new basic skills" reflecting "the demands of the knowledge society … IT skills, foreign languages, technological culture, entrepreneurship and social skills".[18]

Critically, the point of these attempts at educational reform and investment was not merely to provide knowledge industries with the skilled workforce that they increasingly demanded, thereby accelerating growth in productivity and output. Over and above these economic ambitions, knowledge-driven growth was also supposed to address problems of poverty and social exclusion that had arisen during the era of market liberalization.[19]

On the face of it, this might seem somewhat counter-intuitive. After all, many advocates of knowledge-driven growth argued that the rise of the knowledge economy tended to *exacerbate* inequality and social exclusion.[20] Knowledge work allowed skilled individuals who design and program machines to substi-tute their labour for the labour of many other unskilled and semi-skilled work-ers, reaping significant rewards for themselves, but putting the livelihoods of their fellow citizens at risk. Moreover, as the outputs of knowledge work can be replicated at near-zero marginal cost, the economies of scale that knowledge-in-tensive businesses can achieve are an order of magnitude higher than those available to their counterparts in the physical economy. The capacity constraints associated with the production of physical goods – the limits to how many units a given configuration of plant and machinery can produce, the working capital costs of tangible inputs into the production process, the logistics of national and international distribution – do not apply to the "weightless" ideas, designs and content created by knowledge workers. There is thus no obstacle to the most successful computer software company or the most successful author dominating sales in a particular market, to the exclusion of their rivals, and generating correspondingly massive returns, a phenomenon often referred to as "the economics of superstars".[21]

However, advocates of knowledge-driven growth also claimed that social investment in education could counteract these exclusionary dynamics. At the same time as forcing lower-skilled workers into competition with machines, the knowledge economy was also creating demand for skilled labour. People who found themselves displaced could be retrained for more skill-intensive jobs. What's more, these new jobs would generally be higher paid than the work that they replaced. A Treasury report into *Productivity in the UK*, published in 2000 (and featuring a technical appendix dedicated to endogenous growth theory), articulated the logic underlying this position. Higher-skilled work creates more value than less knowledge-intensive work, and thus results in workers receiving higher levels of pay, because in "well-functioning markets" workers will be rewarded "with wages that reflect their productivity".[22] Education increases individual output and thus individual wages, thereby combating poverty and mitigating against social exclusion. If "what you earn depends on what you learn", to quote Clinton's 1992 economic manifesto once more, then a government that helps you to learn also helps you to earn.[23]

Importantly, this meant that education could act as a substitute for more traditional forms of welfare, alleviating unemployment, low pay and inequality through the labour market, reducing the need for government handouts to poorer sectors of society. According to Anthony Giddens, a sociologist often referred to as Blair's "guru" in commentaries of this period, "the guideline is investment in human capital ... rather than the direct provision of economic maintenance".[24] Similarly, in the run-up to the Lisbon summit, the European Commission argued that educational investment would tackle the "under-use of available human resources and the wider costs of wastage in the economy", replacing the fiscal expense of welfare payments to the socially excluded with an active programme of investment in human capital designed to achieve work-based social inclusion.[25]

A surfeit of knowledge jobs

This economic strategy hinged on the assumption that there would be sufficient demand for knowledge workers in the new knowledge economy to meet the increased supply of suitably skilled individuals, therefore enabling the overwhelming majority of citizens to find well-paid, rewarding work commensurate to their new skills. In part, this assumption was simply an extrapolation from existing trends in the labour markets of developed democracies. The share of knowledge-intensive sectors had been increasing over time – recall that Romer had argued that the assumption of "unbounded growth at a constant rate" was justifiable in light of "recent history" – and thus it seemed reasonable to assume that this would continue. In part, the assumed surfeit of demand for knowledge workers was predicated on the belief that businesses operating in knowledge-intensive sectors are highly mobile across borders and make investment decisions based on the supply of skilled individuals in any given location (as well as other factors such as macroeconomic stability and attractive tax rates, discussed in the next chapter). Consequently, by cultivating a highly educated population, countries would be better placed to compete for international investment, thereby securing a larger share of the global market for knowledge workers. In the words of Labour's Peter Mandelson, "decisions about where new investment is made are primarily determined by the skills and attributes of the local population".[26]

However, policy-makers anticipated a further source of demand for knowledge workers, beyond the growth of existing knowledge-intensive industries and the attraction of a disproportionate share of global knowledge investment. Once the supply of skilled workers had increased, businesses and industries that were not particularly knowledge-intensive were expected to find new uses for the new-found knowledge and expertise of the workforce. The governments of developed democracies expressly envisioned what might be described as a "knowledgification" of their labour markets. In *The Work of Nations*, Reich foresaw that existing roles in manufacturing and personal services could be upgraded, enabling their occupants to add more value and thus command higher wages: "Production workers empowered by computers ... have broader responsibilities and more control over how production is organized. They cease to be 'routine' workers – becoming, in effect, [knowledge workers] at a level very close to the production process."[27]

The US Department of Commerce, too, saw substantial potential for converting a diverse range of existing jobs into more knowledge-intensive (and, implicitly, better-paid) roles. In its 1998 report into *The Emerging Digital Economy* it set out how, as machines take over more routine tasks, employees will be redeployed to perform more highly skilled functions, providing better services to their customers:

> Jobs characterized by a transfer of information from one party to another – travel agents, insurance agents, stock brokers, customer service representatives – will likely see routine tasks like order taking disappear,

and more complicated tasks replacing them. For instance, a leisure traveller making plans to go home for the holidays usually knows all the carriers flying that route and simply needs to make the reservation and pay for the flight. That would be a case of order taking, a function as easily performed online as by calling the airline or a travel agent. On the other hand, a couple planning a trip to South Africa might seek the advice of someone who has been to the region, who can recommend hotels in the wine country near Cape Town and safaris in Kruger.[28]

In the UK, Tony Blair was explicit that potential for high-skilled (or at least, higher-skilled) knowledge work was by no means limited to the tech sector. As he argued in his speech to the Knowledge 2000 conference:

> The new knowledge-driven economy is not just about the new, high-tech industries like biotechnology or software development – companies which have built directly on the UK's university and science base. The new economy isn't either just the new technologies like IT and the Internet. It is instead about new sources of competitive advantage. The ability to innovate. To create new products. To exploit new markets. Using whatever means which are appropriate, including IT and E-commerce. And that applies to all businesses, in all sectors. High-tech and low-tech. Manufacturing and services. Businesses in long-established sectors can find ways of using these new approaches to refresh and revitalise their operations.[29]

Underpinning the knowledgification of lower-skilled work was rising societal prosperity, itself a product of the productivity gains arising from rapid technological progress. This rising prosperity, it was hoped, would result in more discerning modern consumers "with differentiated tastes who require firms to develop niche products, to customise and specialise, with quick turn-round times", as Blair claimed in one of his final speeches as prime minister.[30] The differentiation of demand would help to counteract the superstar dynamics inherent to many fields of knowledge work, enabling a plurality of workers to carve out a living as knowledge workers. As Diane Coyle argued in her influential 1997 book *The Weightless World*, "take pop music, a traditional 'winner-takes-all' business ... increasingly, there are even smaller niche markets – the genres of music that play in different kinds of club ... this will limit the tension created by growing income inequality".[31] (At the time of the book's publication, Coyle was in close contact with some of the leading figures in New Labour's younger generation.)[32]

Opportunity, mobility and meritocracy

Education was not, however, just a matter of giving people access to better (and better-paid) work, nor merely about alleviating social exclusion defined in terms of material deprivation. Progressive advocates of knowledge-driven growth also argued that public educational investments could foster equality of opportunity. In contrast to more redistributive notions of equality, this meant allowing market forces to determine the structure of outcomes; however, policy-makers sought to ensure that people could access these outcomes on an equal footing, irrespective of their socioeconomic background and in accordance with their "merit".[33]

In recent years, several commentators have stressed the centrality of meritocracy to Anglo-American progressive politics in the 1990s and 2000s, as well as countries' failure to live up to this ideal.[34] What is less widely recognized is that this meritocratic agenda itself depended on a particular understanding of the knowledge economy. Viewed from a broader historical perspective, the notion that education is sufficient to equalize life chances looks somewhat odd. It ignores the contribution of capital to economic success: whether physical assets such as tools, machines and factories, or financial assets to fund risky new ventures. Consequently, it was only by insisting that economic resources had minimal impact on opportunity that progressives could reconcile meritocracy with an acceptance of substantial economic inequalities, and this is where the rise of the knowledge economy played a vital role.

According to advocates of knowledge-driven growth, in the knowledge economy, knowledge, ideas and skills supposedly become more important determinants of economic success than capital. In the words of Geoff Mulgan (the founder of the UK think tank Demos, who would go on to lead the Number 10 Policy Unit under Blair from 2003 to 2004):

> In the twenty-first-century economy the most valuable things are rarely physical, and it is possible to create wealth almost out of nothing, or rather nothing more than ideas ... Virtual companies are being established without an office and in some cases without even a staff. Others have no easily definable property. Small software companies regularly emerge as if from nowhere to become corporate titans, just as traders now deal on world markets from remote cottages.[35]

The knowledge economy was so dynamic, so mercurial, that even intangible capital such as patents and copyrights would prove to be of only fleeting value to their owners. According to Robert Reich, although "certain intellectual assets will remain even after talented employees depart ... in the high-value economy, such intellectual property often loses its value quite quickly".[36]

What was true of businesses was also true of individuals. As Charles Lead-beater (a sometime adviser to the 10 Downing Street Policy Unit during the Blair years) observed, you do not have to be wealthy in order to compete in the knowledge economy: "everyone with an education can have a go … twenty-five-year-old drop-outs can create best-selling computer games; a nerd fresh out of college can create the Internet's best browser".[37] It is against the backdrop of the declining relevance of capital to economic opportunity that progressives such as Clinton could claim that education and skills trump all other determinants of economic success; that "what you earn depends on what you learn", as opposed to what you own. Under these circumstances – novel when viewed in terms of the history of capitalism – education really *could* play a decisive role in delivering equality of opportunity. As Diane Coyle argued in *The Weightless World*, the "dematerialisation" of economic production is "helping to reduce the costs and difficulty of becoming a superstar … you need an idea, a cheap computer and a telephone".[38]

Implicit in this capital-light vision of the knowledge economy was an assumption about the kind of industries that would dominate in the knowledge economy era. Computer programming was the archetypal knowledge industry, as software is ultimately nothing more than a string of instructions to machines written by highly skilled workers. Other examples of capital-light production were provided by the diverse range of businesses comprising the "creative industries", in which talented knowledge workers could supposedly conjure value out of next to nothing. Film, music, art, fiction and journalism were all deemed to be knowledge-intensive areas with high growth potential; and, much like computer programming, they required little more than some basic equipment to get started, with the real "value" residing in the ends to which that equipment was put to use. New telecommunications technologies enabled the creators of this content to find global audiences for their output. Already in 1993, the European Commission was predicting an explosion in the growth of "audiovisual services" which would create "demand for new programmes", citing the example of the new products supplied through the Minitel network in France (an on-demand text-based service, run via the French telephone system).[39]

Anticipated growth in creative sector jobs played an important role in democratizing the idea of the knowledge economy. For those who could not see themselves as an aeronautical engineer, entrepreneur or investment banker – whether because of lack of specialist skills, start-up capital, elite connections or inclination – positions such as actor, musician, designer, advertising executive, celebrity chef, journalist or novelist offered an attractive alternative, promising workers a heady cocktail of prestige, autonomy and potentially high financial rewards. In the UK context, it is striking how many influential champions of knowledge-driven growth entered politics from a media background: Peter Mandelson worked for London Weekend Television, Ed Balls for the *Financial Times* and Charles Leadbeater for the *Independent*, to name but a few. As such, they were acutely aware of the possibility of transforming creative content into money. To take one particularly notable example, in the mid-1990s, Leadbeater commissioned the reporter Helen Fielding to write a new newspaper column entitled "Bridget Jones' Diary", which went on to become a commercial juggernaut encompassing a string of popular novels and films.

To the degree that wealth ceases to function as a prerequisite for economic success, and the accident of one's birth no longer dictates the opportunities that one enjoys, some people from modest backgrounds will grow up to be the superstars of tomorrow's economy, whereas some people from more affluent backgrounds will find themselves further down the income distribution than their parents (if not necessarily worse off in absolute terms, as a result of increasing prosperity across society as a whole). Advocates of knowledge-driven growth anticipated that this social mobility, facilitated by the capital-light nature of knowledge production, would ameliorate social tensions that might otherwise arise from growing inequality. Danny Quah of the London School of Economics put the argument thus: "at the same time that income inequalities become more extreme, mobility between rich and poor also rises. Societies then are willing to tolerate the increasing inequality because, simultaneously, greater fractions of the poor see opportunity to transit to being rich."[40]

The geography of merit

For social investment in skills and education to equate to equality of opportunity, wealth was not the only accident of birth that the rise of the knowledge economy needed to neutralize. It was imperative that geography, too, no longer dictated life chances. As we saw in Chapter 1, the policy-makers who championed knowledge-driven growth in the 1990s were highly sensitive to the distinctive geographical pattern of prosperity and decline that emerged from the era of market liberalization. They recognized that job opportunities differed dramatically, depending on whether people were based in the major cities where higher-paid service jobs tended to cluster or in economically declining former industrial towns and cities. As Robert Reich observed, in the USA,

> for most of the nation's history, poorer towns and regions steadily gained ground on wealthier areas, as American industry spread to Southern and Western states in search of cheaper labor. This trend ended sometime in the 1970s, as American industry moved on to

Mexico, Southeast Asia, and other places around the world. Since then, most poorer towns and regions in the United States have grown relatively poorer; most wealthier towns and regions, relatively wealthier.[41]

According to a European Commission report published ahead of the 2000 Lisbon summit, in spite of steady growth and rising employment Europe was still characterized by "marked regional imbalances", with unemployment concentrated in "outlying regions and declining industrial areas".[42]

How exactly would knowledge-based growth counteract regional inequality? The answer was through a remarkably similar set of social investments to those undertaken at the national level: investments in education, skills, infrastructure and research. Effectively, policy-makers were trying to harness the same growth dynamics at the subnational level that they believed to apply at the national level: using social investment in spillover-generating education and research as a magnet for more knowledge-intensive jobs, coupled with infrastructure investments that would improve connectivity between locally based firms and national or international markets. Economically underperforming regions were often earmarked for additional social investment (for example, through the European Union's Structural and Investment Funds). Rather than trying to second-guess the market by favouring specific firms or outcomes – the kind of interventionist industrial strategy that progressives might have attempted back in the 1950s and 1960s – the emphasis was on programmes that would improve conditions for local businesses across the board. Money was spent on initiatives such as training schemes, new transport infrastructure, high-speed broadband, basic research programmes and business support (including advice for exporters, international trade missions and lending facilities).

Some advocates of knowledge-driven growth argued that the rise of the knowledge economy offered another mechanism for mitigating regional inequality. They claimed that, owing to the dematerialized nature of knowledge work, knowledge workers no longer needed to gather together in one physical place but could instead "telecommute" into "virtual offices". Consequently, workers in economically marginalized regions would be able to log on and access high-skilled job opportunities offered by companies located anywhere in the world, provided they had access to a high-speed internet connection. As the *New York Times* journalist Thomas Friedman famously put it, "intellectual work, intellectual capital, could be delivered from anywhere. It could be disaggregated, delivered, distributed, produced, and put back together again ... the playing field is being levelled ... *the world is flat!*"[43] Back in 1993, the European Commission was already arguing that new information networks would facilitate "greater flexibility with regard to ... the place of work itself (teleworking)", and that this would reduce the need for "physical mobility", both for work and for consumption.[44] In one of his final speeches as prime minister, Blair outlined a vision of an increasingly dispersed workforce, connected by technology:

> [F]lexibility in respect of where you work, what hours, whether part-time or full-time – is of huge importance. And technology is enabling ever greater choice. The number of homeworkers in the UK is now well over 3 million. The numbers of teleworkers – using a phone and computer to carry out their work – has almost trebled in the last 10 years. Yesterday I spoke with one young woman … who works from home putting together multi-million pound global corporate deals. Another … likes to live in the North West even though much of her work is London-based. Homeworking through the computer allows her to do so.[45]

To be sure, not all advocates of knowledge-driven growth agreed. As we saw in Chapter 1, many early analysts of the knowledge economy took their cue from the US tech boom in Silicon Valley. They pointed out that knowledge-intensive industries tended to cluster in particular city regions rather than fragment across the globe, arguing that face-to-face contact was vital to building trust and sharing knowledge.[46] Yet even to these commentators, it was far from clear whether policy-makers should – or even could – do much to influence the geographical pattern of economic activity and curb the growing disparities between successful internationally oriented city regions and their less prosperous hinterlands. Often the best these hinterlands could hope for was social investment in transport infrastructure, bringing them within reach of those places where knowledge-intensive industries clustered.

Rhetoric versus reality

To what extent did the reality of social investment match the rhetoric adopted by evangelists of knowledge-driven growth? Figure 2.1 shows public spending on education as a percentage of GDP for five developed democracies (Germany, France, Sweden, the USA and the UK), from the late 1980s (or early 1990s in the case of the newly reunified Germany) through to the eve of the global financial crisis in 2007. France, the USA and the UK all displayed increases in public investment in education over this period, rising from around 4.5 per cent to circa 5.5 per cent of GDP. This represented a substantial mobilization of resources relative to prior education spending levels, although still below the levels of educational investment seen in some other developed democracies, most notably Scandinavian countries such as Sweden. (Germany is an outlier: educational

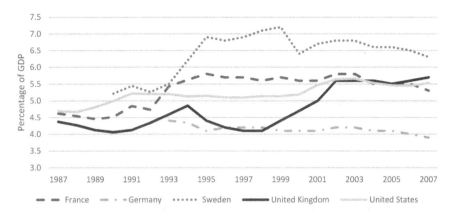

Figure 2.1 Government spending on education as a percentage of GDP, 1987–2007.

Sources: US National Center for Education Statistics (USA); World Bank (other countries pre-1995); Eurostat (other countries 1995 onwards).

spending expanded somewhat later there than in many other developed democracies, trending upwards following the financial crisis.)

Evaluating the scale of these educational investments, it is tempting to argue that they fell short of governments' transformative ambitions (with the possible exception of Scandinavian countries). Progressive advocates of knowledge-driven growth might well conclude that greater levels of investment and more radical reforms were necessary to capitalize on the opportunities presented by the knowledge economy and/or to achieve a greater degree of social inclusion. However, as we will see in Chapter 3, the drive to increase social investment was counterbalanced by other considerations that some policy-makers viewed as equally vital to achieving knowledge-driven growth. These included the imperative to support dynamic markets through low levels of taxation and the imperative to maintain a stable environment for private investment by limiting public borrowing.

Over and above these considerations, however, it is worth noting that the progressive case for social investment still depended on a number of assumptions holding true. It assumed that the rise of the knowledge economy would lead to an abundance of highly skilled work, that enhancing skills would inspire the knowledgification of lower-paid work, that developed democracies would attract a disproportionate share of global knowledge work and that geography and capital would not act as critical determinants of economic success. Were these assumptions to break down, then the link between education spending and knowledge-driven growth would weaken accordingly.

3
TAMING THE MARKET

Social investment was not the only channel through which advocates of the knowledge economy believed that they could affect the pace and quality of growth. This chapter explores how dynamic markets, international openness and a stable macroeconomic framework were also integral to their plans for delivering inclusive prosperity. On the face of it, these aspects of the knowledge-driven growth agenda closely mirror the policy prescriptions of the neoliberal era. Nevertheless, as we will see, the advent of the knowledge economy brought about a change in how such policies were justified and in the results they were expected to achieve. When coupled with social investment, the combination of market liberalization, open borders and tight macroeconomic policies would supposedly advance progressive goals, empowering labour vis-à-vis capital and combating social exclusion. Taking each of these elements in turn, this chapter aims to reconstruct the case for knowledge-driven growth at its most coherent and compelling, the better to understand its limitations and blind spots.

Market dynamism

In the knowledge economy era, in addition to social investment the other crucial ingredient for increasing productivity (and thus prosperity) was competition, which would incentivize individuals and businesses to innovate. As the UK Treasury put it:

> Competition reduces slack and makes a continuous stream of innovations a critical ingredient to business success. It provides strong incentives for firms to adopt best-practice techniques and engage in innovative activity, and hence increases the rate of labour productivity growth. Enterprise also creates competitive pressure as entrepreneurs that start up new firms introduce innovative practices and new technology and challenge incumbents' performance.[1]

Public policy thus had an important role to play in increasing the pitch of market competition: removing impediments to the free play of market forces and reshaping both economy and government to allow the fullest possible expression of market incentives.[2] This also implied that governments would not pursue activist industrial strategies that distorted market outcomes: in the words of the Lisbon Strategy, governments should "further their efforts to promote competition ... shifting the emphasis [away] from supporting individual companies or sectors".[3]

Taxation, regulation and flexibility

Underpinning this agenda was the belief that markets foster innovation by offering financial rewards to successful innovators. Consequently, one means by which governments can stimulate more innovative activity is by increasing the financial incentives on offer, thereby encouraging more entrepreneurs to enter a given market and encouraging incumbents to raise their game. And perhaps the most obvious way in which governments can increase those incentives is by reducing the amount of tax that successful entrepreneurs and businesses need to pay.

The UK government explicitly adopted this approach. According to a 1998 White Paper, *Building the Knowledge Driven Economy*, "many factors contribute to an entrepreneurial culture and some will take time to turn around or are difficult for the Government to influence. One powerful lever that the Government does have is its fiscal policy which can increase the rewards of success."[4] As far as corporation tax and income tax were concerned, this commitment to increasing "the rewards of success" broadly translated into preservation of the status quo. Whereas a left-leaning government might have been expected to raise tax rates on the richest, New Labour maintained the 40 per cent top rate of income tax that it inherited from its Conservative predecessor. It even cut the corporation tax rate slightly, from 33 per cent when it took office to 30 per cent by the time Blair left Downing Street, and two points lower still by 2010. The Blair government was even more proactive in its approach to the tax treatment of entrepreneurs. Advocates of knowledge-driven growth placed a great deal of emphasis on the importance of young start-up companies, deemed to be innovative in their own right and likely to pressurize more established firms to innovate in order to compete.[5] To incentivize entrepreneurship, individuals owning stakes in successful businesses were offered preferential tax rates on capital gains arising from their investments.[6] A similar logic was on display in the European Union's Lisbon Strategy, which described "tax policies" as a key tool for "[improving] the environment for private sector research investment, R&D partnerships and high technology start-ups".[7]

On the other side of the Atlantic, the Clinton administration took a some-what different approach. Clinton's 1993 tax reform saw a modest increase in the rate of corporate tax (from 34 per cent to 35 per cent) and a more substantial move in the top rate of personal income tax (from 31 per cent to 39.6 per cent). Nevertheless, the scale of these tax rises should not be overstated: under Jimmy Carter, the last Democratic president before Clinton, the top marginal rate of income tax stood at 70 per cent. The Clinton administration still subscribed to the view that tax rates of this magnitude would deter the productivity-enhanc-ing efforts of entrepreneurs and innovators, and the overall US tax burden still stood at one of the lowest levels in the Western world.

A further way in which the financial incentives to knowledge creation could be increased was through stronger protection of intellectual property rights. If governments bolster the ability of companies to exploit the knowledge they cre-ate for commercial gain, companies will be more likely to invest in knowledge creation in the first place. Conversely, if competitors are allowed to copy innova-tions without incurring any R&D costs, the financial incentive to engage in inno-vative activity diminishes drastically. At the behest of knowledge-intensive firms, the 1990s saw advanced democracies lead the development of an international framework for the protection of intellectual property, most notably the 1994 agreement on Trade-Related Aspects of Intellectual Property Rights (TRIPS), administered by the newly established World Trade Organization (WTO).

Offering greater financial incentives to successful businesses – both to en-courage the emergence of new start-ups and higher rates of investment and in-novation by established firms – is one way in which public policy might heighten the level of competition in the economy and thereby increase the pace of knowl-edge-driven growth. Alternatively (or additionally), policy-makers might focus on curbing regulations that constrain entrepreneurial dynamism. A statement of principle co-authored by Tony Blair and German Chancellor Gerhard Schröder argued that "[r]igidity and overregulation hamper our success in the knowl-edge-based service economy of the future. They will hold back the potential of innovation to generate new growth and more jobs. We need to become more flexible, not less."[8] The greater the resources businesses expend complying with government regulations, so the argument goes, the less time and money they can devote to their actual operations.

One of the greatest threats to the dynamism of the knowledge economy, in the eyes of its 1990s champions, lay in the overregulation of labour markets: in the rules governing the hiring and firing of staff, the terms on which people could be employed and the rights that they enjoyed as employees. In the knowl-edge economy era, competitive markets were expected to be fast-changing. New innovations might render the business models of entire industries obsolete over-night; rapid shifts in consumer preferences might see demand for one product plummet while demand for another rockets. The faster businesses were able to adapt to these changes, the more productive they would be, and the more dynamic and competitive the economy as a whole would prove. To thrive in this environment, businesses must thus be able to upscale, restructure and downsize rapidly. Traditional labour market regulations – including rules around hiring and firing staff, collective wage bargaining and union representation – were deemed to stand in the way of this dynamism. Instead, as Blair and Schröder argued, "labour markets must ... be flexible".[9]

Anxiety about overregulation of labour markets was particularly acute in continental Europe, not least because continental European labour markets were generally more rigid, more circumscribed by both state and society, than their US and UK counterparts. For many of the European Community's major economies, the early 1990s were characterized by rising levels of unemployment and concerns about the sustainability of the European Social Model (involving generously funded public services and welfare entitlements) in the context of increasing global economic integration.[10] The competitiveness of European businesses seemed to be in question, as rates of GDP growth languished behind those in comparator countries such as the USA and Japan. By relaxing rules around hiring and firing staff, and around the kinds of roles that employers could offer (in particular, allowing for the creation of part-time and/or temporary employment contracts), governments could combat unemployment while simultaneously facilitating the dynamic reallocation of labour to the most productive businesses and sectors in the economy.

Yet, liberalizing labour markets was not politically straightforward, particularly not for the centre-left governments that dominated European politics in the late 1990s and early 2000s. Greater labour market flexibility could be seen as heralding worse working conditions and less secure employment for working-class voters, upon whose support centre-left parties had traditionally depended. How, then, did centre-left advocates of the knowledge economy reconcile flexibility with their progressive aspirations? The answer lies, once more, in the interaction between education policy and the mechanics of knowledge-driven growth. As Blair and Schröder argued, although "having the same job for life is a thing of the past", workers would still enjoy security as a result of reskilling opportunities coupled with buoyant demand for knowledge workers: "lifetime access to education and training ... represent the most important security available in the modern world". Under this new social contract, workers would be rewarded with more lucrative and stimulating work in return for their willingness to accept flexible employment terms and take responsibility for upskilling themselves.[11]

On this account, any reduction in the bargaining power of workers arising from the removal of formal employment rights and the weakening of trade unions would be more than offset by structural changes in the economy, coupled with social investment. The rise of the knowledge economy meant that the onus was on owners and managers of knowledge-intensive businesses to keep their skilled workers content, rather than on skilled workers to demonstrate their value to their bosses. Because demand for knowledge workers was deemed to be buoyant, and because start-up costs in the knowledge economy were believed to be extremely low (because capital was viewed as increasingly unimportant to knowledge-intensive businesses), any knowledge workers who were not well treated by their employers would enjoy a plethora of good exit options. They could go to work for a competitor, or they could strike out on their own. The key to worker empowerment, then, was education, to ensure that workers possessed in-demand skills.[12]

Such reasoning was clearly visible in a report published by Clinton's CEA (then chaired by Joseph Stiglitz) in the run-up to the 1996 presidential election, which concluded that the US government needed to focus on providing people with "security of employability" through a focus on transferable skills, as op-posed to "security of employment", which would stymie the efficient reallocation of labour across the economy.[13] Blair used almost identical language in one of his final speeches as prime minister, arguing that "the challenge today is to make the employee powerful, not in conflict with the employer but in terms of their marketability in the modern workforce".[14] "Employability" and "marketability" compensate for rights as a source of worker empowerment. The same idea could be found in discussions of "flexicurity" within the institutions of the European Union: for example, a 2007 European Commission publication argued that job security "is about equipping people with the skills that enable them to progress in their working lives, and helping them find new employment" not "employ-ment protection legislation". The Commission explicitly framed these reforms in terms of the requirements of "a dynamic, successful knowledge economy", ar-guing that "companies, especially SMEs [small and medium-sized enterprises], need to be able to adapt their workforce to changes in economic conditions. They should be able to recruit staff with a better skills match, who will be more productive and adaptable leading to greater innovation and competitiveness."[15]

Despite this consensus, labour market liberalization came in different forms. Although almost all developed democracies responded to the rise of the knowl-edge economy with liberalizing reforms (or the maintenance of existing liberal policy settings), they set out from different starting points and did not all lib-eralize to the same degree or at the same time.[16] Moreover, liberalization was compatible with quite different approaches to the treatment of workers who found themselves unemployed. On the one hand, some countries adopted what might be described as a "workfarist" model, which assumed that labour market liberalization would itself generate sufficient jobs to ensure workers' "employa-bility", with low levels of unemployment benefits designed to "encourage" people

ˈback into work. This approach was particularly evident in the USA and the UK, countries that maintained the relatively meagre levels of unemployment provision they had inherited from the 1980s (see Figure 3.1). Germany also pivoted in this direction, following the labour market liberalizing Hartz reforms of the early 2000s. Nevertheless, an alternative model, involving higher unemployment benefits, could be found in other developed democracies. This alternative was what the European Commission meant by "flexicurity", arguing that "workers are more prepared to make ... moves" – and thus the dynamism of labour markets will be greater – "if there is a good safety net".[17] There were also differences in the level of support countries extended to the unemployed beyond benefits, with some countries spending substantially more on active labour market policies (training programmes, job-matching services and job search assistance, recruitment incentives, subsidized employment opportunities and so forth) than their peers, and the USA and UK again lagging behind (see Figure 3.2).[18]

Competition policy

If encouraging knowledge-driven growth implied a commitment to competition, in order to increase the pace of knowledge creation in the wider economy, what exactly did the rise of the knowledge economy imply for competition policy, for government intervention to address uncompetitive markets and anticompetitive actions by dominant businesses? On the one hand, emphasizing

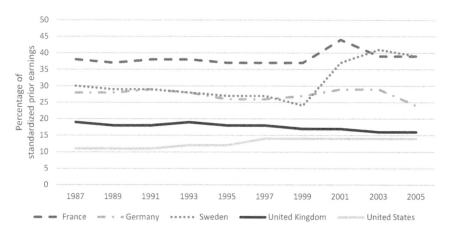

Figure 3.1 Gross unemployment benefits as a percentage of previous standardized gross earnings, 1987–2005

Source: OECD, Historical Gross Replacement Rates.[19]

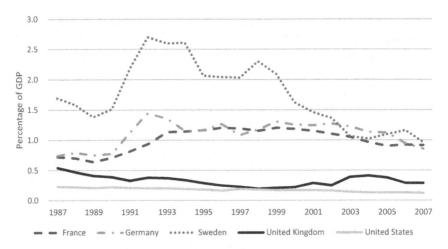

Figure 3.2 Government spending on active labour market policies as a percentage of GDP, 1987–2007

Source: OECD, Public Expenditure on Labour Market Policies (Active Measures).

competition as the driver of productivity-enhancing innovation suggests a zero-tolerance approach to monopoly and market power; on the other hand, competition regulation might be deemed an example of the bureaucratic burdens that government imposes on the dynamism of markets. Indeed, the ambiguity is more fundamental, inherent in the dynamics of knowledge-based growth itself. On the one hand, the minimal start-up costs supposedly associated with knowledge-intensive industries presented lower barriers to market entry, making it easy for new competitors to challenge incumbents with promising new products and ideas. On the other hand, dematerialized production massively increases economies of scale, as additional units of the knowledge inherent in any given product can be created and distributed at near-zero marginal cost, a dynamic that tends to lead to concentrated markets dominated by a handful of large businesses or even by a single company.

How, then, were these tensions resolved? Interestingly, this is one area where there was significant divergence between US and European approaches over the course of the 1990s. The EU tended to stress the benefits of untrammelled cross-border competition, arguing that if this led to knowledge-intensive industries dominated by a small handful of multinationals, then such consolidation was efficient. This logic underpinned European institutions' insistence upon harmonizing markets in telecoms and digital services, removing regulations and subsidies to national champions that might prevent the realization of economies of scale across the entirety of the single market.[20] In the UK, leading figures within New Labour reached a similarly laissez-faire conclusion: even before

Blair's first election victory, Peter Mandelson was arguing that "it would be foolish for competition policy to back every self-styled David against its chosen Goliath ... competition policy needs to focus on abuses of dominance, not on a strong position won fairly in the market-place".[21] The point is well taken: the fact that the winner takes all (or most) in a given market is not necessarily indicative of economic inefficiency. A market structure in which a small number of businesses (or even a single business) dominate can be more efficient than a more competitive landscape in which diverse firms sink significant sums of cash into the development of ultimately very similar products. Under these conditions, almost any concentrated market will be preferable to one in which economies of scale are not permitted to arise; and if that monopoly power is abused, then competitors will presumably emerge to displace the incumbent.

Moreover, policy-makers and commentators alike argued that market dominance was likely to be temporary, on account of the low start-up costs involved in knowledge-intensive industries, which would enable smaller and more agile businesses to take market share away from larger, more bureaucratic incumbents. The techno-optimism of the erstwhile Downing Street adviser Charles Leadbeater was typical of the era: "If knowledge-based industries tend to create monopolies, the government cannot alter that, other than to choose which monopolist we have. The pace of change in these new industries is so fast that monopolies will rarely last."[22] True, some markets might become highly concentrated; however, market dominance was often merited, often efficient and often temporary, as a result of the competitive dynamism of the knowledge economy. Under the auspices of this approach, the UK and other European governments, as well as the European Union itself, would offer minimal resistance to a series of consequential mergers and acquisitions in high-tech industries over the 2000s and early 2010s.

This laissez-faire perspective found adherents in the USA as well: Clinton's Treasury Secretary Larry Summers argued that "the constant pursuit of ... monopoly power" was "the central driving thrust of the new economy".[23] However, in the US context, this anti-interventionist stance proved more contentious than in Europe, creating a fault line between advocates of knowledge-driven growth within the Clinton administration as well as within the wider economic policy community. The risk of monopoly was harder to ignore in the comparatively mature high-tech industries of the US economy, where market concentration and anticompetitive abuses were more than just a theoretical possibility, and claims regarding the inherent dynamism of the knowledge economy could be repudiated by real-life counter-examples. In particular, the dominance that Microsoft enjoyed over the software industry was a major cause for concern among businesses, regulators and policy-makers alike. During Clinton's time in office, the Microsoft antitrust case brought these disagreements to the fore, with prominent figures from academic debates around increasing returns and endogenous growth lining up on both sides of the argument.

Microsoft, Netscape and the browser wars

By the early 1990s, Microsoft was the leading provider of operating system software for home and office computers around the world. The tech giant also boasted a significant market share in lucrative adjacent sectors, such as word processing and spreadsheet applications. This dominance meant that Microsoft reaped massive economies of scale: while the first copy of Windows or Word might cost several million dollars to develop, additional copies could be created for next to nothing. This in turn provided Microsoft with profits it could reinvest into subsequent iterations of its core products (both for development and marketing purposes), allowing it to perpetuate its dominance. Yet in and of itself, such a situation was not necessarily objectionable. In theory, similar economies of scale were available to any rival company capable of developing a similarly popular product, and this competitive threat should have forced Microsoft to keep its prices low and product quality high.

More troubling to economists and regulators was Microsoft's monopolization of network effects, which made market entry significantly harder for would-be competitors. As discussed in Chapter 1, network effects arise when adoption of a particular product, standard or platform by additional users makes the product, standard or platform in question more valuable to other users. The ubiquity of Microsoft's MS-DOS (and, subsequently, Windows) on home and office computers attracted developers to Microsoft's operating systems, resulting in an ever-growing range of Microsoft-compatible software applications, ensuring that future users would continue to gravitate towards Microsoft's operating systems in order to run those applications. A competitor could conceivably develop a superior operating system, but in the absence of a wide range of software developed for that platform, its challenge would not succeed. Purveyors of a new operating system would not only need to convince developers and consumers of the superiority of their software – they would also need to convince them that other developers and consumers would move en masse to the new standard, a coordinated shift that would be highly unlikely in the presence of an established standard.[24]

Furthermore, the fact that Microsoft was a player both in the market for operating system platforms and in the market for applications dependent on those platforms created further opportunities for anticompetitive behaviour. Technologically, Microsoft could rig its operating system in such a way as to ensure that its own applications were more accessible or functioned more smoothly than those of its rivals. Financially, Microsoft could pressurize vendors of new computer systems, which generally came bundled with a pre-installed operating system, to pre-install its Office suite of applications too, whether by offering bulk licensing discounts or even insisting upon joint sales.

Microsoft's business practices had already been scrutinized by competition authorities for a number of years when the so-called "browser wars" of the mid-1990s triggered the US government's most far-reaching legal action yet against the Seattle-based software giant. The seeds of the browser wars were sown by the launch of Netscape Navigator in 1994, which quickly rose to dominate the fledgling market in web browsing.[25] Its user-friendly interface was widely recognized as a key factor contributing to the popularization of the World Wide Web in the mid-1990s, and its business model (free to use for non-commercial purposes, earning revenue through commercial licensing agreements) ensured that a growing number of website developers created pages best viewed in Netscape. In other words, Netscape's initial success created a network effect, whereby increasing numbers of users encouraged web developers to create an increasing number of Netscape-optimized pages, and an increasing volume of Netscape-optimized content encouraged more and more users to adopt the platform.

Yet the competitive threat that Netscape posed to Microsoft reached well beyond the fast-growing browser market. Netscape's success threatened Microsoft's core source of competitive advantage, namely its near-monopoly of PC operating systems. As new protocols and standards were devised for the online world, webpages increasingly began to host not just text and images but applications too: applications that could be run on someone's home computer through their browser, programmed and optimized for that browser's feature set. The browser would act as "middleware": usurping the place of the operating system as the platform through which users accessed applications, and for which developers developed those applications, thereby enabling the browser to enjoy the network effects previously monopolized by Microsoft's operating systems. Indeed, a browser such as Netscape could be designed to run on a range of different operating systems, effectively reducing the operating system to an application in its own right, a commodity to be chosen on the basis of its individual costs and benefits, rather than on the basis of the universe of content to which it would provide access. Netscape's threat to Microsoft was existential.

Microsoft's response was correspondingly aggressive. In May 1995, Bill Gates sent a memo to Microsoft executives that described Netscape as a "new competitor 'born' on the Internet", one that was "pursuing a multi-platform strategy ... to commoditize the underlying operating system" and establish itself as the "key" interface with the underlying hardware for future software developers.[26] In response to this challenge, Microsoft first attempted to persuade Netscape to modify its strategy, to limit the functionality of its Windows-based browsers such that they acted only as an interface to the underlying (Microsoft-owned) operating system, rather than as an independent platform in its own right upon which developers could develop applications. When it became clear that Netscape would not cede its future market opportunities so easily, Microsoft instead concentrated its efforts on developing and promoting its own rival browser, Internet Explorer, while simultaneously seeking to prevent Netscape from gaining market share. To this end, Microsoft included Internet Explorer as part of its new Windows 95 operating system, launched in August 1995. Hardware vendors were prohibited from removing or modifying Microsoft's in-house browser as part of their licensing agreements. In subsequent updates to Windows, Microsoft sought to "bind the [operating system] shell to the Internet Explorer, so that running any other browser [was] a jolting experience".[27] Moreover, Netscape was denied access to technical information about Microsoft's new operating system until a few months before the launch date, pushing back the release of a suitably optimized edition of Netscape Navigator, enabling Internet Explorer to enjoy a spell of uncontested dominance of browsing on Windows 95 machines. Microsoft offered financial incentives to hardware vendors, internet service providers, online portals and online content producers to promote Internet Explorer, in some cases conditioning these incentives on the third party's explicit commitment *not* to promote Netscape Navigator. It even threatened to stop developing Microsoft Office products for the (then ailing) Apple Mac if Apple refused to make Internet Explorer the default browser for all of its new machines. As a result of this pressure, in 1998 Apple dropped Netscape Navigator from the factory configuration of its own Mac operating system.

Legally, the suit that the Department of Justice filed against Microsoft in the spring of 1998 turned on whether these anticompetitive actions violated US antitrust statutes. In April 2000, the District Judge concluded that they did, and two months later he ordered that the software giant's operating systems and applications businesses be split into separate legal entities, capable of competing with each other and forming strategic partnerships with a wide range of rivals. Economically, however, the decisive question was whether or not Microsoft's dominance was in the interests of consumers and the wider US economy. And here, theories of knowledge-driven growth did not provide a conclusive answer.

To some, Microsoft's dominance appeared to be a clear-cut case of monopoly power, which Microsoft then deployed to stifle competition, denying consumers choice between platforms. More concerning from a knowledge economy perspective, however, was the chilling effect that the software giant's actions would have on private sector innovation more broadly. If Microsoft were allowed to use its dominance of the operating system market to favour its own internet platform, then incentives for other software companies to develop new products and platforms that might challenge Microsoft's position (and thus elicit a similarly aggressive response) would be substantially diminished. This would deter innovation, stifling the competitive dynamism characteristic of the knowledge economy, and reducing the range and quality of products on offer to consumers. As Joseph Stiglitz observed, "if the practices that [Microsoft] seem to have been engaged in are not against the law, then the issue is, perhaps the law should be changed".[28]

Other theorists of the new economy played an even more active part in the legal proceedings against Microsoft. W. Brian Arthur was hired by the Department of Justice as an expert adviser on the Microsoft case.[29] When asked about the software giant in a 1995 interview with *Wired* magazine, Arthur observed that:

> [W]hen a high-tech market is dominated by a single company, you end up with fewer new technologies, since competitors with smart new ideas have to battle against the huge advantages of increasing returns … Personally, I don't see pricing as the big issue here. The issue for me is technology. If competitors are shut out of the marketplace, they're keeping their radical innovations out of the marketplace.[30]

The Department of Justice also enlisted Paul Romer to act as an expert on remedy. In his testimony, Romer argued in favour of proposals to split the tech giant's operations into two rival companies. Like Arthur, Romer's primary concern was with the "chilling effect on innovative efforts by all people who might have developed other software technologies that Microsoft found threatening", noting that the removal of this threat "will raise the rate of innovation for the economy as a whole, [creating] a stream of benefits that will persist and grow far into the future".[31]

Nevertheless, the economics profession was far from unanimous in its condemnation of Microsoft's anticompetitive practices. Some objections to the case against Microsoft harked back to earlier ideas about the assumed efficiency of markets and the assumed inefficiency of government intervention. (One academic paper from this period was waggishly entitled "DOS Kapital", capturing the authors' view of the antitrust action as an ideologically dubious intrusion into the free market.)[32] But it was also possible to object to the US government's case against Microsoft using ideas and arguments that were native to the knowledge-based growth regime. Private sector innovation requires public protection of intellectual property, otherwise the financial incentive to innovate will diminish substantially. In a market characterized by strong network effects – that is to say, where adding additional users to the same platform increases benefits for other users of that platform – fragmentation is bad for consumers, and consumers may well find a market supplied by a single monopolist preferable to a market that is superficially competitive but in which networks and network effects are correspondingly smaller. Finally, the massive economies of scale that exist in knowledge-intensive sectors mean that businesses can become ever more efficient as they increase in size, spreading their fixed innovation costs over an ever larger number of customers. Larry Summers, although careful not to address the antitrust proceedings directly in his public statements as Treasury secretary, did state in a contemporaneous speech discussing the "knowledge-based economy" that:

> [W]hen a market is driven by a positive feedback, its efficiency will be directly related to its size. Success will breed success, because it increases efficiency and reduces costs by involving larger networks and by achieving larger production lines over which to amortize the high initial fixed cost ... comparative advantage is yesterday's economics – while today's economics is the importance of global scale.[33]

Summers' not-so-subtle implication was that, in seeking to break up large tech companies in the name of domestic competition and consumer welfare, government might prevent such businesses from achieving the scale necessary to compete internationally, denying the US economy the highly paid knowledge jobs, corporate profits and tax revenues that would otherwise follow.

Ultimately, it was this comparatively laissez-faire approach to regulating the knowledge economy that prevailed in the Microsoft case, and in subsequent US regulation of the tech sector. In June 2001, the appeals court partially overturned the earlier judgement, vacating the lower court's proposed remedies and sending the case back for reconsideration. By this point, however, the Republican George W. Bush had replaced Clinton in the White House, running on a platform that promised a less interventionist approach to regulating competition in the tech sector. On 6 September 2001, following the appeals court ruling, the Department of Justice announced that the new administration no longer sought to break up Microsoft and would pursue a more modest penalty instead.[34] Two months later, a settlement was reached. Microsoft agreed to grant software developers better access to its operating system protocols and hardware vendors more flexibility in their configuration of new Windows-carrying PCs: a far less dramatic outcome than the previously proposed break-up. In short, Microsoft had won, and a precedent for light-touch regulation of competition in the tech sector had been set. Nevertheless, it is worth noting that this conclusion was justified in terms of the benefits of scale in the tech sector rather than in terms of competitive dynamism. The Microsoft case revealed ambiguities in the policy logic of knowledge-driven growth. These ambiguities could have been, and almost were, resolved differently.

Fatefully, at almost exactly the same time as the Microsoft case was reaching its final stages, other developments were unfolding that would shape competition in the tech industry for years to come. Parallel to its antitrust action against the software giant, the US government was also exploring measures to safeguard individual privacy, which would have prevented online firms from amassing vast troves of user data. The 9/11 terror attacks caused the government to alter course, in favour of a collaborative relationship with information-hungry internet companies such as Google.[35] Taken together with the Microsoft ruling, over the space of a few months the federal government laid the foundations for the emergence of data-intensive tech giants that would face minimal restrictions with regard to their market dominance, harvesting of individual data or anti-competitive practices.

International openness

For advocates of knowledge-driven growth, tax reforms, market deregulation and stronger intellectual property rights played a major role in intensifying competition, driving up the pace of innovation in the economy as a whole. But there was a further element essential to this competitiveness agenda: namely, the role played by international markets.

What openness requires: trade, investment and immigration

If heightened competition prompts higher levels of innovation, then allowing overseas businesses access to domestic markets offered another means by which governments could accelerate the rate of knowledge-based growth, exposing domestic businesses to highly efficient international competitors that domestic firms would be forced either to imitate or outpace.[36] In practical policy terms, this meant new international trade deals, both at the regional and global level, and deepening those relationships that already existed. The 1990s saw the creation of the WTO and the ratification of the North American Free Trade Agreement. In Europe, the Maastricht Treaty marked the transition from the European Economic Community to the European Union, paving the way for deeper economic and political integration, including the introduction of a European single currency as a means of reducing the frictions associated with intra-European trade.

Increased competition from overseas was not, however, the sole way in which international trade would improve prospects for knowledge-based growth. In addition to pressurizing domestic businesses to innovate, trade liberalization would also open up overseas markets to domestic businesses, offering export opportunities for domestic firms. Given that the production of knowledge (and thus the output of knowledge-intensive businesses) displays increasing returns to scale, the larger markets created by trade liberalization generate larger incentives for businesses to invest in knowledge production, driving up growth and productivity across the economy as a whole. As Larry Summers argued, "support for international trade becomes that much more important" in the era of the "knowledge-based economy ... because it enables us to take better advantage of the new economies of scale; it allows networks to be larger".[37]

In addition to openness to goods and services imported from overseas, advocates of knowledge-driven growth also stressed the importance of foreign investment. Inward investment would bring not just capital but knowledge too, educating domestic workers and firms in new technologies and business processes.[38] Finally, the international openness that developed democracies needed in order to maximize knowledge-based growth also entailed higher levels of immigration, particularly of higher-skilled individuals. Just as educating the domestic workforce would secure higher levels of investment from knowledge-intensive businesses, so would attracting what the UK Home Office minister Barbara Roche described as "the brightest and best talents" from overseas.[39]

Of course, a permissive attitude towards immigration and investment would only improve productivity where countries were actually attractive to would-be investors and immigrants. To a certain degree, openness itself could serve as a source of attraction. Knowledge-intensive businesses would be more likely to invest knowing that they could draw on talent from anywhere in the world; similarly, global talent would be attracted by the prospect of working for world-leading businesses. But other factors were important too. Social investment in a skilled workforce and a strong research base was deemed to be vital, as were dynamic markets that allowed firms to operate unencumbered by bothersome regulations. Additionally, advocates of knowledge-driven growth argued that knowledge industries were highly sensitive to taxation, as they could relocate across borders much more easily than traditional bricks-and-mortar industries. Knowledge workers, too, were deemed to be internationally footloose. Consequently, both individual and corporate tax rates had to remain low in order for countries to remain attractive.[40]

Developed democracies in the global order

Under these conditions, international openness seemed to be a recipe for higher productivity growth. Yet, such a strategy also carried certain risks for domestic workers and firms. Those unable to keep up would find their salaries and profit margins squeezed or might even find themselves out of work or out of business altogether. Although they might find other, more productive uses for their labour and capital elsewhere in the economy, they could also find themselves straightforwardly displaced, with their future earnings permanently diminished. As we saw in Chapter 2, education and training were supposed to mitigate this risk, empowering people to adapt to economic change and to seize new opportunities to engage in more knowledge-intensive (and thus better-paid) kinds of work. This approach to social inclusion was predicated on an expansion in the volume of knowledge-intensive work available, itself driven in part by an increase in the number of roles available in the global economy and the magnetic pull that social investment in skills was supposed to exert on global knowledge jobs.

Underlying this strategy stood a set of assumptions about the competitive advantages that developed democracies enjoyed relative to their less advanced peers. To early advocates of knowledge-driven growth, these competitive advantages were deemed to lie in the education and innovation systems that developed democracies already had in place (and which they would improve yet further through enhanced levels of social investment), as well as in aspects of their politics and culture that emerging economy rivals would struggle to emulate. On this account, although previous waves of trade liberalization had brought the citizens of developed democracies into competition with lower-cost workers in emerging markets, by specializing in knowledge production developed democracies could dominate the upper echelons of global value chains. Countries might lose manufacturing jobs, but these losses would be offset by new knowledge jobs.[41] In *The Work of Nations*, Reich made the bold claim that, "in principle, all of America's routine production workers could become symbolic analysts and let their old jobs drift overseas to developing nations. The worldwide demand for symbolic analysts is growing so briskly that even under these circumstances real wages would still move steadily upward."[42] Implicit in such analyses was the belief that emerging markets with low labour costs, such as China and India, could not readily reproduce the human capital and societal knowledge that developed democracies had already accumulated. High levels of literacy and numeracy required a comprehensive educational infrastructure of schools and universities, as well as a population that was sufficiently affluent to dedicate time and resources to education rather than to economic activities promising more immediate rewards.[43]

Beyond education and skills, advocates of knowledge-driven growth could point to two further advantages that developed democracies held over their lower-wage rivals. First, developed democracies had strong rule-of-law institutions, which would inspire confidence among would-be investors. In knowledge-intensive industries, where new ideas and inventions might cost billions to develop but where the knowledge they contain can be duplicated for pennies, businesses need public authorities (police, courts and so forth) capable of safe-guarding these costly investments against their rivals. Developed democracies could offer judicial systems with a reputation for political independence, cou-pled with systems of public administration and regulation with comparatively low levels of corruption.

Second, developed democracies offered knowledge-intensive industries a social and political framework in which diversity was protected and in which individuals and businesses were able to experiment with new ideas. Advocates of knowledge-driven growth often asserted that there was an affinity between liberal rights and knowledge creation. The former Downing Street adviser Charles Leadbeater claimed that creative industries thrived in tolerant, liberal, multicultural countries where people are constantly challenged by diverse oth-ers, whereas "settled, stable communities are the enemies of innovation, tal-ent, creativity, diversity and experimentation."[44] According to Joseph Stiglitz, it was difficult to imagine the emergence of the knowledge economy without far-reaching contestation and debate throughout society as a whole, including the political sphere:

> In the actual world, institutions are best structured with openness and
> competition to be robust under the assumption that knowledge and
> virtue are rather less than perfect. That robustness strategy applied to
> social and political institutions leads to the institutions of an open so-
> ciety such as a free press, transparent government, pluralism, checks
> and balances, toleration, freedom of thought, and open public debate ...
> This political openness is essential for the success of the transformation
> towards a knowledge economy.[45]

In a fashion reminiscent of nineteenth-century liberalism, progress was por-trayed as intrinsically linked to individual freedoms. It follows that developed democracies should enjoy a persistent advantage in the knowledge economy era, relative to more illiberal and autocratic competitors.[46]

Macroeconomic stability

Attracting the investment needed to grow the knowledge economy was not solely a matter of offering businesses a workforce of willing knowledge workers coupled with dynamic markets and an open society: it also required stable mac-roeconomic conditions. As economic theorists of endogenous growth had al-ready pointed out back in the 1980s, for businesses to be willing to invest in risky

R&D activities, the proceeds of which might not be realized until several years down the line (if at all), such stability was paramount. The UK's Department for Trade and Industry echoed this analysis in its White Paper *Our Competitive Future: Building the Knowledge Driven Economy*: "Government's first job is to ensure a stable macro-economic environment so business has the confidence to invest for the long term ... Economic instability over the past twenty years has damaged long term investment, growth and employment, by pushing up interest rates and making returns from investment uncertain."[47] Macroeconomic instability means that businesses will undertake less research, as less research appears economically viable, thereby denying the wider economy the productivity gains that such research activities would have produced. Mindful of this, one of the first decisions taken by the incoming New Labour government in 1997 was the transfer of monetary policy-making responsibilities to the Bank of England, thereby preventing UK governments from engaging in short-term monetary stimulus, which would require correction via higher interest rates further down the line.

In addition to monetary policy, fiscal policy too had to help secure investment-friendly macroeconomic stability. Instead of tax cuts and spending increases that inflated government debt levels, public spending had to track incoming public revenues closely. High public debts would signal to individuals and businesses that higher taxes and interest rates lay ahead, deterring them from investing. Within the EU, the 1997 Stability and Growth Pact committed member states to low debt-to-GDP ratios and limited budget deficits. The Lisbon Strategy noted that, "as a result of stability-oriented monetary policy supported by sound fiscal policies in a context of wage moderation, inflation and interest rates are low [and] public sector deficits have been reduced remarkably". These conditions provided the essential backdrop for "the transition towards a knowledge-based economy". Knowledge-driven growth and fiscal responsibility were portrayed as mutually reinforcing: "the opportunity provided by growth must be used to pursue fiscal consolidation more actively and to improve the quality and sustainability of public finances".[48]

Nevertheless, the imperative to balance budgets was in tension with the social investment agenda, as well as with the desire to lower taxes to attract internationally footloose knowledge workers and knowledge capital. Overarching agreement on the importance of knowledge-driven growth thus coexisted with quite differing views on the balance to be struck between these competing priorities. In the UK, for example, this was a source of discord between Tony Blair and his chancellor, Gordon Brown.[49] In the USA, it proved to be an even more contentious issue for the Clinton administration. Whereas Blair's election victories meant he faced minimal resistance to his economic agenda outside his own cabinet, Clinton still had to win over Congress; a task rendered even harder after the Democrats lost control of the House and Senate in the 1994 mid-term elections. Many members of Congress on both sides of the partisan divide still cleaved to the tax-cutting, state-shrinking ideal of Reagan-era economics. Furthermore, Clinton's Republican predecessors had bequeathed him a substantial stock of national debt as well as a widening deficit (testament to the success of their supposedly self-financing tax cuts and their efforts to curb public spending). Ambitious plans for public investment were put on hold, with several of Clinton's economic advisers advocating urgent action to tackle the fiscal crisis, lest market sentiment turn against the fledgling government.[50] A contractionary fiscal policy was also urged by Alan Greenspan, chair of the Federal Reserve, who threatened to raise interest rates to head off inflation unless credible (to him) plans to balance the budget were put into place.[51] Significantly though, these demands for fiscal consolidation could still be framed as integral to success in the knowledge economy era. As Larry Summers argued:

> The advent of a new economy fundamentally changes the stakes involved in the choice of our nation's fiscal policy. When there was less that was profitable to invest in, budget deficits that crowded out private investments were a smaller problem. When financial markets were less sophisticated, less able to move forward and compute the consequences of future fiscal actions for today's long-term interest rates, prospective deficits were less bad and prospective surpluses less good. In a world that is rich with investment opportunities, and where investors are all able instantly to compute the implications of changes of policies five and ten years out – the importance of running a surplus and pursuing prudent policies becomes much, much greater.[52]

Ultimately, the Clinton administration prioritized macroeconomic stability over social investment. Whether this was the best way in which to grow the US knowledge economy is of course debatable, as is the question of whether Clinton could have adopted a more radical social investment agenda given the partisan complexion of Congress. Nevertheless, the economic approach of the Clinton administration was still couched in the language of knowledge-driven growth, at least in public. In private, some of Clinton's economic advisers were more sceptical about the knowledge economy's long-term prospects, suggesting a further reason for resisting ambitious social investments. According to Alan Greenspan, Larry Summers "worried ... that the President was getting carried away with the promise of information technology – as though the United States had never gone through periods of rapid technological progress before. 'Too yippity about productivity' was how Larry once described Clinton's techno-optimism."[53] Nevertheless, many Clinton-era economic policy-makers were more positive about knowledge-driven growth, including even "lifelong libertarian Republican" Alan Greenspan, who "disagreed [with Summers] about the Internet's potential".[54] While Reich worried that fiscal contraction would kill the social investment necessary for inclusive knowledge-driven growth, and Summers worried that the benefits of knowledge-driven growth were being oversold, others such as Greenspan believed that fiscal contraction was conducive to the long-term growth of the knowledge economy.

The trade-off between social investment, macroeconomic stability and the market dynamism supposedly associated with lower tax rates would prove to be a constant feature of political debate in the knowledge economy era, often reflecting deeper ideological tensions within and between different political parties. Even before the global financial crisis and its aftermath heralded a celebration of "expansionary austerity", the governments of many developed democracies – including the USA and the UK – erred in favour of a relatively conservative approach to social investment. There were exceptions to this rule: countries such as Sweden and Finland engaged in higher levels of public investment in education and R&D than many of their peers over the 1990s and into the 2000s, albeit offset by correspondingly high taxes, reflecting a commitment to limited deficit levels in the pursuit of macroeconomic stability as per the EU's Stability and Growth Pact.[55] Such countries regularly featured at the top of European rankings showing levels of employment in high-tech industries or shares of high-tech goods and services in overall exports. They also enjoyed relatively high rates of GDP growth over this period and displayed greater resilience in the face of the global financial crisis.[56] These success stories suggest that the shortcomings of the knowledge-driven growth agenda elsewhere might be attributable in part to the prioritization of low taxes over social investment, a point we return to in Chapter 10.

Review

In its heyday, the rise of the knowledge economy appeared to offer policy-makers a way of harnessing dynamic markets to further progressive ambitions while simultaneously defending a larger state as a means of delivering a more competitive and prosperous market-based society. To its advocates, knowledge-driven growth had the potential to address a range of social ills: promising to combat poverty, equalize opportunity, empower workers and overcome exclusion on the basis of geography or socioeconomic background. Underpinning these expectations stood a number of assumptions about the mechanics of the modern economy: about the abundance of knowledge jobs available, the competitive advantages that developed democracies enjoy relative to emerging economies, the internationally footloose nature of knowledge jobs and knowledge industries, and the declining relevance of capital and place to economic success.

At the same time, however, the knowledge economy concept was far from monolithic. Despite widespread consensus about the desirability of knowl-edge-driven growth and the core components of a knowledge-driven growth strategy, this did not preclude disagreement about the details. Policy-makers argued about whether to break apart digital monopolies or whether to promote national champions, whether "the world is flat" or whether knowledge-intensive businesses tend to cluster together, whether to adopt a workfarist model of lib-eralized labour markets or whether to invest in social safety nets and workforce activation policies. Although the USA and the UK gravitated towards a vari-ant of knowledge-driven growth in which social investment was constrained by concerns about the impact of higher taxes on market dynamism and higher deficits on macroeconomic stability, this was not the only possibility available to policy-makers; indeed, even within the UK and the USA, this approach to knowledge-driven growth was contested. Chapter 4 shows how these ideas con-tinued to be debated – and applied – long after the concept of the "knowledge economy" had fallen out of fashion.

4
CONTINUITY AND CHANGE

A case could be made that the knowledge economy era ended with the bursting of the dot-com bubble in 2000, or the attack on the twin towers in 2001, or the collapse of Lehman Brothers in 2008. Certainly, each of these epochal events undermined the heady optimism of the 1990s, with its bold predictions of increasing returns to individuals, firms and countries willing to specialize in the production of knowledge. Routine elections, too, brought changes in the political guard: over time, the centre-left parties and politicians who bestrode the political scene in Europe and North America at the end of the twentieth century gave way to rivals on the right.

This chapter will show how, despite all this flux, the economic strategies pursued by developed democracies remained remarkably stable. Although they seldom referred to "the knowledge economy", politicians and policy-makers of diverse partisan loyalties continued to espouse a vision of knowledge-driven growth, advancing a policy programme based around social investment, market dynamism, macroeconomic stability and international openness, at the foundations of which lay certain assumptions about the mechanics of the modern economy. True, they modified this agenda in line with their partisan leanings, as well as in response to changing global circumstances. Nevertheless, for mainstream politicians and parties, continuity triumphed over change, albeit with diminishing expectations about what these knowledge-driven growth strategies would actually achieve.

Rightward shift

The election of George W. Bush saw marked changes in the tone and focus of US policy. The terrorist attacks of 11 September 2001, and the bellicose response that these atrocities elicited from neoconservative hawks within the Bush administration, meant that political debate during this period was dominated by foreign military adventures and domestic security measures rather than comparatively pedestrian questions of economic growth. Moreover, older market-driven accounts of growth had remained highly influential in the USA, sustained during Clinton's presidency by advocates in Congress and right-leaning think tanks, upon whose work and personnel Bush-era economic policy-makers regularly drew. Nevertheless, despite this ideological shift, the rhetoric of knowledge-driven growth persisted, and Bush's economic agenda can be seen as a species of knowledge-driven growth strategy.

Perhaps the most obvious example of this was the fact that Bush's flagship policy initiative outside the "war on terror" focused on education. The "No Child Left Behind" Act aimed at improving outcomes for schoolchildren, through mandating regular student assessments in order to monitor school standards and enabling parents to choose alternative education provision where schools persistently failed to achieve a certain level of performance. Although Bush himself rarely invoked the knowledge economy, the idea that technological change required more educated workers did feature prominently in his discussions of educational reform. As he observed in a 2004 speech, "technology is changing, and it races through our economy, but work skills don't change as quickly. And that's the challenge we face. We've got to make sure we get people trained."[1] The priority Bush attached to education can be seen in his first presidential budget. Amid an otherwise archetypal example of neoliberal policy reform – cutting growth in public spending and lowering taxes across the board (as opposed to the more targeted tax cuts on entrepreneurial activity typical of knowledge-driven growth) – Bush's *Blueprint for New Beginnings* nevertheless found the money for a large increase in federal funding for elementary and secondary education.[2] As is common with US presidential budget proposals, these ambitious plans were watered down as they passed through Congress, but the US education system remained a recipient of additional funds, alongside more conventional conservative spending priorities such as defence.

Much like Clinton, Bush saw inequality in terms of a skills gap. In a 2006 speech on the state of the economy in New York, he acknowledged that "some of our citizens worry about the fact that our dynamic economy is leaving working people behind", arguing that "the reason [for this] is clear … we have an economy that increasingly rewards education, and skills because of that education". Consequently, the solution to income inequality lay in social investment: "the key to rising in this economy is skills – and the government's job is to make sure we have an education system that delivers them". He went on to celebrate federal funding for education, training and research "to make sure that we stay on the cutting edge of change".[3]

Bush's pick to succeed Alan Greenspan as chair of the Federal Reserve, Ben Bernanke, echoed the President's logic, declaring in a 2007 speech that, "as the larger return to education and skill is likely the single greatest source of the long-term increase in inequality, policies that boost our national investment in education and training can help reduce inequality while expanding economic opportunity". At the same time, Bernanke emphasized the importance of market dynamism and international openness to success in the modern global economy: "policy approaches that would not be helpful, in my view, are those that would inhibit the dynamism and flexibility of our labor and capital markets or erect barriers to international trade and investment".[4] This is not to argue that Bush-era economic and educational policy was identical to that of Clinton's Democrats: faced with the budget surplus that Bush enjoyed in his first year in office, as opposed to the deficit that Clinton inherited from his Republican predecessors, the Democrats might well have prioritized higher levels of social investment over lower taxes. Nevertheless, the continuities in rhetoric and analysis are striking.

Continuity also prevailed over change in Europe. By 2005, centre-right leaders had replaced their centre-left counterparts in several of the countries that had originally signed up to the Lisbon Strategy; the ranks of the European Council had also been swollen by the accession of ten new member states in 2004. Yet in 2005, with the centre-right in power in 14 out of the 25 EU member states, the European Council nevertheless agreed to a relaunch of the Lisbon Strategy, reaffirming the importance of knowledge-driven growth. Although what became known as "Lisbon II" represented a subtle re-ranking of the original strategy's priorities – emphasizing growth and employment over social cohesion, reflecting the EU's rightward political reorientation as well as policy-makers' understanding of the evolving global context – it simultaneously reaffirmed the logic and the assumptions of the knowledge economy era. Productivity remained the overarching goal, driven by a combination of liberalization and supply-side social investments in areas such as research, education and infrastructure, within a framework of macroeconomic prudence. The European Council argued that government resources must be redeployed "in favour of support for certain horizontal objectives such as research and innovation and the optimization of human capital", while still insisting that "sound macroeconomic conditions are essential to underpin the efforts in favour of growth and employment".[5]

Admittedly, around the margins, there was a degree of debate about some of the mechanisms driving knowledge-based growth. For example, a 2004 report published by the European Commission's High Level Group on the Lisbon Strategy (commonly referred to as "the Kok report", after the group's chair, the former Dutch Prime Minister Wim Kok) queried the earlier neglect of "the traditional industrial strengths of the European economy". In contrast to the notion that countries could specialise entirely in the weightless work of knowledge production, it stressed the interdependence of manufacturing and innovation: "industrial growth and productivity since industrialisation have always been underpinned by advances in technologies ... [and conversely] a vigorous knowledge economy necessarily needs a strong high-tech manufacturing sector making high-tech goods at the frontier of science and technology".[6]

European policy-makers were also reassessing the competitive challenge posed by emerging markets. Whereas the knowledge economy discourse of the 1990s tended to view lower-wage countries such as China and India as a threat to low-value-added industries and lower-skilled workers in developed democracies, by the mid-2000s there was a growing awareness that they might vie for a share of higher-skilled work too. As the Kok report argued:

> China, industrialising with a large and growing stock of foreign direct investment together with its own scientific base, has begun to compete not only in low but also in high value-added goods ... India's challenge is no less real – notably in the service sector where it is the single biggest beneficiary of the "offshoring" or "outsourcing" of service sector functions with an enormous pool of educated, cheap, English-speaking workers.[7]

Nevertheless, the appropriate response to these challenges was to double down on knowledge-driven growth: "Europe has to develop its own area of specialisms, excellence and comparative advantage which inevitably must lie in a commitment to the knowledge economy in its widest sense".[8] Thomas Friedman made an almost identical point in his international bestseller *The World Is Flat*, published at around the same time as Lisbon II. While noting that the likes of China and India were already making inroads into the knowledge economy, Friedman argued that there would still be plenty of knowledge jobs to go round: "the bigger the market, the more new specialties and niches it will create ... *there is no limit to the number of idea-generated jobs in the world*".[9]

Financial crisis

In the EU and the USA, knowledge-driven growth strategies bridged party-political divides and survived changes in government, indicating a paradigm that was firmly embedded within policy-making circles and which enjoyed widespread acceptance within the broader public sphere. These strategies would also survive the onset of the global financial crisis. At least initially, policy-makers tended to treat the credit crunch that began in 2007 and reached its most acute stage in September 2008 as a shock originating in the financial sector. In their eyes, it reflected problems with regulatory oversight and business practices on "Wall Street" rather than any problem with how the economy worked on "Main

Street". Consequently, it required a rethink of the policy framework governing the financial services sector but did not necessitate a wider reappraisal of the mainstream economic agenda. To quote President Obama's inaugural address, delivered in the depths of the crisis: "Our workers are no less productive than when this crisis began. Our minds are no less inventive, our goods and services no less needed than they were last week, or last month, or last year. Our capacity remains undiminished."[10]

The fact that knowledge-based growth was not widely perceived to be implicated in the crisis meant that it was easy for policy-makers to see it instead as a *solution* to the economic slump. As Peter Mandelson – recalled to government in October 2008 by the new Prime Minister Gordon Brown – wrote in his autobiography, "competitiveness, innovation, the 'knowledge economy' – all these had been cast into starker relief by the economic crisis, and mattered even more now than when I had promoted them at the DTI [Department of Trade and Industry] a decade earlier. If ever there was a time for government to do all it could to encourage a diversified economy, making our GDP less reliant on the financial services, this was it."[11] Mandelson's remark is somewhat misleading: it portrayed knowledge-intensive industries as an alternative to financial services, whereas previously financial services had been viewed as an integral part of the UK's knowledge economy. For example, according to the Treasury's *Science and Innovation Framework 2004–2014*, the category of "high-growth, knowledge-driven sectors" included "careers in science *as well as financial services and consultancy*".[12] Leaving that subtle rebranding exercise aside, Mandelson seemed to be calling for a more interventionist approach to knowledge-driven growth than Labour had pursued under Blair, although the interventions in question still primarily involved social investment in education, infrastructure and research. As such, it marked a doubling down on the supply-side agenda of the preceding decade, a quantitative rather than a qualitative shift:

> Government would have to help in those areas where businesses and technologies would not, or could not, take the lead because market signals or incentives were not strong enough: areas like … high-calibre research; the commercialisation of inventions and innovations; training and skills programmes to create a world-class workforce; and infrastructure improvements to underpin a competitive economy.[13]

On the other side of the Atlantic, Barack Obama was another longstanding devotee of knowledge-driven growth. Even before the financial crisis hit, in an address to the newly created Hamilton Project in Washington, DC in 2006, he argued that: "One thing that we all know is that when you invest in people, people will prosper. When you invest in education and healthcare and benefits for working Americans, it pays dividends throughout every level of our economy."[14] Heaping praise on his audience, many of whom were heavily involved in the Clinton administration, Obama argued that "the economic statistics of the nineties ... speak for themselves – income growth across the board, 22 million new jobs, the lowest poverty rate in three decades, the lowest unemployment in years". To the extent that he disagreed with the public policy agenda that Clinton had pursued, the disagreement was one of emphasis rather than analysis. Querying how we "deal with the losers in a globalized economy", Obama observed that "there has been a tendency in the past for us to say, well, look, we have got to grow the pie, and we will retrain those who need retraining. But, in fact, we have never taken that [retraining] side of the equation as seriously as we need to take it."[15] In essence, Obama was claiming that Clinton's agenda had foundered owing to insufficient levels of social investment rather than any more fundamental flaw. This view was reflected in his choice of economic policy team, which included prominent figures from the Clinton era such as Larry Summers.

Obama and his administration would invoke the knowledge economy repeatedly once in office too: in the context of USA–Mexico relations,[16] improving access to publicly funded research and data[17] and intellectual property protections for US-based businesses.[18] However, educational reform and investment formed the centrepiece of Obama's knowledge economy agenda, as it had for Clinton before him. As with many progressive advocates of knowledge-driven growth, Obama believed that better education would improve US productivity, output and living standards. At the same time, it would enhance social mobility, enable marginalized demographics to participate fully in society and cut the waste of welfare dependency:

> [W]e know that the success of every American will be tied more closely than ever before to the level of education that they achieve. The jobs will go to people with the knowledge and skills to do them – it's that simple. In this kind of knowledge economy, giving up on your education and dropping out of school means not only giving up on your future, but it's also giving up on your family's future and giving up on your country's future ... high school dropouts are more likely to be teen parents, more likely to commit crime, more likely to rely on public assistance, more likely to lead shattered lives. What's more, they cost our economy hundreds of billions of dollars over the course of a lifetime in lower wages and higher public expenses.[19]

In concrete policy terms, this implied higher levels of funding for schools and universities as well as reforms to ensure that that money was well-spent, increasing government intervention in failing schools. However, like Clinton before him, Obama's ambitions were hamstrung by Congressional opposition. New educational spending constituted a relatively small proportion of Obama's 2009 stimulus package, and from 2011 onwards the Republican-controlled House of Representatives, influenced both by anti-government ideology and partisan calculation, resisted new spending initiatives originating from the other end of Pennsylvania Avenue. Given the obduracy of the opposition, it is perhaps unsurprising that Obama's rhetoric increasingly focused on what the US government should be doing rather than what it was doing; rhetoric that was still framed in terms of "flat-world" thinking about the knowledge economy:

We live in a 21st century global economy. And in a global economy, jobs can go anywhere. Companies, they're looking for the best-educated people, wherever they live, and they'll reward them with good jobs and good pay. And if you don't have a well-educated workforce, you're going to be left behind. If you don't have a good education, then it is going to be hard for you to find a job that pays a living wage … Here's what I think we should do as a country … First of all, we've got to give every child an earlier start at success by making high-quality pre-school available to every 4-year-old in America … We should give every student access to the world's information … We need to bring down the cost of college and give more young people the chance to go to college … We need to redesign more of our high schools so that they teach young people the skills required for a high-tech economy.[20]

Within the European Union, too, the global financial crisis prompted a doubling down on policies designed to promote knowledge-driven growth rather than a reappraisal of the knowledge economy agenda itself. "Europe 2020" – the successor to the Lisbon Strategy – was officially adopted by member states in 2010. It interpreted the financial crisis as "a wake-up call, the moment where we recognise that 'business as usual' would consign us to a gradual decline, to the second rank of the new global order".[21] Nevertheless, the broken model of "business as usual" was not knowledge-based growth but rather the persistent failure to implement knowledge-based growth strategies. The crisis had not altered the diagnosis of Europe's weaknesses:

Europe's average growth rate has been structurally lower than that of our main economic partners, largely due to a productivity gap that has widened over the last decade. Much of this is due to differences in business structures combined with lower levels of investment in R&D and innovation, insufficient use of information and communications technologies, reluctance in some parts of our societies to embrace innovation, barriers to market access and a less dynamic business environment.[22]

Indeed, if anything, Europe's competitive position had worsened. In addition to lagging behind the USA and Japan in the growth of knowledge-intensive sectors of the economy, the challenge from emerging markets was becoming increasingly acute: "countries such as China or India are investing heavily in research and technology in order to move their industries up the value chain and 'leapfrog' into the global economy … [putting] pressure on some sectors of our economy to remain competitive".[23]

Perhaps unsurprisingly, believing itself to be confronted by the same pathologies as before the crisis, the European Commission proposed the same policy solutions. Europe's top priority was "smart growth: developing an economy based on knowledge and innovation".[24] And this was to be achieved by a familiar array of initiatives: increasing R&D spending; improving education systems; offering adults access to retraining and lifelong learning opportunities; completing the single market by harmonizing laws and regulations, to provide European companies with larger economies of scale; accelerating the roll-out of high-speed internet to create a Europe-wide customer base for the digital sector. Of the five key performance targets mentioned in the new Europe 2020 strategy, two ("research and innovation" and "education") reflected the ongoing prioritization of social investment, and two ("employment" and "combating poverty") were depicted as consequences of social investment rather than independent policy priorities in their own right: "better educational levels help employability and progress in increasing the employment rate helps to reduce poverty. A greater capacity for research and development as well as innovation across all sectors of the economy, combined with increased resource efficiency will improve competitiveness and foster job creation."[25]

The austerity years

Although the first responders to the global financial crisis resorted to ideas of knowledge-driven growth and social investment, it might be argued that their successors adopted a different approach altogether: austerity. Faced with the costs of bailing out the banking system, coupled with reduced tax receipts because of the ensuing economic slump, policy-makers across the developed democratic world turned to austerity measures to "fix" the public finances. In the eurozone, the governments of countries such as Greece, Ireland, Portugal and Spain faced a sovereign debt crisis in which they were unable to borrow in order to meet their existing spending commitments or refinance their debts, let alone embark on new social investment programmes. The "Troika" of the European Central Bank, the European Commission and the International Monetary Fund (IMF) demanded spending cuts and tax rises in return for emergency funding. In the UK, 2010 saw a general election campaign fought amid widespread media coverage of events in Greece, resulting in a Conservative-Liberal Democrat coalition government pledging to cut the deficit by slashing public expenditure. In the USA, the Tea Party movement propelled Republicans to take control of the House and many state-level legislatures, blocking the Obama administration's stimulus efforts in Congress and subverting them within individual states through countervailing spending cuts.[26]

At first glance, the austerity movement might be interpreted as a resurgence of the neoliberal agenda of the 1980s, a rolling back of the state in order to make space for market-driven growth. This interpretation has a great deal of merit. Although technically austerity is ambivalent between spending cuts and tax rises as a means of closing budget deficits, the reforms pursued in the wake of the global financial crisis focused primarily on reduced expenditure to achieve fiscal consolidation, slashing government funding for social programmes. The austerity agenda drew inspiration from academic economists intellectually aligned with the political right, such as Alberto Alesina, Carmen Reinhart and Kenneth Rogoff (the last of whom was an adviser to John McCain's 2008 presidential campaign). In the USA and the UK, austerity was championed by successors to Reagan and Thatcher, in the Republican and Conservative parties respectively.[27]

Yet – at least in its European manifestations – austerity politics also recognized the imperatives of knowledge-driven growth. The "Europe 2020" strategy already sought to reconcile fiscal consolidation with its broader agenda of education and innovation:

> [T]he consolidation of public finances in the context of the Stability and Growth Pact involves setting priorities and making hard choices ... [T]he composition and quality of government expenditure matters: budgetary consolidation programmes should prioritise "growth-enhancing items" such as education and skills, R&D and innovation and investment in networks, e.g. high-speed internet, energy and transport interconnections ... The revenue side of the budget also matters and particular attention should also be given to the quality of the revenue/tax system. Where taxes may have to rise, this should, where possible, be done in conjunction with making the tax systems more "growth-friendly".[28]

The European Commission was not merely paying lip service to knowledge-based growth: the conditions imposed on eurozone countries seeking bailouts tended to reflect these commitments, with tax rises focused around consumption rather than income. True, public sector pay cuts did impact upon state-funded education and research, although overall these budgets tended to be spared the brunt of the consolidation efforts.

In the UK, David Cameron's rebranding of the Conservative Party involved the wholesale adoption of the rhetoric of knowledge-based growth. Education was deemed to be vital to social inclusion. As Michael Gove, then shadow secretary of state for children, schools and families, claimed in 2009:

> The central mission of the next Conservative Government is the alleviation of poverty and the extension of opportunity. And nowhere is action required more than in our schools. Schools should be engines of social mobility. They should enable children to overcome disadvantage and deprivation so they can fulfil their innate talents and take control of their own destiny.[29]

A 2007 Conservative Party policy paper echoed the now-familiar diagnosis of global competition in knowledge-intensive industries, with education and skills viewed as the key determinants of success for individuals and countries alike:

> [G]lobal change is placing an ever higher premium on intellectual capital ... For those nations equipped to adapt globalisation also promises the chance to extend wealth and opportunity to more citizens. Countries, and individuals, who are highly-skilled will benefit hugely as more and more opportunities open up for their talents to be used. But those nations and individuals without high levels of skills will lose out, as jobs and opportunities increasingly move elsewhere.[30]

Of course, invocations of knowledge-driven growth did not necessarily translate into policy action. Across the USA and Europe, rolling back the state in the name of fiscal consolidation squeezed out social investment in the wake of the global financial crisis, even though austerity was self-imposed, in the case of countries such as the UK and the USA, with their own sovereign currencies, which were able to borrow or create money at minimal cost in terms of interest rates or inflation; or collectively self-imposed, in the case of members of the European single currency. It might plausibly be argued that champions of austerity were simply adopting the language of knowledge-driven growth for propagandistic purposes, disguising a neoliberal policy agenda in progressive clothing. Even were this the case, however, it would still testify to the enduring appeal of knowledge-driven growth rhetoric among policy elites and the general public.

Moreover, as we have seen, a fiscally conservative approach to knowledge-driven growth was foreshadowed in the debates of the pre-crisis era. From its inception, the knowledge-driven growth agenda was accompanied by a macroeconomic analysis that implied that too much borrowing would crowd out private sector expenditure on innovation; that higher taxes would encourage knowledge-intensive businesses to invest elsewhere; and that increased inflation (and the interest rate rises needed to combat it) would deter firms from embarking upon R&D projects that only yield dividends over the medium to long term. Austerity could be framed in terms of the knowledge economy's need for macroeconomic stability, even though in actual fact austerity tended to stifle growth, in turn requiring higher levels of borrowing and higher taxes than would have otherwise been the case, thereby undermining the very conditions deemed conducive to knowledge-driven growth.[31]

As the limitations of austerity became increasingly apparent over the 2010s, mainstream parties of the centre-left and centre-right sought to distance themselves from it, promising higher levels of social investment. Under Ed Miliband, the Labour Party fought the 2015 general election on a manifesto that declared "the economy is not creating the productive, high-skilled and well-paid jobs that we need to raise living standards". It outlined an economic strategy based around investing in "world class infrastructure" (including "affordable, high speed broadband"), creating "knowledge clusters" of private enterprise based around universities and providing training rather than benefits for "young people who do not have the skills they need".[32] Hillary Clinton's 2016 presidential election campaign frequently referenced the knowledge-intensive advanced manufacturing sector, which it portrayed as "responsible for high-paying, high-skilled jobs, and [as] a long-term driver of innovation". Clinton's campaign noted, in an echo of endogenous growth theory, that these jobs "create spillover benefits throughout the economy". Although advanced manufacturing was highly internationally mobile, businesses could be enticed to move to or remain in the USA via "tax relief" targeted "to encourage investment in hard-hit areas", the promotion of "regional hubs" bringing together universities and businesses "to develop world-leading technologies", and public investments in "the skills and training of America's workforce".[33] In France, social investment and high-tech growth was key to Emmanuel Macron's centrist agenda too: his 2017 economic plan pledged a €15 billion investment in skills, "to give everyone the opportunity to retrain for the jobs of the future and fast-growing industries".[34] While seeking to distance themselves from the squeeze on social investment associated with austerity, all these programmes still reaffirmed the importance of macroeconomic stability, emphasizing how new investments would be financed through modest tax rises, modest borrowing and/or cuts to spending in other areas; always with an eye on remaining "attractive" to knowledge-intensive industries that were assumed to be internationally mobile and wary of committing to countries with too high tax rates or deficits.

To summarize, even after the heyday of the knowledge economy concept in the late 1990s and early 2000s, knowledge-driven growth continued to be seen by policy-makers as a source of well-paid jobs, rapid productivity gains and social inclusion, provided governments made the necessary social investments and pursued the necessary reforms. To be sure, policy elites' views changed in light of changing circumstances. Growth expectations diminished following the bursting of the dot-com bubble and the global financial crisis, and over time policy-makers became increasingly anxious about the competitive challenges posed by emerging economies such as India and China. Nevertheless, the economic strategies that politicians of diverse partisan loyalties have championed in diverse developed democracies from the 1990s onwards share many features in common. These strategies posit that economic growth will increasingly depend on the growth of knowledge-intensive industries. They insist that knowledge-intensive firms are highly mobile, and that countries must invest in education in order to attract and retain knowledge-intensive businesses, while also offering them a stable macroeconomic environment and flexible labour markets. And they contend that progressive aspirations for social inclusion can best be achieved by broadening access to education and training, enabling the socially excluded to acquire skills that will allow them to access well-paid work opportunities.

PART II

The knowledge economy in crisis

5
THE CRISIS OF GROWTH

"Work hard. Have fun. Make history." Amazon's motto is emblazoned across its Seattle offices, alongside other motivational slogans such as "build yourself a great story" and "try something new". Much like the business it houses, Amazon's campus has expanded over time in new directions and into new spheres, including three interlocking geodesic domes that run along Lenora Street between 6th and 7th Avenues. Before the pandemic hit, Amazon's Seattle premises were home to over 50,000 staff, many of them well-paid knowledge workers who benefited not only from generous salaries and stock options but also from fussball tables, craft classes, a rooftop dog park and film previews. Amazon employees work in cutting-edge fields such as cloud computing, artificial intelligence, language processing and the design of new consumer electronics, while Amazon also invests heavily in the creation and distribution of digital content such as TV dramas and documentaries. Amazon's success story seems to epitomize the rise of the knowledge economy, as predicted by earlier advocates of knowledge-driven growth.

Yet there are other ways in which Amazon epitomizes the rise of the knowledge economy, reflecting facets of knowledge-driven growth that this previous generation of techno-optimists either failed to predict or sought to downplay. Amazon, like the knowledge economy era itself, does not only generate high-skill, high-pay employment but also an abundance of less skill-intensive, lower-paid work in warehouses and on the streets. Modern managerial techniques are not exclusively a matter of break-out rooms and brainstorming spaces, craft classes and dog parks; lower down the income distribution, these techniques might involve optimizing the number of orders processed, the miles of warehouse corridors covered or the directions followed by delivery drivers, while minimizing time lost to sick leave and comfort breaks.[1]

Amazon also epitomizes the ambiguous impacts of the rise of the knowledge economy on labour markets in advanced capitalist democracies. Emerging economies such as India and China now compete with developed democracies for knowledge work: Amazon's single largest office building in the world opened in

Hyderabad in 2019, with its occupants working in fields such as machine learning and new payment technologies. Moreover, in addition to creating new jobs – for computer programmers, network architects, delivery drivers and warehousing staff – Amazon also seeks to automate these tasks, replacing workers with machines. These advances are most obvious in routine low-skilled work, through the increasing use of robots within Amazon's warehouses, and through Amazon's experiments with drones and remote-controlled delivery vehicles. But Amazon has also played a pivotal role in automating higher-skilled work, reducing demand for highly skilled network architects and web developers through the user-friendly cloud-computing services it offers to businesses.

Finally, Amazon epitomizes the competitive dynamics of the knowledge economy era. Its early successes have allowed it to dominate the world of e-commerce. Would-be challengers do not simply need to replicate its extreme economies of scale but also recreate the networks of customers and vendors Amazon has cultivated, each attracted by the other, as well as the vast troves of consumer data that its operations continue to generate on a day-to-day basis. Moreover, in addition to creating a rival e-commerce and logistics service, these would-be competitors would also need to reckon with the interlocking ecosystem of other services offered by Amazon, such as consumer electronics and digital content subscriptions. Competing with Amazon requires deep pockets, to finance both the development of a rival platform and the accumulation of users, much as Amazon's emergence has itself proved to be highly capital-intensive.

In Part I, we saw how a previous generation of policy-makers conceptualized the rise of the knowledge economy and how they sought to reconfigure public policy in light of this understanding. We also saw how this policy agenda has proved highly resilient, continuing to inform mainstream political and economic thinking in developed democracies through to the present day. Over the next four chapters, we will explore the ways in which the realities of growth over the last three decades have called into question these economic strategies, beginning with a survey of the economic performance of developed democracies over the last 30 years and a reassessment of the competitive dynamism of the knowledge economy.

Secular stagnation

Had history ended in 2007, the preceding 15 years could have been read as a vindication of the knowledge-based growth regime. Academics and central bankers hailed the long period of low interest rates and steady economic growth as "the Great Moderation", an era in which the tools and techniques of economic management were finally able to tame the business cycle.[2] The burst of productivity growth that began first in the USA in the mid-1990s, before spreading to other developed democracies, seemed to testify to the emergence of a "new economy" in which growth was not limited by conventional constraints such as the scarcity of capital or labour. This new economy proved remarkably robust, even when confronted by economic shocks such as the Asian financial crisis of the late 1990s or the bursting of the dot-com bubble in the early 2000s. Policy-makers such as the UK Chancellor Gordon Brown could claim with some plausibility to have abolished the economically and socially damaging pattern of boom and bust that had typified the preceding decades.[3] The knowledge-based growth regime, with its emphasis on sound macroeconomic management and social investment, seemed intellectually irrefutable and politically unassailable.

Needless to say, the global financial crisis undermined the credibility of these claims in dramatic fashion. Following the crisis, economic performance in almost all developed democracies has been woeful by almost any recent historical benchmark. Table 5.1 shows average GDP per capita growth per year for a range of developed democracies from 1961 onwards, divided into four distinct epochs: the era of the mixed economy (ending with the collapse of the Bretton Woods agreement on currency flows that underpinned international commerce during the postwar reconstruction); the era of market liberalization (ending with the start of Clinton's presidency in 1993); the era of the early knowledge economy (ending with the financial crisis); and the inter-crisis era (culminating in the Covid-19 pandemic). Obviously, any such division is somewhat arbitrary, and different divisions would lead to somewhat different results. What is undeniable, however, is that growth in the inter-crisis era has been markedly lower than in any of the preceding periods; a product of both the scale of the decline caused by the financial crash and the weakness of the subsequent recovery.

Table 5.1 Average annual growth rates of GDP per capita, selected countries

	UK	USA	Germany	France	Sweden
Mixed economy (1961–73)	2.97	3.01		4.59	3.53
Market liberalization (1974–92)	1.77	1.84	2.37	1.97	1.36
Early knowledge economy (1993–2007)	2.59	2.15	1.32	1.55	2.63
Inter-crisis era (2008–19)	0.43	0.97	1.14	0.52	0.69
Combined knowledge economy era (1993–2019)	1.63	1.62	1.24	1.09	1.77

Source: World Bank, Indicator: NY.GDP.PCAP.KD.ZG; data for Germany from 1971.

But not only did the global financial crisis mark a turning point in the fortunes of knowledge-driven growth; it also called into question the nature of the prosperity that preceded it. To many commentators, the global financial crisis recast the growth of the previous 15 years as a mirage. Viewed from 2007, the economies of developed democracies had generally performed well over the era of knowledge-driven growth (the figure for Germany was heavily affected by the costs of reunification). But when we take a long-term average of growth rates for the knowledge economy era inclusive of the inter-crisis years, we see that average economic performance for this period considered as a whole is generally below the average level recorded for previous growth regimes. (The only exception out of the five countries selected is Sweden, which enjoyed exceptionally high rates of growth during the heyday of the knowledge economy as well as below-average rates of growth during the era of market liberalization, including a major financial crisis at the start of the 1990s.)

Economists have described this pattern as indicative of "secular stagnation". The term is most prominently associated with Larry Summers, who we encountered earlier as a senior economic adviser to both President Clinton and President Obama. Over a string of papers and talks, Summers has argued that not only is the post-crisis growth record "disturbing" but also that the growth enjoyed in the decade leading up to the crisis was unsustainable, premised on increasing household indebtedness rather than higher productivity:

> It is now clear that the increase in house prices ... (that can retrospectively be convincingly labelled a bubble) was associated with an unsustainable upward movement in the share of GDP devoted to residential investment ... And this made possible a substantial increase in the debt-to-income ratio for households ... I would suggest to you that the record of industrial countries [since the late 1990s] is profoundly discouraging as to the prospect of maintaining substantial growth with financial stability.[4]

Admittedly, Summers had long been a sceptic when it came to knowledge-driven growth, arguing that Clinton was "too yippity about productivity", as we saw in Chapter 3. But he is far from alone in critically reappraising the knowledge economy era. Many commentators have noted that the boom years of the 1990s and early 2000s were predicated on easy access to cheap credit. When lenders began to doubt the collateral on which much of this credit growth was based – in particular, the value of US housing – this spending no longer appeared sustainable, and nor did the business profits and individual income to which it had given rise. The political economist Colin Crouch has aptly described this pattern of economic stimulus through household debt as "privatised Keynesianism", an economic model wherein individuals rather than the state borrow money to compensate for shortfalls in demand, thereby keeping output and employment levels high.[5] Even the export-oriented economic models of countries such as Germany ultimately depended on demand from elsewhere, demand that was often fuelled by credit-creating financial markets rather than broad-based productivity growth in the importing countries.[6]

How, then, can we explain the comparatively poor growth rate of the knowledge economy years, once we factor in the housing bubble and the ensuing decade of crises? To answer this question, it is worth reminding ourselves why the knowledge economy was supposed to achieve a higher rate of growth in the first place. Competition was integral to this account: the intensity of competition was supposed to encourage ever greater levels of investment in socially valuable innovation, which would push up the productivity and profits of innovative companies while simultaneously generating new ideas and knowledge that would "spill over" into the wider economy, driving up growth. This competitive dynamism was in turn a product of the low barriers to entry typical of knowledge-intensive sectors of the economy – sectors in which "everyone with an education can have a go", in which small companies can access global markets, in which all you need is "an idea, a cheap computer and a telephone" – as well as by the scale of the rewards on offer to successful entrepreneurs. However, if this competitive dynamism were *not* to emerge, if barriers to entry were higher than advocates of knowledge-driven growth anticipated, then the link between the rise of the knowledge economy and rapid economic growth would be weakened.

Competition and the knowledge economy

The archetypal business of the knowledge economy era was a software company: a company whose employees produced nothing other than knowledge, in the form of instructions for computers to follow, which once developed could be reproduced and distributed again and again at near-zero marginal cost. Barriers to entry in the digital sector so conceived are extremely low. No production line or distribution network is needed: only imagination, skill and a personal computer. Aside from the admittedly substantial investment in human capital needed to train software developers, the capital costs of the software industry appear minimal.

In the digital sector, many of these assumptions appear to hold true today. Admittedly, the modern software industry is much more sophisticated than its 1990s counterpart, and its outputs are correspondingly more complex. As a result, development teams typically number in the hundreds if not thousands for major new releases by established software studios. Nevertheless, there is also a steady stream of games and applications developed by individuals operating on their own; and (in theory at least) entrepreneurs requiring more resources should be able to find financial backing for their endeavours from some source or other. At this level, dynamic competition appears to be the norm.

Yet, as the internet has become increasingly central to the new digital economy, traditional software development – in which companies use the knowledge work of their employees to produce clearly defined standalone products, which they then sell to paying customers – accounts for a decreasing proportion of overall value creation in the rapidly expanding digital sector. While the archetypal businesses of the digital sector today still produce code – such as Facebook's app or Google's search algorithm – their operating model is markedly different to that of a 1990s software company. In many instances, the software that these tech companies produce is provided for free, or at a heavily discounted price, with profits flowing from the sale of a panoply of other services to consumers and businesses: premium versions of free applications, cloud hosting and processing facilities, marketing insights, advertising space, payment processing and so forth. And often, what makes this code valuable to paying and non-paying customers alike are the data that underpin it, data that are curated by these platforms and derived primarily from users themselves (whether in the form of consciously created content, such as Facebook posts, or in the form of records of past behaviour, used in the optimization of recommendation-producing algorithms).

On the face of it, this might appear to be evidence of market dynamism in action. Competition forces businesses to reduce their prices ever lower, ultimately leading to a situation in which people receive digital services in exchange for personal data rather than cash payment. Only highly efficient businesses, delivering products that will appeal to a wide range of consumers, are likely to succeed in such an environment. Although this might discourage potential rivals from even attempting to enter areas dominated by successful incumbents (so markets may appear non-competitive), the dominance of these incumbents will only last as long as they remain efficient and their products remain attractive. On this account, dynamism is secured by the *threat* of competition: such businesses will probably spend significant amounts on innovation year after year in order to keep their operations lean and their user numbers high.

There is some merit to this account, superficially at least. Today's leading tech companies do indeed spend significant amounts on R&D. The world's five largest tech companies, as measured by market capitalization, are also among the world's biggest investors in research. In 2018, Amazon, Alphabet, Microsoft and Apple all ranked in the top ten companies globally by R&D expenditure, with Facebook slightly further down in fourteenth place.[7]

But does this reflect competitive threats to the core operations of these firms or a desire to expand into new sectors? On closer examination of the business model of today's tech giants, there are good reasons to doubt the level of competition they face in their primary markets. Arguably the main reason for this is the network effects that many of these businesses enjoy. As mentioned in Part I, network effects arise when adoption of a particular product, standard or platform by additional users makes the product, standard or platform more valuable to other users. A classic example of such effects is the telephone network, whereby each additional household that chooses to connect to the network makes that network a more useful means of communication for every existing telephone owner, as they can all now contact a larger proportion of the population. Network effects (or "positive network externalities") are clearly evident in social media and content-sharing platforms such as Facebook, Instagram and YouTube, where people want to share (or have the option of sharing) content with as many friends and acquaintances as possible while also having the ability to consume shared content from as wide a social circle as possible too. Similarly, as a consumer seeking a taxi ride or short-term rental accommodation, I will look first at the platform with the most taxi drivers and accommodation suppliers registered with it; as a taxi driver or accommodation supplier, I will gravitate towards the platform that attracts the most consumers. These platforms are known as "two-sided markets" in the economics literature.[8]

Network effects also arise in more subtle ways in other parts of the digital economy. While at first glance, browsing for content via Google Search, movies from Netflix or physical goods from Amazon's own product listings (as opposed to the two-sided market of Amazon Marketplace) might not seem to involve a network effect, in actuality they do. Every time a particular search query is entered, and a particular result selected (be that result a webpage, a movie or a product), the platform in question gathers insight into how relevant these options were to that user, allowing them to refine their recommendations for future users (whether all future users, or more specifically future users with a similar behavioural profile).[9] As platforms accumulate these data from an ever larger user base, they should become better and better at making relevant recommendations, which should make them more and more attractive to their users: the hallmark of a network effect.[10] True, these "second-order" network effects operate somewhat differently to more conventional network effects. With social networks and online marketplaces, additional users create additional value for existing users by enlarging the *quantity* of possible connections between users (including connections to the content, services and/or products that users might supply to each other). By contrast, network effects such as those seen in "recommender" algorithms create additional value by improving the *quality* of the match between an individual user and the content, services and/or products that she may wish to consume (which may or may not be supplied by other users).[11] Nevertheless, the point remains that network effects provide incumbents in many digital market sectors with advantages that go beyond economies of scale alone.

This represents a profound shift from the value creation model assumed by many earlier advocates of knowledge-driven growth, one that has serious implications for the level, or even the possibility, of competition within a particular market. Whereas skilled computer programmers were central to the archetypal business of the old knowledge economy, for present-day platforms such as Facebook, Google, eBay and Uber, it is users themselves who are vital to value creation: whether by providing content directly to other users, by generating data and behavioural insights that digital platforms can market to other businesses, by consuming advertising content or by buying and selling goods and services on which the platform earns commission. (Commentators remarking on this shift in the mid-2000s described it as the advent of "Web 2.0", typified by mass online participation, often mediated through user-friendly platforms that have made it easier for the less technically minded masses to participate.)[12]

Consequently, lack of users, and the costs of cultivating a user base large enough to make such a business model viable, act as substantial barriers to entry in the new digital economy, in addition to more familiar concerns about ever-expanding economies of scale. Far from the capital-light business models envisaged by knowledge economy enthusiasts in the 1990s, today's most prominent internet start-ups burn through millions upon millions of dollars of venture capital investment in an attempt to grow their user base, till they achieve sufficient scale to dominate their chosen segment of the digital economy.[13] Needless to say, many fail in the attempt, and some will achieve scale only to find that the network effect they cultivated is not as powerful a differentiating factor as they had hoped. Nevertheless, without access to capital, such efforts are almost always doomed from the get-go. This means that competition is less intense in the digital sector than once appeared likely, as the capital necessary to build networks of sufficient scale to compete is a scarce resource, acting as a filter limiting the numbers of would-be competitors.

Markets characterized by strong network effects display a tendency towards concentration. As network effects benefit users, users will gravitate towards platforms that already have an established user base, and which are likely to continue recruiting them in future. Consequently, the literature on markets characterized by strong network effects emphasizes the importance of early-mover advantage, as well as the tendency of such markets to "tip" decisively in favour of one competitor at a certain point in their life cycle.[14] Once this tipping point has been reached, it is extremely difficult to dislodge an incumbent. Users must be encouraged to switch from the old platform, which means the new platform cannot just be technically superior or cheaper or more user-friendly: it must promise people access to the same or better networks too, a hard sell so long as the incumbent is providing a minimally satisfactory service. (Incumbents sometimes use other tactics to maintain their dominance too: for instance, contracts that prohibit any vendor wishing to use their platform from advertising goods and services on rival platforms at lower prices, or short-term changes in pricing and service levels to stifle any potential challenger.)[15] Moreover, it is often *efficient* for these markets to be concentrated: because users derive greater benefits the more other users subscribe to the same platform or standard, a situation where the user base is fragmented across multiple different platforms or standards is likely to be suboptimal from the perspective of users.

Market concentration has implications for the pace of innovation. Once a business has established network effects and economies of scale in a particular sector, competitive threats will recede, and the pressure to innovate will reduce. But more than that: established networks of users offer today's tech giants substantial advantages in emerging network-intensive sectors of the digital economy, allowing them to imitate and overtake new companies and products. The fact that the Android user base can be easily enlisted into any new Alphabet offering, or that the likes of Google and Facebook already possess a vast compendium of data that can be used for personalization and optimization purposes in new contexts, means that anyone considering a start-up venture that depends on creating significant network effects may be deterred from doing so.[16] In effect, the first-mover advantages that tech giants enjoy in their existing domains of operation give them an advantage *over* first-movers in adjacent sectors, potentially stifling innovation and restricting consumer choice. At the same time, the existence of these as-yet uncolonized adjacent sectors helps to explain large tech firms' ongoing appetite for high levels of R&D spending.

It is little surprise, then, that the proliferation of network effects created as the tech sector seeks to challenge, restructure and coordinate more and more areas of the economy as a whole – communication, transportation, retail, entertainment – has been accompanied by the emergence of a handful of large platform companies, offering integrated services across a wide range of domains.[17] This is not to say that the "Big Five" of Amazon, Apple, Alphabet, Microsoft and Facebook are the only businesses capable of innovating in today's digital economy. However, through their combined dominance of operating systems (both for mobile phones and computers), online search, cloud computing, digital advertising, social networking, collaborative working, instant messaging and e-commerce, these companies control much of the infrastructure on which wider social and economic activity is predicated in the digital era and benefit from correspondingly massive numbers of active users. Any innovative new business launching in the digital sector today will almost inevitably depend on the infrastructure provided by one or more of these companies; a dependence which gives these tech giants a significant head start in any sector in which they choose to compete.

Beyond digital

What about other sectors of the economy? It was already apparent in the heyday of the knowledge economy that many knowledge-intensive industries outside the IT sector required a level of capital investment that belied the notion that knowledge workers need little more than an education in order to succeed. In advanced manufacturing and life science sectors, for example, businesses require deep pockets in order to finance the costs of large-scale research teams, laboratories, prototypes, safety trials and so forth. The financial sector, too, requires substantial capital reserves on the part of new entrants.

Reflecting such barriers to entry in many high-growth knowledge industries (and in increasingly knowledge-intensive traditional industries), the rise of the knowledge economy does not appear to have heralded an era of competitive dynamism. If anything, data suggest that, over recent decades, many industries in many developed democracies have become steadily more concentrated, with a smaller number of larger incumbents capturing ever greater market shares.[18] Analyses published by both the IMF and the OECD find evidence of growing market power across many advanced economies, with leading firms better able to command higher mark-ups on their variable costs over time.[19]

Admittedly, some economists point out that market concentration is not necessarily problematic and may simply reflect the reallocation of resources and revenues to more productive firms.[20] Even so, this picture of economies dominated by a smaller number of large (if perhaps highly productive) firms seems to be a far cry from the dorm room dynamism anticipated by a previous generation of policy-makers and a return to a more familiar pattern of "big beats small". Even if the causality runs in the opposite direction, and "big has beaten small", there is no guarantee that small will be able to beat big in the future. In both the USA and Europe, the rate of business churn has been falling since before the financial crisis, reflecting a slowdown in the kind of start-up activity that was supposed to spur knowledge-driven growth.[21] This suggests that high barriers to entry in the knowledge economy era do not exist solely in sectors dominated by today's tech giants.

Correspondingly, analysis of young, high-potential start-up businesses provides evidence of a decline in entrepreneurial success. Using data from the USA, a team of economists writing in 2016 noted a reduction in the proportion of new businesses that exhibited growth rates far above average (a pattern typical of successful start-ups).[22] Prior to 2000, the distribution of growth rates was skewed towards the positive end of the distribution, driven by a significant number of high-growth outliers; by 2007 the distribution had almost normalized, and the trend continued through to 2011. This decline in "skewness" was particularly pronounced in sectors often seen as fundamental to the new economy: high-tech, knowledge-intensive industries such as software development and computer hardware manufacture. An OECD study looking at data from 18 advanced economies drew similar conclusions, noting a downward trend in start-up activity in most countries surveyed from 2001 onwards (the UK bucked this trend, at least prior to the crisis, but still saw a decline in the proportion of micro-businesses that succeeded in scaling up between 2001 and 2007).[23] Follow-up work concluded that the most productive firms in the services sector were recording profit levels consistent with market power, indicating a lack of competitive pressure.[24]

Significantly, these trends appear to pre-date the financial crisis, suggesting the declining dynamism of the knowledge economy era cannot be dismissed as merely a consequence of the crash. To be sure, the crisis (and the way in which governments responded to it) have not helped. Post-crisis, central banks dramatically reduced borrowing costs to stimulate the moribund global economy, a development which some commentators claim has slowed the pace of innovation by keeping "zombie" businesses afloat on a cushion of cheap money.[25] Had these businesses been allowed to go to the wall, so the argument goes, the capital and labour tied up in them would have been redeployed more productively, pushing up the growth rate. Nevertheless, the decline in entrepreneurial activity evident before the crisis suggests there may be a more fundamental problem with the supposed dynamism of the knowledge economy itself.

Perhaps this should not be too surprising. After all, early theorists of the new economy recognized that new technologies required deep pockets, displayed significant economies of scale and often benefited from network effects. Add to this mix the fact that customer data can be weaponized as a source of competitive advantage, benefiting businesses that have the largest customer base, and it seems reasonable to expect consolidation and concentration rather than competition as industries become increasingly knowledge-intensive.

Maybe we should not be bothered by these developments: perhaps start-up style innovative activity has merely been displaced and now takes place within dominant firms operating at the technological frontier rather than in the wider economy. After all, competition does still occur between these firms: competition between Apple and Alphabet today is no doubt preferable to the lack of competition over which Microsoft presided in the 1990s. Nevertheless, this vision of competition in the knowledge economy era is a pale imitation of the competitive dynamism that an earlier generation of policy-makers believed would drive a step-change in productivity growth. It indicates that investors and inventors alike increasingly believe that innovative activity is less likely to succeed outside today's dominant businesses. If that is the case (or even if it is only believed to be the case), it will dampen the prospects of knowledge-driven growth, assuming we accept – as Paul Romer argued during the Microsoft antitrust case – that "in many industries, new entrants are a critical source for the innovations that take technology in fundamentally new directions".[26]

Moreover, other data suggest that innovative activity concentrated within dominant firms is a poor substitute for innovative activity in the wider economy. The political economist Herman Schwartz cites the growing size of cash holdings over which large corporations preside, as well as their penchant for using these cash holdings to buy back their own shares, as evidence that today's dominant businesses are only reinvesting a limited proportion of their profits. This indicates that they are not under particularly intense pressure to innovate, which Schwartz attributes to the growing importance of intellectual property rights to their business strategies.[27] The monopolization of intellectual property rights enables these businesses to dictate terms to other firms in their supply chains (to extract "monopoly rents", in the economics jargon), depressing the profit margins of these other firms and hence depriving them of funds that they might otherwise have used for productivity-enhancing investments.[28]

Aggregate-level investment statistics also testify to a lack of competitive dynamism in the knowledge economy era. On average, total public and private spending on R&D in OECD countries increased modestly from 2.1 per cent of GDP in 2000 to 2.4 per cent of GDP in 2018. While this figure conceals some

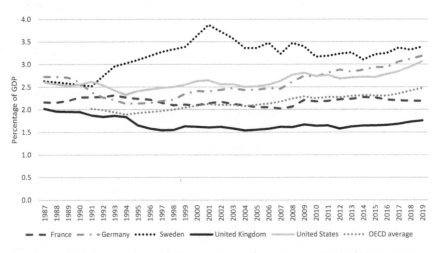

Figure 5.1 Gross domestic R&D spending as percentage of GDP, 1987–2019

Source: OECD, Indicator: GDEXPRD.

variation between countries and over time (see Figure 5.1), it is hardly indicative of a dramatic expansion in knowledge production. Those levels of R&D investment look particularly poor when viewed alongside the falling cost of borrowing over this period, as central banks lowered interest rates in an effort to stimulate economic activity. Using data from a range of EU countries and the USA, the economists Jonathan Haskel and Stian Westlake have highlighted that investment growth in the weightless intangible assets of the knowledge economy era (defined broadly to include not just software and new product designs but also training, marketing and business process improvement) slowed sharply as a proportion of GDP after the bursting of the dot-com bubble, and again after the onset of the global financial crisis. On both occasions, levels of intangible investment grew at lower rates after the crash than they had done before.[29]

In sum, far from heralding a new age of rapid knowledge-driven growth, the knowledge economy era to date has been characterized by sluggish levels of growth, particularly once the global financial crisis is factored into the equation. The competitive dynamism that policy-makers once predicted appears to have given way to an era in which incumbents dominate, in which innovation and disruption increasingly presuppose substantial financial resources, as well as other pre-existing advantages such as established user networks and intellectual property rights. Growth in knowledge investment appears to be stalling, further contributing to economic stagnation.

6
THE CRISIS OF WORK

The rise of the knowledge economy not only promised a new model of growth, with innovation building upon innovation to drive productivity ever higher. Critical to its appeal was the promise of a surfeit of highly paid, highly skilled jobs; at least for those developed democracies enlightened enough to adopt an economic strategy centred around social investment. True, even optimistic advocates of the knowledge economy recognized that technological progress would lead to changes in the nature of work and to the loss of certain types of routine jobs. However, they anticipated that the knowledge economy would generate proportionately more new opportunities for better work, and consequently that technological and economic change could improve the lot of the overwhelming majority. The new jobs created would not only be well remunerated but would also provide workers with cognitively stimulating problems to solve and the autonomy necessary to think creatively about solutions.

This prediction was premised on the expectation that knowledge-intensive industries would continue to grow their workforces as the knowledge economy expanded, and that developed democracies that invested in educating their citizens would be well positioned to secure a disproportionate share of this jobs growth. It also depended on the "knowledgification" of existing jobs, with a better-educated workforce capable of adding more value (and thus commanding higher salaries), even when employed in what had historically been lower-skilled roles and industries.

The high-skill, high-wage economy

Has the expansion of high-skilled work that earlier advocates of the knowledge economy once promised taken place? In a word, yes. Over the last three decades, developed democracies have seen knowledge workers account for an increasingly large proportion of the overall workforce. More and more people are employed as scientists, architects, software engineers and management consultants; more and more people work in knowledge-intensive sectors such as finance, education and healthcare. Data compiled by Maarten Goos, Alan Manning and Anna Solomons for a selection of EU countries show that, between 1993 and 2010, employment rates in higher-skilled occupations such as corporate managers, healthcare professionals and engineers did indeed increase across the board.[1] More recent research by the OECD, using the same classification system but covering more countries and a longer time period, confirms these trends (see Figure 6.1).[2] The rise of the knowledge economy has offered many workers who would previously have ended up in mid-skilled employment the chance to move up the value chain and into more skill-intensive roles.[3]

Productivity growth, too, is consistent with people moving into more and more knowledge-intensive (and thus productive) occupations. However, here the trend appears to be one of ongoing productivity growth rather than a dramatic step-change coinciding with the rise of the knowledge economy, suggesting that rapid productive innovation has been a persistent feature of the postwar era rather than something distinctive to the last 30 years (see Figure 6.2). Moreover, the rate of productivity growth in many developed democracies has decreased since the global financial crisis, indicating a slowdown in technological progress in spite of the emphasis that national governments and supranational institutions have placed on knowledge-driven growth. Admittedly, this slowdown might be attributed to global macroeconomic conditions post-crisis and policy choices such as austerity rather than to any fundamental failing of knowledge-driven growth. Yet, as we have seen, austerity was at the very least compatible with the cautious approach to government borrowing, spending and taxation emphasized by many earlier advocates of knowledge-driven growth.

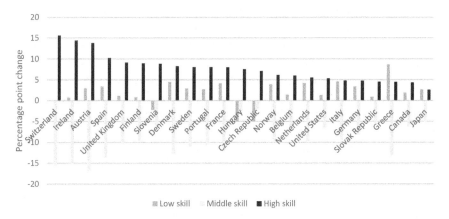

Figure 6.1 Percentage change in share of total employment by occupational skill level, 1995–2015

Source: OECD, Employment Outlook (2017).

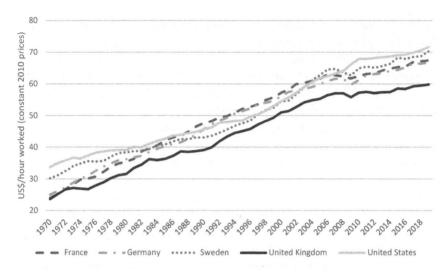

Figure 6.2 GDP per hour worked (constant prices 2010), 1970–2019

Source: OECD, Indicator: GDPHRWKD.

The rhetoric of global competition, prudence and living within one's means was easy to repurpose in defence of spending cuts following the financial crisis.[4]

More problematic even than the recent slowdown in productivity growth, from the perspective of the high-skills, high-pay theory of the knowledge economy, is that the expansion of knowledge work and associated productivity gains have *not* been consistently accompanied by a corresponding increase in median wages. This trend predated the financial crisis, and it even predated the 1990s' enthusiasm for the knowledge economy. From the 1980s onwards, in many advanced democracies, average workers' salaries have become increasingly "decoupled" from rising societal productivity levels.[5] And, despite the hope that better-educated workers would be able to command higher wages in an era of knowledge-driven growth (reflecting the additional value that their improved skills generated and the increasing bargaining power that owners of skills enjoy relative to owners of capital in an economy geared to produce ideas rather than things), these trends have continued unabated. While there may be more knowledge jobs than ever before, the average worker does not appear to have reaped the benefits. Why?

Explaining wages

At first glance, the decoupling of wages from productivity growth appears to be incompatible with the rapid expansion of knowledge work. If more and more people are entering into higher-earning occupations, surely wages should increase, as early advocates of the knowledge economy predicted? Yet if we look back to Figure 6.1, the expansion of more knowledge-intensive roles at the top of the income distribution is not the only trend of note. Significantly, this expansion has coincided with a decline in the share of the labour market accounted for by medium-skilled, medium-paid occupations: jobs such as clerical workers and semi-skilled machine operators, whose tasks are increasingly performed by machines (for example, by software that streamlines the back-end office processes of many businesses, or by production line robots replacing factory workers) and/or by workers overseas. And while in most (but not all) countries this decline has been primarily compensated for by an increase in higher-skilled work, in almost all cases it has also been accompanied by an expansion in the proportion of people employed in lower-paid occupations (such as security guards, retail workers and carers), a phenomenon that economists have described as "job polarization".[6]

Consequently, if the proportion of higher-paid roles is expanding, but median wage growth has stalled, one possibility is that insufficient knowledge-intensive jobs are being generated to improve the lot of the average worker. In analyses of median wage trends, everything hinges on the location of the median individual: our average worker, sat right at the middle of the income distribution. If they are fortunate enough to secure one of the expanding range of knowledge-intensive jobs, then median wages should rise; if not, then median wages might stagnate or even fall. Although the expansion of higher-skilled work has tended to outweigh the expansion of lower-skilled work at the aggregate level, it may yet fail to reach our median individual, as they remain in a medium-skilled job or even slide into a lower-paid occupation.

Another explanation of this apparent paradox could be that our average worker *has* moved to a higher-skilled occupation, but they are not receiving a substantially higher salary as a result. Perhaps the increased supply of skilled individuals has reduced the wage premiums that higher-skilled workers can command. Perhaps changes in the distribution of wages *within* particular job types mean that a small proportion of people in those occupational categories are enjoying substantially larger rewards but the vast majority are not.[7] (We return to this point in Chapter 7, when we examine the relationship between education and social inclusion in the context of so-called "superstar" effects.)

Whichever of these explanations of rising wage inequality holds – and the answer appears to differ from country to country as well as over time[8] – they both problematize the understanding of knowledge-driven growth that rose to prominence in the 1990s, and which continues to justify social investment policies today. Most obviously, if the rise of the knowledge economy is not generating enough knowledge work to compensate the majority of workers for the loss of medium-skilled jobs, then its desirability begins to look somewhat doubtful. But even if there are plenty of knowledge jobs to go round, unless they are well paid, then they will no longer appear quite as desirable as they once seemed, particularly if the flexibility demanded of knowledge workers requires sacrificing the security, stability and clear career progression that previous generations enjoyed.

Diminished opportunities

Why might the knowledge economy be generating fewer well-paid jobs than previously anticipated? To answer this question, it is worthwhile returning to some of the assumptions and predictions made in the heyday of the concept. One major source of knowledge work was supposed to be the "knowledgification" of existing jobs. Roles such as sales clerk, factory worker and travel agent would all become more knowledge-intensive, so the reasoning ran, which would enable the workers in question to add more value through their labour and earn a greater share of the rewards as a result. The sales clerk might learn a new language, helping their company to expand into overseas markets; the factory worker might study engineering, enabling her to identify efficiency gains on the production line; the well-travelled travel agent would be able to make superior recommendations to his clients.

Yet, far from experiencing an expansion of creativity, autonomy and knowledge-intensity, for many lower-skilled workers the rise of the knowledge economy has had the opposite effect, making their work more routine and reducing their independence, providing fewer opportunities for them to exercise skills that would differentiate themselves and "add value". In their book *Capitalism without Capital*, innovation scholars Jonathan Haskel and Stian Westlake point out that one of the knowledge products of the new economy is knowledge about human activity: knowledge about optimum paths for people to follow through a warehouse, for instance, or the fastest way to serve coffee to your customers. New technologies make it increasingly easy to monitor how humans are behaving relative to these standards. This leads to workplaces that are highly proceduralized, with prescriptive rules and thoroughgoing surveillance systems to ensure compliance with said rules.

The result has been a bifurcation between business activities that *create* new knowledge and business activities that *deploy* newly created knowledge on their workforce. The former are deemed to require flattened management hierarchies, fluid organizational structures and individual autonomy, enabling workers to interact, learn and experiment, thereby identifying new ideas and opportunities: think of Amazon's Seattle campus, complete with fussball tables and juice bars. By contrast, the latter are increasingly hierarchical and authoritarian, with behaviours increasingly prescribed and proscribed: think of Amazon's warehouses, in which workers are equipped with tracking devices that monitor their movements.[9] Consequently, instead of witnessing the knowledgification of lower-skilled occupations, on average the knowledge economy offers such workers fewer opportunities for individual skills to make a difference to output, which means those skills cannot generate greater returns for the person who possesses them (or for their employer). In a detailed analysis of low-paid work in industries such as call centres, hotels, food processing, retail and healthcare, the social scientists Caroline Lloyd and Ken Mayhew found limited evidence of recruiters in the UK reporting skills shortages, suggesting that initiatives to improve skills would not improve the prospects of workers in these sectors.[10]

These developments have consequences for social mobility too. The disappearance of medium-skilled, medium-paid jobs across the economy as a whole has removed many of the roles that lower-skilled people traditionally moved into once they had acquired enough experience or training. Job polarization, in effect, takes away the ladders that were previously in place to allow people to progress into higher-skilled (if not necessarily highly skilled) work. Moreover, the qualities required in lower-skilled settings may differ markedly from those required in high-skilled settings: adherence to rules and the constitution of an ox, in the case of an Amazon warehouse, versus the blue-skies thinking required to "build yourself a great story" in Amazon's Seattle offices. Experience in the former environment does not necessarily demonstrate aptitude for the latter, even before we account for social prejudices both overt and tacit. Lloyd and Mayhew's study of low-paid work in the UK highlighted how these jobs offered minimal scope for career progression once people were in-post: even managers who themselves had risen up the ranks admitted that such a feat was extremely unlikely for new joiners to their organizations, as a result of "delayering" (the removal of mid-tier supervisory work) and an increasing tendency to recruit externally for more senior management roles.

The business models of the new economy have also directly replaced some forms of paid knowledge work with machines. Managerial-level jobs overseeing delivery staff or maintenance workers are increasingly threatened by the rise of digital platforms that coordinate personnel using algorithm and customer feedback instead of middle-class employees. The consolidation of once-dispersed workforces into single-platform networks – such as TaskRabbit and Helpling – acts as a substitute for more localized network businesses and the entrepreneurs who once created and oversaw them. The human input required by a hundred different taxi firms – with their distinctive call centres and business support functions, their distinctive owner-operators, investors, accountants and managers – can be substantially reduced by the likes of Uber and Lyft.

A different dynamic, yet equally damaging to the quantity of knowledge work available, occurs in platforms that curate user-generated content for consumption by other users. We saw in Chapter 2 how the media and the creative industries were supposed to act as a major source of new opportunities in the knowledge economy era, as new technologies made it ever easier for people to create and distribute their own films, music and text. Although creative industries have indeed expanded since the 1990s, there has also been a countervailing tendency for people to produce content for free and to consume freely produced content. On platforms such as YouTube and TikTok, Facebook and Instagram, WordPress and Tumblr, most users receive minimal financial compensation for the content they create; they are instead rewarded with free access to platforms, to content-creation tools and to the networks those platforms offer for sharing that content. Review and rating platforms such as TripAdvisor, or sales platforms that provide significant opportunities for user feedback such as Amazon and Airbnb, also receive content for free from their users, and provide that content for free to other users, making their money instead from targeted advertising and market intelligence and/or by taking a cut of sales made in light of that knowledge. The 1998 US Department of Commerce report on *The Emerging Digital Economy*, cited in Chapter 2, hoped that travel agents rendered redundant by the digitalization of booking procedures might find new work providing people with "the advice of someone who has been to the region, who can recommend hotels in the wine country near Cape Town and safaris in Kruger".[11] As it transpires, while such information is indeed valuable, that value accrues to businesses that succeed in extracting it from people for free (such as TripAdvisor, founded in 2000). People provide this information, not for money but rather for the pleasure of sharing knowledge on a user-friendly and high-profile platform, for the satisfaction of rewarding good and punishing bad suppliers, for the status that online recognition conveys and/or in the hope of becoming so influential a voice that paid opportunities for content creation will follow. It is little surprise, then, that the media sector – which has traditionally paid people to create content, which has often relied on advertising for supplemental income and which includes advertising and marketing jobs under its auspices – has been profoundly affected by the rise of digital platforms funded primarily by advertising revenues.[12] Research into UK recruitment patterns indicates that the number of graduate-level media vacancies has fallen by two-thirds in the 12 years from 2007 to 2019, more than in any other sector.[13]

Arguably, it was always thus. From the early days of the internet onwards, much content creation and curation was done for free, by hobbyists and enthusiasts keen to showcase their skills and share their knowledge. Social theorists debated whether this should be understood as an anarcho-communist gift economy, in which altruistically motivated people volunteered ideas and information, or a new mode of capitalist production in which workers were conned into producing things without compensation.[14] In the 1990s, America Online appointed thousands of "community leaders" from among its customer base to moderate chat rooms and assist other users; in 1999, a group of disgruntled volunteers sued AOL for violation of minimum wage laws, a case that the internet provider eventually settled out of court in 2009 for a reported $15 million.[15] Nevertheless, the advent of Web 2.0 marked a step-change in the prevalence of such arrangements, as an ever higher proportion of the world's population came online and as businesses responded by providing users with ever more opportunities to publish as well as to consume digital content.

Parallel to this explosion of uncompensated content creation, citizens of the web have proven themselves remarkably reluctant to pay for digital content that is *not* given away for free, striking a further blow to the viability of content creation as a reliable source of paid knowledge work. The same technologies that enabled individuals to distribute their content at near-zero marginal cost also made it possible for individuals to distribute other people's content at near-zero marginal cost.[16] After its launch in June 1999, the peer-to-peer file-sharing service Napster rapidly became notorious as the public face of music piracy. Despite its legal travails and subsequent bankruptcy, it inspired a series of successor platforms, and a range of similar channels persist to this day (albeit often in harder-to-find corners of the dark web). The easy availability of pirated alternatives pushed down the prices that music labels, film studios and book publishers felt able to charge for their products.[17] This in turn allowed content aggregators to emerge, offering legal access to vast libraries of copyrighted content in exchange for competitively priced subscription fees: the likes of Spotify and Netflix, for example. This process of digital disruption has led to a substantial decline in the revenues that recording artists make from their recordings, with revenues from streaming significantly lower than historical revenues from sales of physical or digital copies of music. Content creators that give away their content for free need large audiences in order to make a living out of advertising revenues alone and often have to supplement their income in other ways (for example, through live performances). As a result of these shifts, the idea that a sizeable number of knowledge workers will be able to earn a living by creating content for "smaller niche markets" appears doubtful, contrary to the predictions of earlier advocates of knowledge-driven growth.[18]

Even IT jobs are not safe from retrenchment in this brave new digital world. The mass adoption of cloud computing – in which websites, databases and software applications are increasingly stored on and operated through remote servers – has allowed businesses to outsource many of their IT functions. Whereas in the recent past, firms employed specialists to manage server hardware and software on-site, now it is increasingly cost-efficient for businesses to rent hardware and software from the cloud, using a smaller local staff to procure, configure and administer these remote services. Even high-tech start-ups with no shortage of computer-literate employees – such as Airbnb, Slack and Uber – adopt such outsourcing strategies.[19] And the cloud-computing market is dominated by familiar names: in early 2020, the top three providers by revenue were Amazon Web Services, Microsoft Azure and Google Cloud Platform.

Globalization, automation and work

For many advanced economies in the 1990s, the point of aggressively targeting knowledge-based growth was to compensate for the loss of jobs to lower-wage economies, particularly in the manufacturing sector. Yet, the above examples highlight how technological progress does not always imply an increase in the volume and value of knowledge work available. Historically, the impact of technological progress on labour markets has always been ambivalent, at least over the short to medium term. From the early days of the industrial revolution onwards, new technologies have often acted as substitutes for human labour. The introduction of Hargreaves' spinning jenny and Arkwright's water frame, for example, reduced the amount of labour needed to produce yarn from cotton fibres; machine operatives also required fewer skills than cottage artisans, who had to master every stage of the production process themselves. Workers do not just compete against other workers in cheaper labour markets: they also compete against the machines produced by innovative knowledge work. Advances in knowledge can substitute for the skills and knowledge of existing workers.

With the benefit of hindsight, something similar appears to have been happening in advanced democracies over recent decades. Although in the knowledge economy debates of the 1990s, technological progress tended to be portrayed as generative of new, high-skilled job opportunities, which could act as a substitute for semi-skilled jobs in sectors such as manufacturing that were being lost to globalization, a growing body of evidence suggests that it may have been technological progress itself that was primarily responsible for the decline of traditional semi-skilled jobs in developed democracies. While advanced economies have shed manufacturing jobs and emerging economies have increased them (as a proportion of overall employment), manufacturing jobs account for a smaller share of *global* employment today than they did 30 years ago, which is indicative of the efficiency gains associated with automation.[20] Within advanced economies such as the USA and the UK, although manufacturing jobs have declined, manufacturing output has increased. This implies that the labour that remains in this sector is becoming more and more productive, because of the adoption of new technologies, the development of new techniques and investment in new machinery.[21]

In short, the replacement of workers by machines (in which the emergence of the knowledge economy is complicit) plays at least as large a role in the decline of traditional manufacturing industries as the replacement of workers by cheap foreign labour (for which the emergence of the knowledge economy was supposed to compensate). An IMF study of subnational employment patterns over the period 1999 to 2016 concluded that regions specializing in industries exposed to higher degrees of automation experienced larger and more persistent increases in unemployment than regions specializing in industries exposed to higher degrees of overseas competition. These "automation shocks" translated to lower wages and productivity over the longer term, whereas regions that experienced "globalisation shocks" saw labour force participation rates rebound relatively rapidly.[22] Instead of offering a solution to industrial decline, the rise of the knowledge economy appears to have accelerated it.

Such trends should not come as a surprise. Many of the innovations of the last 30 years have enabled individuals and organizations to produce the same output with less labour, and less skilled labour, than they required before. For example, increasing automation of factory production lines obviates the need for expert machinists. The computer revolution, and the widespread adoption of spreadsheets and databases, has reduced demand for skilled clerical workers. It should not be forgotten that, for much of the twentieth century, the term "computer" itself was primarily used to describe a kind of job vacancy rather than a kind of office equipment.[23] As mentioned above, digital platforms increasingly substitute for managerial labour. The shift to online commerce has cut demand for front-office and back-office staff across the entire economy, as consumers and businesses increasingly input data into internet-based forms themselves, which are then processed and passed on to the fulfilment stage without manual intervention. Significantly, many of the jobs that have been replaced by technology could themselves be considered knowledge jobs – at least, entry-level knowledge jobs – from the perspective of an earlier era, as they required literate, numerate and articulate staff.

Needless to say, the automation of tasks previously performed by salaried labour brings benefits as well as costs. From the perspective of skilled knowledge work, technological progress means that new jobs are created in designing, constructing, programming and maintaining the machines that displace labour. Moreover, the fact that more output can now be produced for less labour should mean that prices fall, increasing the quantity of output sold, and improving the lot of consumers by leaving them with more cash with which to purchase other products.[24]

Nevertheless, this effect is unlikely to offset the impact of the labour losses entirely. At the level of an individual sector, there are very few goods or services for which demand is so elastic that it expands in lockstep with productivity increases (and corresponding price decreases), such that existing employment levels will always be maintained through the sale of additional units. Admittedly, those who have been automated out of a job in one sector can go and seek new employment in another, and there should be more demand for these other goods and services, now that technological progress has increased overall societal income, and cheaper automatically produced products leave consumers with more cash in hand. However, even the expansion of demand for other more labour-intensive goods and services may not leave workers better off. In their 2018 paper, "Artificial Intelligence, Automation and Work", the economists Daron Acemoglu and Pascual Restrepo demonstrate that technological advances that enable us to perform existing tasks more efficiently, substituting capital (machines) for labour in one part of the economy, mean that displaced labour is forced to compete against other labour across a narrower range of tasks, pushing down wages. As a result, *absent any countervailing force*, such technological advances will reduce labour's share of national income, rendering workers worse off relative to owners of capital.[25] True, productivity gains may mean that workers can afford to buy more goods and services with their wages than they did before, as those goods and services are becoming cheaper to produce, so they may be better off in terms of their absolute purchasing power. However, even this is not guaranteed, if productivity growth is disappointing.

Here, then, is an alternative (and potentially complementary) explanation for the decoupling of wages from productivity growth. In addition to median wage growth stalling because of growing wage inequality (because our median worker has not secured a role in a knowledge-intensive sector, owing to job polarization, or because that role is not highly paid, owing to growing wage inequalities within knowledge-intensive sectors), we might also be witnessing disappointing wage growth because tasks historically performed by workers are increasingly performed by machines and algorithms. This labour-displacing dynamic means that productivity gains will accrue disproportionately to owners of capital rather than to owners of labour.

The resurgence of capital

Is there evidence of such a shift? For much of the twentieth century, many economists assumed that the share of overall output accruing to capital and labour respectively was fixed, subject only to minor fluctuations from year to year; and for much of the twentieth century, available data appeared to support this conclusion.[26] More recently, however, the stability of these national income shares has been called into question. Even before the financial crisis, mainstream economists working for international institutions such as the European Commission and the IMF noted that the labour share appeared to be trending downwards in the early years of the new millennium.[27] In his landmark work of 2013, *Capital in the Twenty-First Century*, the French economist Thomas Piketty drew on a wealth of historical data (focusing in particular on the USA, UK, France and Germany) to argue that this ratio only appeared to be constant during the years of the postwar settlement, and that in developed democracies the share of national income accruing to capital (and its owners) has been trending upwards at the expense of labour from around 1980 onwards. As a result, the wealthiest have been getting ever wealthier, relative to their poorer peers.

The finding that the capital share of national income is increasing in many parts of the developed world is now well established in the economics and public policy literature (although there is considerable debate as to its underlying causes, and the role of housing wealth in particular, a point we return to in Chapter 7). Both the OECD and IMF report downward trends in the labour share of national income in advanced economies.[28] However, the trend is not universal: different measurement approaches reach different conclusions, as do different time horizons, and there is still substantial year-on-year variation.[29] This makes it difficult to conclude that changes in labour–capital shares play an essential part in the decoupling of median wages from productivity growth in the knowledge economy era as we have defined it, starting in the mid-1990s. For example, according to OECD analysis, in France and the UK labour shares of national income were broadly stable between 1995 and 2014 (registering a modest uptick of 0.9 per cent and 0.4 per cent respectively); Sweden even saw a substantial increase in its labour share (of 3.6 per cent).[30]

Nevertheless, at least for countries that saw labour shares plateau (as in France and the UK) or fall (as in the USA, Germany and the majority of other OECD countries), these trends are still deeply problematic for the account of the knowledge economy advanced during the heyday of the concept. Whether labour shares are moving downward or broadly stable, either way they suggest that the rise of the knowledge economy did not empower workers, who were supposed to find their skills and their ingenuity ever more essential to the production of knowledge-intensive goods and services. According to advocates of knowledge-driven growth, the transition to the knowledge economy should have rendered non-human forms of capital (cash, buildings, plant, machinery, even intellectual property) relatively insignificant compared to the productive contributions made by skilled knowledge workers. Under these circumstances, skilled labour should have been able to strike a comparatively favourable bargain with capital owners, thereby skewing national income decisively in its favour. Trends in labour shares over the knowledge economy era suggest that this has not happened.

It might be argued that the analysis of the dynamics of the knowledge economy was correct, and the problem lay rather with the implementation of the knowledge-driven growth agenda. The analysis of rising wages and worker empowerment only ever applied to *skilled* workers. Consequently, if the labour share falls, this might indicate a failure of social investment, a failure to equip workers with the skills demanded by the knowledge economy. The fact that several Nordic countries that adopted knowledge-driven growth strategies involving comparatively high levels of social investment tended to see labour shares rise rather than fall provides some support for this argument (a group that included not just Sweden but Denmark and Finland too). However, when data for a larger range of established European democracies are compared, the correlation between social investment in education by the state and changes in the labour share looks weak (see Figure 6.3).[31]

Moreover, labour disempowerment (or at least, minimal evidence of labour re-empowerment) is consistent with other features of the knowledge economy. Many knowledge-intensive businesses remain highly dependent on capital, whether in the form of robots, laboratories or expensively cultivated networks of active users. Where that capital is not readily duplicated – for example, where it is fenced off by intellectual property protections or consists of singular network effects – only so much labour will be necessary to exploit it, and increasing your workforce will yield diminishing returns. By contrast, with traditional capital goods such as plant and machinery, once the point where labour produces diminishing returns is reached, it is always possible for you (or your competitor) to buy more machines for labourers to operate.

As we will see in Chapter 10, whether the weakened bargaining position of labour in the knowledge economy era is a product of inadequate social investment, or whether it is related instead to a lack of demand for skilled knowledge workers and the comparatively strong bargaining position of capital, has

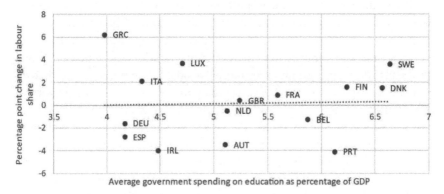

Figure 6.3 Change in gross labour share of output relative to average government education spending as percentage of GDP, EU-15 countries 1995–2014

Sources: OECD (labour share), Eurostat (education spending).

profound implications for public policy. Whatever the root cause, however, it means that "the employee" has not, on average, been made "powerful ... in terms of their marketability in the modern workforce", as earlier advocates of knowledge-driven growth contested.[32] This matters, because this empowerment was supposed to substitute for formal employment protections, such as active trade unions and legally enforceable employee rights. Without such empowerment, the liberalization of labour markets seems more like a recipe for precarity than "flexicurity". Indeed, several analyses attribute recent shifts in national income from labour to capital primarily to the policy changes and power imbalances associated with labour market liberalization, rather than to technological change.[33]

New tasks for labour

This dystopian picture of growing unemployment and economic inequality is, however, only part of the story of technological progress. Innovation also introduces entirely new goods and services to the economy, demand for which generates entirely new sources of work and employment. Over the twentieth century, labour-saving innovations in the largely unremunerated domestic sphere – for example, the invention of the washing machine, vacuum cleaner and dishwasher – exemplify how new markets arise for new technologies, creating new salaried jobs in the process. Technologies that complement leisure time, such as the automobile, television or computer games console, or increase quality and length of life, such as advances in healthcare, also fit this pattern, creating new tasks for labour to fulfil. And effective demand for all of these new goods and services is made possible by rising income levels, with automation – rendering existing tasks possible with less labour – a key factor in making people affluent enough to increase and diversify their consumption. An increasing amount of labour (often comparatively highly skilled labour) is needed to carry out the tasks of designing new products and executing new processes, manufacturing and operating new machines, and devising and delivering new services. Acemoglu and Restrepo posit that these labour-generating technological advances could counteract the downward pressure on wages created by labour-displacing inventions.[34] Consequently, most mainstream economists argue that automation tends to replace jobs but not work, not demand for labour in general; or at least, that automation has tended to do so to date, when viewed over a sufficiently long time horizon.[35]

However, the point remains that not all technological advances generate new tasks, and there may be periods in history where labour-displacing technologies dominate over innovations that generate new tasks for labour.[36] Moreover, for any given individual or community, there may be a significant gap in both time and space between the displacement of labour and the creation of new work opportunities: opportunities that may also require lower skill levels, or very different skillsets, to the jobs that have been lost. For any given individual, there is a risk that opportunities compensating for displacement of their existing job will not arise within an accessible labour market within their lifetimes, or that these opportunities will require skills that it would be uneconomical for said individual to acquire at that point in their life cycle. The automation of manufacturing jobs in developed democracies over the last 40 years offers a striking example of these dynamics.

Nor is it necessarily the case that labour-generating innovation will inevitably reassert itself. The American economist Robert J. Gordon argues that the labour-generating innovations of the twentieth century may have been a historical one-off.[37] The automation of much domestic labour – through the supply of electricity, gas, water and sewage infrastructure to households, and through the introduction of household appliances – satisfied an age-old set of demands, with a transformative impact on people's lives (particularly the lives of women).[38] The economic impact of innovations such as smart homes, coordinated by the internet of things, may prove to be mild by comparison, in terms of the range of new products and services that will be created, in terms of the clamour for such novelties and in terms of the time they will liberate both for paid labour and for leisure. If this is the case, then knowledge-driven growth could generate fewer jobs than it destroys, as it allows existing tasks to be performed with less labour without identifying (enough) productive new ways for labour to be deployed. Recall that Romer's model of endogenous growth, discussed in Chapter 1, assumed the possibility of endless innovation: Gordon's rather more pessimistic history of technology challenges this assumption.

True, both of these possibilities are equally speculative. Someone surveying the history of technological progress in 1870 might have concluded that we had reached a point where people's wants were satisfied, or that they were imminently satisfiable subject to wider adoption of existing technologies and a suitable rearrangement of social forces (for instance, via the revolutionary overthrow of the ruling class). Their conclusions would have been reasonable but wrong. We cannot be sure what our technological future holds over the long run. Nevertheless, we can examine current trends for some insight into the outlook for the next few years, to assess whether labour-displacing or labour-generating technologies are in the ascendant.

Perhaps the most prominent technologies reconfiguring the world of work today involve machine learning and artificial intelligence. These algorithms "learn" by looking at large sets of data, often gathered from human activity: for instance, large collections of images tagged by humans on the basis of what they contain, large collections of text produced by humans sending messages to one another, large collections of text translated by humans from one language to another and large collections of sensor data gleaned from humans driving vehicles equipped with sophisticated cameras and lasers around busy city streets. Some futurists confidently predict that we are not far from the point where advanced computers will be able to substitute entirely for human thought processes in a wide range of fields.[39] In so doing, artificial intelligence could potentially automate a vast range of activities presently performed by human labour, displacing routine manual workers and knowledge workers alike. For example, new sensor technologies, and the data that they yield, make self-driving cars and lorries a real possibility, threatening the livelihoods of the millions of people employed as taxi and haulage drivers today. Already, algorithms can execute highly skilled tasks such as writing newspaper copy, sifting through vast swathes of documentation in preparation for legal cases and diagnosing tumours from medical imaging, with results often indistinguishable from or better than those produced by human knowledge workers.[40] As far back as 2013, the consultancy firm McKinsey was predicting that the increased automation of knowledge work could lead to computers substituting for between 110 million and 140 million full-time knowledge workers by 2025.[41]

While such predictions may prove overstated, the point still stands that a (potentially substantial) proportion of the tasks that people perform for payment today are under threat of imminent automation, a list that includes knowledge-intensive tasks as well as comparatively unskilled ones. And while these developments will require additional knowledge workers to write algorithms and design machines, the net impact of substituting robots and software for tasks currently performed by human labour will be to reduce employment opportunities overall and create increasing competition for what opportunities remain. In other words, even though the amount of knowledge work available may expand, this is not guaranteed; and even if it does, increased competition for said knowledge work, arising from dwindling opportunities in the wider labour market, may see salaries for the average knowledge worker fall (particularly if coupled with social investments designed to increase the supply of knowledge workers, and thus the competition for these jobs; a point we discuss in Chapter 7). Only to the extent that innovation simultaneously identifies new goods and services (such as novel healthcare treatments or new consumer products), the demand for which will lead to the redeployment of human labour, can growth in well-paid knowledge work be secured. Worryingly, in the short term at least, innovations in the area of artificial intelligence appear to focus on *replacing* existing human labour, rather than on generating novel tasks for human labour to perform; which is hardly surprising, given many of these algorithms have been "trained" by human labour to replicate human labour.[42] True, new products and services that use artificial intelligence are also being invented, creating entirely new tasks for human labour to perform, but it is not clear how much labour these new products and services will require or for how long.

To the extent that labour-displacing dynamics dominate, we should expect the ongoing development of the knowledge economy to empower owners of capital rather than knowledge workers. Consequently, even though declines in the labour share of national income have generally been modest over the knowledge economy era to date, the stability of labour–capital shares cannot be taken for granted over the longer term. The introduction of new technologies in the field of robotics, automation and artificial intelligence has the potential to tilt the distribution of national income further in favour of capital. There is no guarantee that any given wave of technological progress will be predominantly labour-generating rather than labour-replacing. As the economist Carl Frey notes in his 2019 book *The Technology Trap*, for the majority of the nineteenth century, the productivity advances of the industrial revolution were accompanied by wage stagnation, as new technologies reduced demand for labour and for the skilled labour of artisans in particular.[43] The artificial intelligence revolution may see the same dynamics repeat themselves, over the medium term at least.

The advent of artificial intelligence also looks set to strengthen the bargaining position of capital relative to labour at the level of individual businesses, too. As we have already seen, many of the competitive advantages enjoyed by today's dominant tech businesses derive from what they own rather than from whom they employ. Ownership of network effects, economies of scale, vast troves of historical data and the means of collecting vast troves of data on an ongoing basis provide today's tech giants with an advantage that challengers can only replicate by acquiring similarly large networks of users and similar portfolios of synergistic products (operating systems, email, cloud-computing facilities, social media, mapping applications, autonomous vehicles, payment services, online stores for apps and entertainment content, and so forth). Crucially, today's tech giants enjoy a significant head start in the development and deployment of the next wave of artificial intelligence technologies, because the datasets and user networks that they already possess are ideal for training artificial intelligence algorithms. Without similar resources, innovation in the field of artificial intelligence is all the more challenging.

Consequently, for an individual starting out in the tech sector today, joining one of these businesses is often more attractive than starting up on one's own. Once on the payroll, the threat that you could simply take your knowledge and expertise to a rival, or start up a competitor business in your own right, feels rather hollow, given that you cannot take users and data with you when you leave, to say nothing of any intellectual property that you generated while in-post. (Infamously, when one of the founders of Google's autonomous vehicle project sought to broker a move to Uber, he found both himself and his new employer at the centre of a string of court cases for theft of trade secrets.) Even if you do opt to go it alone, you may struggle to attract venture capital funding, as potential investors will be aware that an established tech giant could mimic your business model using their existing data and user base, forcing you out of the market before you have achieved the scale necessary to compete. In short, your labour will be worth less to potential employers and investors, however highly skilled you are, however innovative your ideas. The exit options that were supposed to empower labour in the knowledge economy era are less viable in high-tech markets where capital (physical, financial and/or intangible) plays a pivotal role. The resurgence of capital does not merely dampen the competitive dynamism of knowledge-intensive industries; it also means that knowledge workers will receive lower returns for their labour than would otherwise be the case.

7

THE CRISIS OF INCLUSION

What of the broader moral and political case for knowledge-driven growth, predicated on its ability to deliver social mobility, equality of opportunity and a fairer distribution of economic rewards? In light of the shortfall of knowledge work already identified, it should come as little surprise that the inclusivity of knowledge-based growth has fallen short too: if being included means securing a well-paid knowledge job, then there are not enough of these jobs to go around. Even if we define inclusion more modestly, as the ability to access these jobs on an equal footing, it is unclear whether policy-makers have delivered. A 2018 report into social mobility by the OECD noted that opportunities for people to move up and down the income distribution have decreased across the developed world since the 1990s, with the highest earners more likely to remain highly paid and the lowest earners more likely to remain poorly paid than they were two decades before, with your parents' education and occupation increasingly decisive in shaping your own life chances.[1]

This chapter explores why the social inclusion agenda has faltered. It begins by examining the uneven geographical distribution of opportunity, before turning to the relationship between education and economic success. Does what you earn really does depend on what you learn? Or are other factors – access to capital and social networks, for instance, or the competitive structure of certain knowledge-intensive sectors themselves – to blame for rising inequality?

The landscape of opportunity

Knowledge-based growth was seen by some of its 1990s advocates as a solution to the problem of regional economic divergence, and in particular to the loss of jobs in former industrial heartland regions arising from globalization. Yet, far from reversing these trends, the knowledge economy era has witnessed a further deepening of regional economic inequalities. For example, in the USA, whereas prior to 1980 cities with lower wages saw faster wage growth (and thus convergence with their more affluent counterparts), post-1980 this trend has stalled, with some higher-wage cities – such as Boston, New York and San Francisco – pulling further away from the pack.[2] Similar patterns are replicated across western Europe.[3]

Why has this happened? Much as academic theorists of endogenous growth and increasing returns originally anticipated (in contrast to many cheerleaders of the knowledge economy among the political class and the professional commentariat), knowledge-intensive businesses have tended to cluster together in large cities and their surrounding regions. This in turn attracts would-be knowledge workers to the areas in question, whose presence then attracts more knowledge-intensive businesses, in a mutually reinforcing dynamic. This process results in massive differences in economic output per capita between different parts of the same country. The OECD estimated that, in 2016, output per capita in the most productive small region of the USA was about five times that of the least productive. This ratio was higher still in Germany, and highest of all in the UK, where the per capita GDP of the City of London was over 23 times that of the Isle of Anglesey, a difference that was quite literally off the scale (see Figure 7.1).[4]

Moreover, the economic advantages of living in these thriving city regions are not restricted to those working in high-value knowledge industries. Workers who supply in-person services – ranging from security to spas, from restaurants to retail, from performance art to personal training, from healthcare to hairdressing – also stand to benefit. Buoyant demand for knowledge workers results in tighter labour markets, meaning that salaries are generally higher across the board. Added to that, well-paid workers typically consume more in-person

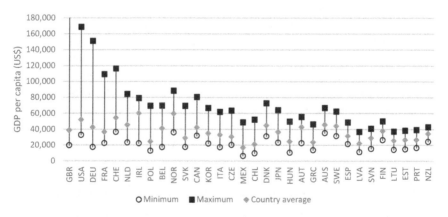

Figure 7.1 Regional disparities in GDP per capita, 2016.

Source: OECD, *Regions and Cities at a Glance* (2018). Scale as per OECD report.

services, and are willing to pay a higher price for them, than their poorer counterparts. (Indeed, the desire to be close to consumption opportunities, as well as job opportunities, explains in part why certain cities are particularly alluring to these workers.)[5] Service providers enjoy greater demand for high-end (and correspondingly more expensive) services, as well as the ability to charge higher prices for equivalent services relative to an economically declining area. This translates to higher productivity levels in the services in question, in more affluent regions.[6]

Of course, the plethora of work (and consumption) opportunities available in thriving city regions means that increasing numbers of people want to live in them. And cities also provide their residents with opportunities that transcend the transactional: social networks of friends and partners working in diverse industries can be sustained more easily in places where a diverse range of employment opportunities are available. As more and more people are attracted to these economically thriving areas, and those who are employed in them secure higher and higher salaries, house prices and rental charges rise. Low interest rates and quantitative easing (targeted central bank purchases of financial assets, aimed at boosting economic activity) have further inflated asset prices, including the price of housing stock. Before the pandemic in Germany, house prices in the seven largest metropolitan areas – Berlin, Hamburg, Munich, Cologne, Frankfurt-am-Main, Stuttgart and Düsseldorf – consistently grew at a faster rate than prices elsewhere in the country, despite already being above the national average to begin with.[7] In the UK, rises in the cost of housing in London have far outpaced increases in other regions.[8] From 1993 to 2018, inflation-adjusted house prices in US cities such as Los Angeles, Seattle and Boston almost doubled (in the case of San Francisco, they more than doubled); whereas in cities such as Chicago, Detroit and Houston, real house prices on the eve of the pandemic were much as they were when Clinton first took the presidential oath of office.[9] These rises in housing costs have tended to outstrip rises in wages, making these areas increasingly inaccessible, both for newcomers and for longstanding residents who do not already own an equity stake in the local property market. A study of internal migration patterns in the UK found a smaller proportion of people moving regions for work in 2016 than in the late 1990s and early 2000s, suggesting that, despite increasing disparities in the wages on offer in different regions, workers are less willing or able to move to places where pay (and thus, in theory, productivity) is highest.[10]

Indeed, the increases in the share of national income accruing to capital rather than labour that have been apparent in many developed democracies over recent decades – mentioned in Chapter 6 – may owe more to the evolution of housing costs than to the capital intensity of knowledge work. Drawing on data from the G7 countries, the economist Matthew Rognlie has argued that increases in the capital share of national income are almost entirely attributable to increases in the share of national income accruing to owners of housing.[11] Housing and land shortages in property hotspots push up rents, increasing the share of national income received by the owners of housing. As the housing sector is highly capital-intensive – only a relatively small amount of income from property goes to pay the labour costs of repair and maintenance workers – this leads to a larger capital share of national income overall.

Note that this is *not* to say that capital (or the lack thereof) presents no obstacles to participating in the knowledge economy. Rather, it implies that one way – perhaps the major way – in which capital obstructs entry in knowledge-intensive sectors is by increasing the price of accommodation in city regions where potential knowledge workers can access knowledge jobs, and where potential entrepreneurs can access networks of venture capital investors and business partners as well as robust local demand. Such barriers still curtail the competitive dynamism of the knowledge economy and increase social exclusion, as people are shut out of opportunities because of insufficient funds, insufficient creditworthiness or the simple reluctance to risk what limited funds they have (or can borrow) in the hope of being successful in their chosen field. Not every aspiring actor can afford to wait tables in Los Angeles, New York or London while they wait to be discovered, and only the most privileged few can afford to do so indefinitely.

What of the advent of the virtual office, the technological revolution that was supposed to spread well-paid knowledge work to economically marginalized communities? Up until the Covid-19 pandemic (the implications of which are discussed in more detail in Chapter 10), it is fair to say that reports of the death of the office had been greatly exaggerated. Although there was a growing tendency for knowledge workers to work from internet-enabled locations other than their offices, few could be described as outright telecommuters. The UK's Office for National Statistics reported that, as of 2019, only around 1.7 million people (around 5 per cent of the workforce) worked mainly from home.[12] Data from the European Working Conditions Survey show a gradual upward trend in home working across the continent: in 2005, 5.8 per cent of survey respondents worked from home all or almost all the time, while in 2015, 13.1 per cent reported working from home daily or several times a week.[13] But overall, the pre-pandemic data seem to suggest that, although workers did spend increasing amounts of time working from home, home working was not a substitute for work performed in an office, studio or laboratory but rather a complement to it. In the USA, around a quarter of workers worked from home some of the time in 2017–18, but only slightly more than half of this group ever worked exclusively from home (as opposed to combining home work with work on-site in an office or similar), and only around half of those individuals again did so regularly (once a week or more).[14] In the UK, well over a quarter of the workforce reported at least some level of home working, although the overwhelming majority of these individuals did not work mainly from home.[15] These working patterns meant that knowledge workers still needed to reside relatively close to their main place of work, pushing up property prices in places where knowledge-intensive businesses clustered.

This should come as no surprise. As we saw in previous chapters, many early theorists of the knowledge economy were sceptical about the potential for knowledge work to free itself from the fetters of physical place. Study after study pointed to the importance of interpersonal connections to the growth of knowledge industries.[16] Within workplaces, casual social interactions and chance encounters add up to dense networks of trust and knowledge-sharing; in urban areas, the same patterns are replicated outside offices, within and between entire industries. Although the enforced isolation of the Covid-19 pandemic pushed people to engage with remote working technologies to an unparalleled extent – and doubtless accelerated the trend towards hybrid home working – these technologies are still an imperfect substitute for face-to-face contact.

The race between education and technology

There is, however, one respect in which advocates of knowledge-driven growth might claim that their predictions were vindicated. The rise of the knowledge economy has seen economic rewards for the best educated increase, suggesting that "what you earn" does indeed depend upon "what you learn". The victory is a Pyrrhic one, to be sure, as the point of the prediction was to argue for greater educational investment, enabling more and more people to enjoy a share of those economic returns, whereas since the early 1990s the opposite has occurred, with economic rewards becoming ever more concentrated at the very top of the income distribution. During the knowledge economy era, almost all developed democracies have experienced sharp increases in wage inequality, irrespective of their social investment strategies and approach to labour market liberalization.[17] Nevertheless, the very existence of increasing economic rewards that are concentrated among the best educated makes at least a *prima facie* case for more social investment, as a means of combating social exclusion.

One of the most prominent explanations for increases in income inequality over recent decades dovetails neatly with the knowledge economy narrative of the 1990s. On this account – described in the economics jargon as "skill-biased technological change" – technological progress drives up demand for skilled workers, who invent, improve and apply new technologies to deliver improvements in productivity. All else being equal, this will increase the salaries of skilled workers, leading to a widening wage gap between skilled and unskilled members of the workforce, causing economic inequality to rise. This trend can, however, be mitigated, to the extent that the supply of skilled workers keeps pace with the expanding demand for their skills – for example, through widening access to high-quality public education.

In their aptly titled book, *The Race between Education and Technology*, the economists Claudia Goldin and Lawrence Katz argue that this model explains a large proportion of the fall and rise of inequality in the USA over the course of the twentieth century.[18] In the early 1900s, occupations that required higher levels of schooling – such as clerical work – paid significantly better than those that did not. However, the spread of publicly funded, widely accessible high school education dramatically increased the supply of skilled workers, as did the expansion of higher education following the Second World War. This left the US workforce well placed to adopt and adapt the new technological innovations of the twentieth century; it also meant that inequality was kept in check, as the supply of skilled workers rose in line with demand, limiting the wage premiums they could command relative to their lower-skilled peers. From around 1980 onwards, however, growth in the supply of college-educated workers slowed. As a result, the wages commanded by college-educated workers have risen over this same period.

Interestingly, Goldin and Katz note that the growth in *demand* for the college-educated appears to have slowed in the 1990s: something that they struggle to reconcile with the rapid spread of IT and workplace reorganization in this period, but which provides further evidence that the rise of the knowledge economy has not been accompanied by a rapid explosion in the number of knowledge jobs available. Indeed, had the ranks of the college-educated continued to expand from 1980 to 2005 at the same rate as between 1960 and 1980, Goldin and Katz conclude that slower demand growth would have led college-educated workers' wages to *fall* relative to those of their lesser-skilled peers, reducing inequality.[19]

The policy conclusion that follows is that governments that want to reduce inequality must increase the supply of suitably trained workers, which, as we saw in Chapter 2, is precisely what many mainstream political figures have been seeking to do over the last 30 years. (Katz himself served as chief economist of the US Department of Labor during the first Clinton administration, under Robert Reich.) To quote Alan Greenspan, reflecting on inequality in the USA in 2007:

[T]he shortfall of the supply of advanced skills relative to the demand for them is pressing the wages of skilled workers higher relative to the wages of the less skilled. There is no compelling reason why the pace of innovative ideas, which often come in bunches, should be immediately matched by a supply of skilled workers to implement them. The insights that advance cutting-edge technologies emerge from a very small part of that workforce ... [In the years preceding the First World War, striking income disparities] were driven by a substantially larger concentration of wealth than exists today. Much of the income concentration of those days reflected interest, dividends, and capital gains from that wealth, rather than wage and salary differentials. In contrast, the income concentration of today owes more to the generation of high incomes from work spurred by the imbalance between the demand for skilled workers and their available supply.[20]

How does this analysis fit with the evidence? In the US labour market, the best educated have indeed seen their wages rise by the highest amount over the last four decades. In a 2011 paper, Daron Acemoglu and David Autor noted that wage increases enjoyed by college graduates outstripped those enjoyed by their less educated peers from about 1980 onwards, that those who attended graduate school fared even better and that their less educated peers experienced a fall in their real wages over the same time period. This pattern was particularly pronounced among male members of the workforce.[21] The increases in wage premiums for the better educated appear to confirm the notion of a race between education and technology, reflecting high demand for advanced skills in the knowledge economy era, but a failure to expand supply accordingly. The decline in wages for lower-skilled workers suggests the labour-displacing effects of automation discussed in Chapter 6, as these individuals compete against one another to perform a narrower range of tasks.

Is income inequality primarily a skills issue, however? If it is, we might expect that the education and training decisions of individuals, households and governments over the knowledge economy era would begin to erode the premium associated with higher education. The UK offers an interesting test of these hypotheses. From the early 1970s to the late 1980s, the number of students attending university in the UK remained relatively stable, at around 15 per cent of the age group in question. However, between 1988 and 1996, while US higher education participation rose modestly, participation rates in the UK almost doubled. Around a third of college-age students in the UK were attending university by the mid-1990s.[22] By 2018, the government estimated that over half of all young people in England participated in higher education by the age of 30.[23] According to the "race between education and technology" hypothesis, such a boom in the supply of university-educated graduates should see a reduction in the wage premium that these educated individuals command. Yet, looking at earnings data for this cohort as they entered the job market in the years preceding the global financial crisis, the labour economists Ian Walker and Yu Zhu concluded that the wage premiums commanded by college graduates were broadly stable. The increase in the supply of graduates did *not* seem to reduce the inequality between graduates and non-graduates.

What *did* emerge from their analysis, however, was that the top-earning graduates (those in the upper quartile) saw an increase in their wage premiums, with stagnation or decline in the returns to higher education for graduates further down the income distribution (consistent with the additional supply of educated labour reducing the wages such graduates could command). Looking across 15 European countries and the USA, Pedro Martins and Pedro Pereira found that wage premiums for education were highly dispersed: at the very top of the distribution, the best educated saw significant gains from their education, but people with apparently similar education levels saw substantially lower wage premiums too.[24] In other words, even where the expansion of education appears to be keeping pace with technology, other dynamics might also be at play, restricting competition for the best-paid jobs, competition that would otherwise keep the university wage premium in check.

This is not surprising, given lack of education is clearly not the sole factor preventing people from accessing highly paid jobs. Social networks are an important source of information about job opportunities and career paths, providing insight into the skills and aptitudes that aspirant workers need to convince recruiters that they possess: information that formal education often struggles to supply. To the extent that those in more highly paid occupations tend to socialize with other highly paid workers (and their offspring), as communities become increasingly stratified along economic lines, the pool of likely candidates for vacancies diminishes.[25] Conversely, individuals with the intellectual aptitude to succeed, but who lack the "right" socioeconomic, ethnic or cultural profile, might conclude that such careers are not for the likes of them. The absence of softer skills – so-called "cultural capital", referring to the language and frames of reference deployed by dominant social groups – may also act as an informal obstacle to higher-pay work for individuals from socially excluded backgrounds.[26]

Added to this, for admission to many well-paid and high-profile careers, experience is essential. Over the last two decades, many young workers in Europe and North America have had to acquire this experience by doing unpaid or low-paid internships in sectors ranging from media to law and finance, effectively subsidizing their own subsistence while they work. For individuals from wealthy homes, the risks associated with this investment might be tolerable; for people from poorer backgrounds, the combination of upfront expenditure and uncertain return often deters them from applying in the first place.[27] Access to money (or the lack thereof) thus restricts the supply of candidates from certain backgrounds into these industries, reducing competition and pushing up salaries from where they would be were education the sole prerequisite for success. And this is before we factor housing costs into the equation: as we have already discussed, would-be well-paid workers generally need to base themselves in cities with an abundance of better-paid jobs, and this comes at an increasingly prohibitive cost as house prices and rental costs soar, privileging the already local and/or the already wealthy.

A further factor that helps to bulwark earnings inequality, despite increases in the supply of skilled workers, lies in the structure of advanced economies. Many fields in today's technologically advanced societies display "superstar effects": the phenomenon by which demand is concentrated on the top performers in a particular market, which we encountered back in Chapter 2.[28] This trend is particularly evident in competitive sports: at the end of the day, there can only be a certain number of players on the pitch, course or court at any one time, and so two extremely good players are usually no substitute for one who is among the very best in the world. But similar dynamics can be observed anywhere where people are willing to pay significantly more for marginal gains in performance. Only one medical team can operate on you at any one time; only one legal team can fight your case. Consequently, if one surgeon is twice as likely to save your life than another, you will probably be willing to pay more than twice the price for her services (assuming you can afford to do so); if one law firm is twice as likely to win a suit that will save your business than another, the premium they command will increase accordingly, especially if your opponent is also bidding for their services.

Crucially, the rise of the knowledge economy exacerbates these dynamics, extending them into ever more fields. If there is a decisive advantage to being first mover in a particular digital market, then the ability to develop a platform that attracts early adopters within six months might well prove infinitely more valuable than the ability to develop an identical platform within 12 months. Increasing the supply of skilled software engineers – the number of teams competing for the first-mover advantage – is thus unlikely to erode the premium that the most efficient team can command (although it may alter who gets to command it). Similarly, the first group of researchers to patent a particular innovative design for a drug or microchip will reap the rewards, potentially leaving slower rivals working on the same technology empty-handed. In the winner-take-all situations typical of the casino of technology, individuals and organizations that offer marginal improvements in the chance of victory can command fees vastly in excess of those with very similar skill sets. To the extent that these dynamics prevail in a given sector, a greater supply of skilled workers will only have a marginal impact on the unequal structure of rewards. (It also follows that, in many instances, these rewards could be significantly reduced – for example, by higher taxes – without substantially altering the outcome, from the perspective of wider society: the platform, drug or microchip will still get invented, the court case will still be fought, the football match will still be played.)

We would also expect persistent inequality among producers whose output can be reproduced and distributed at near-zero marginal cost once it has been created, as is the case with computer software, books, video, music, sports broadcasts and other digital (or digitizable) content. The best authors, computer programmers and rock stars can expect to earn substantially more than their peers.[29] Technological advances and global economic integration have increased the of the markets that they can service, driving up their earnings in the process. Even though the average member of the public might view their output as only marginally better than that of their rivals, the fact that it is deemed marginally better by many means that it will be bought first, in preference to other alternatives. Limited consumption time means that the market for second-rate entertainment is far smaller than that for blockbusters of film, art, sport and literature. Moreover, massive economies of scale mean that such products can often undercut their less popular peers on price too.

The wrong kind of education?

This is not, however, to suggest that more and better educational investment has no role to play in decreasing inequality and improving social mobility. True, increases in the graduate wage premium might be driven by other factors in addition to supply and demand for educated labour, reflecting broader shifts in economic structure associated with the rise of the knowledge economy: such as the emergence of superstars and winner-take-all dynamics, as well as the rationing of opportunity to people who combine education with particular social, economic and geographical advantages. However, we should still consider the possibility that the way in which university-level education has expanded has not addressed the demand for skilled labour.

Scholars have posited a number of reasons why this might be the case. First, the average underlying ability of the expanding numbers of students now accessing higher education may be lower than it was in the past.[30] Second, there is the possibility that the expansion in higher education has brought about a decline in the average quality of university tuition. A third potential explanation is not related to the quality of students or the education they receive but rather to the subject matter that they study. Perhaps today's graduates are not acquiring the skills that employers want, taking degrees in the arts, humanities and social sciences instead of science, engineering and maths.[31]

It is thus plausible that some of the wage inequality associated with educational differences could be reversed by more and better public investment in education. There is evidence of an undersupply of graduates with particular skills, and a better standard of education (not just at the university level but also in schools and early years), focused on the skills shortages of knowledge-intensive industries, should increase competition for highly paid knowledge work and thus reduce the wage premium such workers can command.[32] Obviously, lack of education is not the only factor involved in limiting social mobility: competition for higher-paying jobs is also constrained by experience and geography, cultural capital and social networks. Assessing the relative impact of these various factors is extremely difficult, owing to the lack of sufficiently detailed micro-level data. But let us assume for the sake of argument that the non-educational effects are small, or that other policy interventions could be used to address them. Would we then be able to combat inequality and improve social mobility through educational investments alone, as progressive advocates of knowledge-based growth have so often assumed?

The answer, importantly, might still be no. To the extent that inequality is a product of superstar effects and winner-takes-most dynamics, additional competition will have little impact on the scale of rewards available at the top. And to the extent that knowledge-intensive industries tend towards concentrated market structures, with high barriers to entry – as substantial capital investment is needed to develop knowledge-intensive products and cultivate active users, data troves, network effects and economies of scale, and as successful businesses monopolize valuable intellectual property and proprietary platforms – increasing the supply of skilled labour may serve primarily to reduce the payroll costs of the incumbents rather than benefiting workers. In this scenario, while social investment might reduce wage inequality (increasing the supply of highly skilled workers, thereby reducing the premium they can command relative to their less educated peers), it might also allow the employers of highly skilled workers to pay lower salaries, increasing the proportion of revenues that end up in the hands of founders, senior managers and early investors. This would in turn cause the labour share of national income to decline relative to the capital share, exacerbating inequality because of the highly concentrated ownership of capital. Education – even the right kind of education – might not overcome the structural inequality inherent in the knowledge economy era, at least as it has developed to date.[33]

8
THE NEW WORLD ORDER

What of the internationalism of the knowledge economy? As we saw in Chapter 3, the politicians, academics and commentators who championed the idea of knowledge-based growth often stressed the importance of international openness to success in the new economy. This was partly because, on their analysis, there was no alternative: globalization (itself abetted by the computing and telecommunications revolution of the 1980s and 1990s) had made labour, capital and ideas internationally mobile, and this was a reality to which countries would simply have to adapt. But it was also because, they conjectured, policies that actively sought to deepen international openness and international ties would enable countries to steal a march on their rivals in the global knowledge economy. Removing obstacles to international investment would help to attract knowledge-intensive overseas businesses, providing domestic workers with opportunities to work for (and learn from) firms at the cutting edge of the global technological frontier. Removing obstacles to international trade would provide domestic consumers with higher-quality (and lower-cost) goods and services while simultaneously exposing domestic industries to efficiency-enhancing competition, allowing them to incorporate the latest technologies and techniques into their own output. Removing obstacles to international immigration – at least for highly skilled workers – would enable technologically advanced, high-wage countries to cream off the most innovative, educated and skilled workers from the rest of the world, further consolidating their lead in knowledge-intensive industries.

Underpinning this optimistic internationalism was a particular analysis of the competitive advantages of developed democracies in the knowledge economy era. This analysis assumed that the presence of a highly educated workforce, combined with high-quality infrastructure and robust rule-of-law institutions, would enable developed democracies to act as a magnet for knowledge work (and the businesses that create it): an advantage that their lower-wage rivals would find difficult to replicate. The same high wages that put advanced economies at a comparative disadvantage in fields such as mass manufacturing should enable these self-same countries to attract and retain highly skilled talent from overseas. And, in an era where knowledge is key, democracies that encourage the free movement of ideas within and across borders (including the products, individuals and firms who embody them) should be well placed to stay at the cutting edge of the global knowledge economy. Moreover, even if workers in emerging markets could compete for knowledge-intensive jobs on the same terms as their counterparts in developed democracies (as Thomas Friedman claimed in *The World Is Flat*), rising global prosperity would ensure a surfeit of demand for new forms of knowledge work.

In this chapter, we evaluate whether international openness has contributed to the prosperity of developed democracies in the ways that advocates of knowledge-based growth originally anticipated, or whether the picture is more nuanced. We begin by scrutinizing the competitive advantages of developed democracies in the global knowledge economy, particularly vis-à-vis their emerging market peers. We then explore whether free trade and openness to international competition more broadly are necessarily beneficial to the growth of knowledge-intensive industries – and also whether knowledge-intensive industries have necessarily proved as internationally mobile as they once appeared. The chapter concludes by examining the question of immigration, in terms of both its economic impacts and wider sociopolitical ramifications.

The lure of education, liberalism and the rule of law

Just how critical were the supposed competitive advantages of developed democracies to success in the knowledge economy era? And just how hard was it for emerging economies to replicate those advantages? Perhaps the most obvious point to note is that, if knowledge-based growth is desirable, and if investment in education will enable a given country to capture a disproportionate share of global knowledge jobs, then many countries will adopt this policy approach simultaneously, thereby neutralizing the relative advantage any individual country can gain. Such strategies might still be advisable to maintain one's relative share of knowledge work, particularly if knowledge work as a whole is increasing in value and volume across the global economy. But the response of other countries to the same incentives will in all probability limit the scale of the benefits on offer.

Critically, this applies to emerging economies as well as developed democracies. Countries such as India and China have sought to capitalize on the knowledge economy in their own right, diluting the impact of pro-knowledge policies in the developed democracies. By prioritizing investment in skills, these countries have witnessed an explosion of knowledge work, with comparably

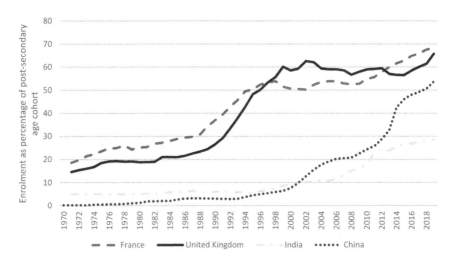

Figure 8.1 Tertiary education enrolment as percentage of post-secondary age cohort, selected countries, 1970–2019

Source: World Bank/UNESCO Institute for Statistics, Indicator: SE.TER.ENRR.

educated knowledge labour often available at a lower cost than in more advanced economies. Figure 8.1 shows how China and (to a lesser extent) India have increased the rate of tertiary education enrolment from the dawn of the new millennium onwards, with enrolment levels in China now rivalling those in the UK and France.[1]

Moreover, multinational corporations are alive to these possibilities, structuring supply chains to take into account the price of knowledge work in different jurisdictions. Educated workers in less affluent countries tend to be cheaper than educated workers in higher-income countries.[2] Tech companies indigenous to emerging economies are increasingly supplying goods and services produced via knowledge work to domestic, regional and global markets. The international political economy of knowledge-based growth thus offers a further explanation as to why workers in developed democracies have not seen the abundance of lucrative knowledge jobs that they were once promised. Developed democracies compete for knowledge jobs not only against each other but against emerging economies too, although this competition is not quite the free-for-all predicted by the likes of Thomas Friedman, as we will see later in this chapter.

Outside education, advocates of knowledge-based growth in developed democracies anticipated that the culture and institutions of liberal democracies would be a further source of competitive advantage in the knowledge economy era. Tolerant, open, liberal, multicultural societies supposedly excelled in creativity and innovation, cultivating knowledge-based growth, whereas "settled, stable communities are the enemies of innovation, talent, creativity, diversity and experimentation. They are often hostile to outsiders, dissenters, young upstarts and immigrants … that kind of community is the enemy of knowledge creation, which is the well-spring of economic growth."[3] Such accounts of knowledge-based growth echo the self-congratulatory certainties of the post-Cold War era: that open societies are uniquely adaptable, representing the historical end point of political-institutional progress.[4] Yet, the link between liberal freedoms, democratic contestation and knowledge-based growth has proved to be tenuous at best. The case of China offers ample evidence of this disjoin. Over the last decade, China has developed a set of world-leading tech businesses such as Alibaba, Tencent and Baidu. It has also cultivated a competitive advantage in highly promising high-tech industries of the future, such as green technologies and artificial intelligence.[5] This economic transformation has not been accompanied by a shift towards Western-style liberal democracy, as Western champions of China's WTO accession hoped back in the late 1990s and early 2000s. If anything, China has cultivated these highly successful knowledge industries while moving towards a more authoritarian model of government. Indeed, a lack of liberal qualms regarding privacy, surveillance and data collection might be an advantage when developing data-hungry technologies such as artificial intelligence algorithms.

What of the rule-of-law institutions that were supposedly vital to making investments in knowledge commercially viable? The very replicability that makes knowledge potentially so valuable – the fact that the same idea, recipe, design or program can be reproduced countless times at near-zero marginal cost and deployed simultaneously by countless users across the world – can also render it deeply unprofitable, if the originator of that knowledge has no way of restricting its use to fee-paying customers.[6] Books, fashion labels, trademarks and many medicines can be reproduced relatively inexpensively; even sophisticated technologies such as microchips or new materials can be reverse-engineered, given suitable facilities. If countries want to encourage knowledge work, they must therefore safeguard the intellectual property rights of domestic knowledge workers and knowledge businesses, not just at home but also abroad.

This analysis lay behind the development of international intellectual property rules, most notably the TRIPS agreement, which came into force in January 1995, to be administered and enforced by the newly created WTO. TRIPS reflected developed democracies' commitment to their own knowledge-intensive industries, potentially disadvantaging less developed intellectual property-importing countries. However, by making participation in the international trade system contingent upon respect for intellectual property rights, advanced economies left developing countries with little choice. Arguably, it was only the prize of WTO membership that incentivized an intellectual property-importing country like China to adopt a more robust approach towards intellectual property rights over the course of the 1990s.[7]

Yet, the cooperative structure of TRIPS and other international intellectual property protections are inherently precarious. It is rational for countries seeking to cultivate their own knowledge-intensive industries to police domestically created intellectual property strictly, and to demand exacting protections from international partners for their knowledge-intensive exports, while simultaneously soft-pedalling on enforcement of the intellectual property rights of overseas companies (provided they are able to pursue this strategy without sanction). China in particular has been widely condemned for such conduct over recent years, with ready availability of counterfeit goods in many parts of the country, sometimes sitting side by side with their more expensive genuine counterparts.[8] If knowledge-intensive businesses cannot enforce their intellectual property rights effectively across the globe, or if they have to pay a premium to do so, then this will mean the profits to be gained from operating at the technological frontier will be correspondingly lower than advocates of knowledge-based growth once anticipated. Similarly, if consumers in developed democracies have to pay a premium for innovative products and leading brands, while consumers in emerging markets can free-ride because of lax intellectual property enforcement, this places the former group at a relative disadvantage. From both a business and consumer perspective, then, the economic advantages that knowledge-based growth brings to developed democracies will not be as great as once they seemed.

International trade, investment and network effects

Openness to trade in new products, and to investment by overseas companies, were also widely supposed to position developed democracies at the forefront of knowledge-driven growth. Innovative new goods and services would act as a model for domestic companies, who would be forced to build superior rival products, or who would use these innovations to enhance the efficiency and productivity of their own operations. Alongside capital investment and jobs, overseas companies would also bring new technologies and know-how, thereby improving the skill level of the domestic workforce.

This logic works well for many high-tech goods and services, so long as international trade does not undermine other socially desirable outcomes, such as environmental protections, minimum employment standards and human rights (a point we return to in Chapter 10). However, where the strategies of multinational firms revolve around seizing first-mover advantage, harnessing network effects and economies of scale that make them all but unassailable by would-be domestic challengers, openness to foreign investment and foreign products may simply translate into foreign ownership of monopoly rents. These rents are the additional value that dominant businesses can extract from the wider economy on account of their exclusive ownership of a scarce resource, such as the network effects associated with digital platforms.[9] Conversely, obstacles to overseas investment in such sectors or overseas supplies of such services can make it easier for domestic champions to emerge, granting them time to achieve critical mass in their own right. In recent years, a number of Chinese tech companies have been able to achieve dominant positions – domestically and regionally – in markets such as search (Baidu), e-commerce (Alibaba) and social media (Weibo and WeChat), markets that in North America and Europe are dominated by US tech giants. It is an open question whether these Chinese companies would have enjoyed such success had the Chinese government not placed barriers in the way of competition from overseas tech firms. Similarly, the success of domestic taxi-hailing apps in countries such as Iran (Snapp), India (Ola) and Spain (Cabify) may owe something to the regulatory barriers in place in this particular market sector, granting domestic businesses a vital reprieve from overseas competitors such as Uber.

Should we care about the emergence of domestic challengers, or is this simply a vestigial nationalistic reflex, a relic from a less globalized era? To be sure, the citizens of one country can gain from businesses based in another, and not just in their capacity as consumers of cheaper, better services but also in their capacity as employees of, or even investors in, such businesses. In a world where capital flows freely across many borders, where workforces are spread across many locations, does it even make sense to speak of businesses as "belonging" to one state or another? Governments can benefit from overseas businesses too, from taxing sales, salaries and profits generated by a given business within their jurisdiction, irrespective of where in the world it happens to be headquartered. Yet, in most cases, the lion's share of the economic rewards accrue to the home country of these multinational businesses. As a general rule, they retain large, well-paid workforces in their countries of origin. And although shares in publicly traded multinational companies are owned by investors from all over the world, the founders and early investors who own substantial proportions of stock tend to be based predominantly in the businesses' home locations. In terms of taxation rights, too, the benefits to having knowledge-intensive overseas companies operate in your jurisdiction are limited: for decades, multinational corporations have sought to locate intellectual property in tax havens and structure their international operations such that as much profit as possible is attributed to this property, to the ultimate benefit of shareholders rather than tax authorities.[10]

These gains to the citizens of other countries might be forgivable if the businesses in question were contributing to the economic growth of the countries in which they operate (and/or to which they sell) in other ways. To the extent that a knowledge-intensive company's investment in a given economy spills over to increase the productivity of the workforce as a whole, and to the extent that its products encourage emulation and competition that enhance the welfare of consumers in general, then there are clearly benefits to the economies in which they operate too. But if the software and systems underpinning their services are relatively straightforward – if their main selling point is their network effects, the ability to access people and the content, goods, services and data-driven insights that other people produce – then the case for a protectionist approach looks substantially stronger.[11] Not only would this mean more wages, profits and taxes for the domestic economy in question, it would also mean more data. As we saw in Chapter 6, access to data (and the people who generate it) is crucial to the development of many advanced artificial intelligence applications. Consequently, countries who want to compete in the coming wave of digital innovation need to think not just about educating workers and attracting investors but also about how domestic knowledge industries are going to accumulate the users and the data they need in order to innovate.

International mobility, international cooperation and the race to the bottom

Early advocates of knowledge-based growth tended to view knowledge-intensive industries, and the knowledge workers comprising them, as hyper-mobile. New ideas can be produced anywhere in the world, so the argument ran, and knowledge-intensive businesses are unencumbered by the physical capital that typified a previous generation of businesses: plant, machinery, factories and so forth. Even where knowledge businesses ultimately do need such facilities, physical manufacturing can be split off from knowledge production and located wherever costs are lowest: "Designed by Apple in California" but "Assembled in China", to quote the back of one of the most iconic products of the knowledge economy era. Without physical investments to tether them to particular locations, knowledge businesses could in theory relocate to wherever in the world they identified workers sufficiently skilled to meet their needs. But this also meant that they could relocate in response to other factors as well, including higher tax rates, macroeconomic instability or uncertain access to other markets. On this account, the rise of the knowledge economy exerts a disciplining influence over policy-makers, forcing them to keep taxes, spending and borrowing low while also maintaining international openness, or else face the economic consequences of knowledge-intensive businesses relocating to other jurisdictions. The same dynamic also applies at the level of individual workers.

Where tax rates are too high, or other social and economic conditions are unsatisfactory, highly skilled individuals will migrate to countries where they are treated better.

These arguments featured prominently in the early policy debates of the knowledge economy era, and their logic was reflected in the policy approaches that governments adopted.[12] But it is increasingly questionable whether knowledge-intensive businesses – and the knowledge workers they employ – are as footloose as policy-makers once feared. In their 2019 book, *Democracy and Prosperity*, Torben Iversen and David Soskice draw on the literature on agglomeration effects in thriving city regions to argue that knowledge industries are not highly mobile but rather "geographically embedded in the advanced nation-state".[13] The same increasing returns that attract certain types of knowledge worker and knowledge-intensive business to particular locations mean that individuals and companies alike stand to lose by moving elsewhere. Particular industries become rooted in places where they can access not just workers with relevant expertise but also suppliers, customers, investors, lawyers, accountants and so forth; particular individuals become rooted in places where they can access diverse employment opportunities.

Superficially, it might seem that other major cities can replicate these benefits, thus placing them (and the nations in which they are based) in competition with one another. However, the degree of specialization typical of advanced economies means that even apparently similar activities in different locations may not substitute particularly well for each other. Complementarities between workers and businesses, customers and suppliers, as well as the broader institutional structure of a particular place (its educational establishments, its regulatory framework, its financial system), mean that knowledge work carried out in one location cannot be easily transplanted to another. Automobile manufacturers in the USA might focus on different technologies, deploying different techniques, to their counterparts in Germany; software engineers in Berlin might be grappling with a different range of problems to their counterparts in Munich. Consequently, a business that wanted to shift some of its knowledge-intensive activities from one location to another would in all likelihood need to relocate a substantial proportion of its current workforce as well, to ensure that they could then transfer their specialized tacit knowledge to employees in the new location, as well as relocating specific workers from the wider ecosystem of suppliers, investors, professional advisers and so forth that support that activity. The UK's departure from the EU offers a useful illustration of this point: despite the dire predictions of financial services industry bodies, the number of jobs that shifted from London to other European financial centres has to date been minimal, reflecting the difficulty of coordinating the movement of an entire sector. Individual knowledge workers are often reluctant to relocate. Even internationally mobile immigrants become rooted in particular locations, not just because of job opportunities but also because they develop personal relationships, start families and create homes, activities that form dense social networks and attachments to particular neighbourhoods and cities. Friends you haven't met yet are a poor substitute for those you have.

Such effects serve as a counterweight to the tendency of knowledge jobs to flow to skilled workers in emerging markets (or rival developed countries, for that matter), where labour costs might be cheaper, taxes lower or regulations more favourable. Empirical evidence suggests that, once established, knowledge-intensive research activities tend to remain concentrated in particular locations even in the face of rising costs.[14] Indeed, some early theorists of the knowledge economy explicitly acknowledged as much: for example, in *The Work of Nations*, Robert Reich noted that "symbolic-analytic zones cannot easily be duplicated elsewhere on the globe. While specific inventions and insights emanating from them traverse the globe in seconds, the cumulative, shared learning on which such ideas are based is far less portable."[15] Nevertheless, the interpretation of the knowledge economy that rose to prominence in policy-making circles placed more emphasis on a global competition for capital and talent, obsessing about the risk of falling behind as a result of excessive taxation, borrowing and regulation.

This "flat-world thinking", the notion that knowledge-intensive businesses can credibly threaten to relocate in response to developed democracies' economic policy decisions, has been further undermined by another development: a deepening of international cooperation, at least among certain groups of countries. Taxation offers a particularly interesting case study of this phenomenon. The international order assumed by early theorists of the knowledge economy was one in which atomized nation states were locked in competition for highly skilled individuals and for investment by knowledge-intensive businesses. This meant that tax rates on mobile factors of production (capital and individuals) were destined to fall, with countries forced to recalibrate their tax systems (shifting the burden of tax on to the likes of consumption and property, which are less mobile), to reduce their public spending (shifting the burden of public service provision on to private-paying individuals) or both. This was reflected not just in falling tax rates, particularly on corporate profits, but also in widespread acceptance of the terms on which international markets chose to supply capital. These terms included the extensive use of offshore tax havens, allowing profits to be shifted to locations where they were taxed at even lower rates (if they were taxed at all). While in theory, countries could choose whether or not to accept these terms, in practice any country doing so unilaterally would cut itself off from an important source of international finance.

This analysis presupposed a world of nation states competing against each other in a race to the bottom, with governments and citizens unable or unwilling to challenge the status quo. However, the global financial crisis of 2007–8, and the fiscal crises that it precipitated, have triggered a sea change in global international tax cooperation. The political economists Rasmus Corlin Christensen and Martin Hearson hypothesize that the confluence of the crisis with the increasing prominence of the digital economy made the status quo fiscally and politically unsustainable. Governments, faced with the costs of dealing with the financial crisis, could no longer tolerate tax avoidance to the same degree, particularly not from an increasingly important sector of the economy. The growth of the digital sector also increased public awareness of such tax avoidance practices: awareness that tipped easily into hostility against a backdrop of austerity, when average citizens were seeing their own tax burdens increase and public services slashed. Consequently, from the financial crisis onwards, governments adopted a more confrontational approach towards tax avoidance, both multilaterally and unilaterally.[16] Evidence of this new-found desire to tax footloose individuals and capital can be found in the creation of the Common Reporting Standard in 2014, which saw financial institutions providing information about the dealings of non-resident account holders to the tax authorities in their countries of residence, closing down opportunities for tax avoidance and evasion (particularly on the part of high-net-worth individuals). It can also be seen in the sharing of information about profits reported and taxes paid by multinational corporations between tax authorities in different jurisdictions – so-called country-by-country reporting – which is vital to understanding companies' tax avoidance strategies, identifying loopholes that allow profits to go untaxed.[17] Unilateral actions include the introduction of the Foreign Account Tax Compliance Act in the USA, the Diverted Profits Tax in the UK or France's digital services tax. Such unilateral actions in turn prompt greater support for international cooperation, even among multinational corporations who are the targets of such multilateral initiatives, as they begin to perceive a single harmonized set of rules as the "least bad" option available to them. While these moves fall short of the policies that many tax justice campaigners would like to see implemented, they may still constitute the beginnings of a shift in the global governance of taxation.

Immigration

The internationalism of the knowledge economy era was also reflected in many developed democracies' openness to immigration over this period. Immigration was supposed to give countries that embraced it a competitive edge, improving the quality and quantity of human capital available and thus making these countries more attractive to knowledge-intensive businesses. While rhetorically, countries tended to emphasize openness to high-skilled immigration, in practice many countries simultaneously encouraged or at least tolerated lower-skilled migration too. In part this was a consequence of established international agreements, such as the freedom of movement enshrined within EU law. In part, it was a consequence of "diaspora effects", as the formation of immigrant communities within advanced economies facilitates further migration from less affluent countries, with intra-family and intra-community ties providing would-be immigrants with advantages in formal immigration processes, as well as better information about those processes and more opportunities to circumvent them.[18] The embrace of multiculturalism in general was also seen as part of the openness of the knowledge economy: the liberal attitudes that were supposed to incubate innovation, creativity and knowledge exchange. Furthermore, mass immigration was tolerated by governments, businesses and households keen to keep a motivated low-wage workforce at their disposal.[19]

It is worth emphasizing that immigration was supposed to benefit indigenous populations. Openness to high-skilled migration in particular was meant to attract knowledge-intensive businesses to invest in a given country, confident that they could recruit the most talented individuals to staff their operations, irrespective of where in the world these individuals originated. These immigrants would bring with them expertise, ideas and practices, which the domestic population could then learn from, appropriate and develop. But even lower-skilled migration was supposed to benefit the average consumer, by addressing labour shortfalls in particular industries (for instance, healthcare and the construction sector) and doing jobs (such as seasonal agricultural labour) that indigenous workers were unwilling to perform, given the often onerous demands and low pay on offer. Net migration was also supposed to address the sustainability of developed democracies' welfare states, as longer life expectancy coupled with declining birth rates conspired to reduce the share of indigenous working-age individuals within the population at large, and thus the tax revenues that underpin services such as health and social care.

These economic benefits have for the most part been realized. In many developed democracies, it is difficult to imagine how large sections of the public and the private sector could operate without ready access to migrant labour. Numerous studies have demonstrated how immigration into advanced economies – highly skilled and lower skilled alike – has tended to increase productivity and wage levels across the board.[20] However, these economic benefits have been unevenly distributed, with the gains focused on higher-skilled workers and more affluent households, which is unsurprising, as these parts of society are best placed to reap the profits generated by immigrant employees or purchase goods and services produced in whole or part with immigrant labour. Lower-skilled workers have seen smaller positive impacts on their wage levels, and some analyses even show immigration forcing down the wages of lower-skilled groups.[21] This is consistent with lower-skilled indigenous workers finding themselves in competition with immigrants, bidding down the salaries they might otherwise command and/or the working conditions on which they might otherwise insist. Such competitive dynamics are hardly surprising, especially given that many migrants to developed democracies enjoy the added incentive of earnings that are substantially higher in purchasing power terms than they are for indigenous workers, when remitted back to countries of origin where the cost of living is lower.

This means that immigration could quite easily be experienced as a net negative by parts of the domestic population, particularly if it imposes other economic, social and psychological costs beyond those captured by productivity and wage levels. Those costs might take diverse forms. For example, immigration might reduce incentives for governments and businesses to upskill indigenous workers, reducing their earning potential.[22] The presence of groups who (perfectly reasonably) prefer to interact in their first language, with other speakers of that language, could lead to a decline in social solidarity within local communities.[23] Differences in culture and ethical values can be a source of conflict, and can require costly processes of individual adjustment and interpersonal negotiation to resolve. A wealth of evidence suggests that higher levels of immigration lead to lower public support for redistributive policies, reducing the social transfers and public services on which lower-paid workers and economically struggling regions disproportionately rely.[24] Added to this, governments might fail to expand local public services to cope with localized population increases associated with migration.[25] For some citizens of developed democracies, the impacts of immigration have been far more ambiguous than advocates of international openness once claimed.

Review

The chapters in Part II have highlighted numerous shortcomings in the understanding of the modern economy on which the policy agenda of knowledge-driven growth was predicated, a policy agenda that emphasized social investment, dynamic markets, fiscal prudence and international openness. On this account, national prosperity depended first and foremost upon cultivating high-tech businesses oriented towards a global market. Yet, as we have seen, policy-makers seem to have overestimated the knowledge economy's productivity-enhancing potential. Certainly, economic growth in the developed world has been sluggish at best over the last 30 years, when viewed as a whole. Market concentration and the enduring importance of capital – in particular, finance, intellectual property and data – have constrained the entrepreneurial dynamism of knowledge-intensive sectors, at least relative to the expectations of policy-makers in the 1990s and early 2000s.

Even if that productivity-enhancing potential were to be realized, knowledge-driven growth might still occur without generating a particularly large number of intellectually and financially rewarding job opportunities. In the absence of a surfeit of knowledge work to be done, the "security of employability" supposedly guaranteed by one's skills is a poor substitute for the security of employment that was provided by legal protections and trade union activism in the era of the mixed economy, before those safeguards were dismantled in the service of market liberalization.

Efforts to achieve laudable goals such as equality of opportunity and social inclusion through social investment, particularly investment in education, have also disappointed. Success in many parts of the knowledge economy turns less on what you learn than on access to capital, social networks and thriving local labour markets. Moreover, the structure of opportunity in the knowledge economy – particularly in sectors typified by superstar effects and substantial economies of scale – means that if anything the gulf between the richest and the rest has widened, making it even less likely that well-meaning educational initiatives can bridge that gap. Wealth and poverty alike are becoming progressively more persistent across generations, and there are reasons to fear that higher-paying jobs may become increasingly scarce, as artificial intelligence algorithms increasingly substitute for tasks currently performed by highly skilled individuals.

The benefits of international openness, too, are more ambiguous than they once seemed. The competitive advantages of developed democracies, characterized by strong rule-of-law institutions and liberal freedoms, are less pronounced than they appeared in the immediate aftermath of the Cold War. In markets where substantial first-mover advantages and network effects dominate, openness to international investment begins to look like a questionable strategy. Immigration into developed democracies can impose social and economic costs, at least on some parts of the indigenous population.

All in all, the policy agenda of knowledge-based growth and the understanding of the knowledge economy on which it was premised have proved to be flawed in several important respects. In turn, those flaws have meant that this policy programme has failed to deliver for many of its earlier supporters. In Part III, we will explore the political ramifications of this failure, and whether these policy shortcomings are surmountable. Chapter 9 examines how the election-winning consensus that formed around knowledge-driven growth has unravelled, creating space for new political movements to emerge, while Chapter 10 assesses how the economic and political problems of the knowledge economy era might be overcome.

PART III

Beyond the knowledge economy

9
POLITICAL BACKLASH

Since the global financial crisis, many developed democracies have experienced seismic political upheavals. Knowledge-driven growth strategies – and their champions in the political establishment – today stand on unstable electoral ground. Centrists of both the left and the right have seen their vote share eroded. Party systems that just a few years ago appeared frozen have suddenly become fluid. New political movements and organizations have seized votes, seats and even government office from their better-pedigreed rivals. In other cases, outsiders have contested the leadership of mainstream parties, posing serious challenges to candidates favoured by established party hierarchies and powerbrokers, and on occasion even emerging victorious. These outsiders pose serious challenges to diverse aspects of the knowledge-driven growth agenda: calling into question everything from its commitment to international openness to its celebration of dynamic markets, from its vision of prudent macroeconomic policy to its insistence that social investment will suffice to tackle problems of inequality and exclusion.

In Part I, we explored how the knowledge-driven growth agenda came to dominate economic policy debate and practice in developed democracies from the early 1990s onwards. In Part II, we examined the diverse ways in which that knowledge-driven growth agenda has fallen short. In this chapter, we unpack the political implications of those shortcomings. The chapter begins by revisiting the idea of the knowledge economy as a growth regime: a set of economic policy ideas and assumptions that are underwritten politically by a distinctive coalition of supporters. It identifies three groups who have been particularly badly affected by the shortcomings of knowledge-driven growth, and thus who are particularly likely to withdraw their support from the status quo: younger people, lower-paid and/or lower-skilled workers, and residents of regions undergoing relative economic decline. The chapter goes on to examine electoral data showing declining levels of support for the political mainstream, as well as evidence that these declines are particularly pronounced among the three groups that our analysis predicts. The chapter concludes by comparing this analysis to alternative accounts of the outsider insurgency, showing how it is compatible with these rival explanations but also how it is complementary to them, filling in their gaps and resolving their inconsistencies.

Fragmentation

As outlined in Chapter 1, a growth regime consists of two components. It denotes a set of ideas about the causal mechanisms underpinning economic growth, on the back of which governments base their policy choices. It also denotes a broad-based coalition that underwrites this paradigm politically, encompassing the expert community of policy-makers and commentators, academics and think tanks, rival politicians from other mainstream parties and groups within wider civil society. Ultimately, a broad range of people accept the dominant policy paradigm as tolerably conducive to their individual interests and to the common good (as they understand it). Assuming this coalition holds together, over time the ideas and policies it supports become widely accepted as a starting point for social and economic problem-solving. Gatekeepers to the policy-making community (in academia, the media and the bureaucracy) increasingly use these ideas to evaluate the expertise of would-be experts. These ideas also shape the terms of political discourse, as politicians of diverse partisan affiliations increasingly recognize that they must couch their economic vision in these terms if they are to garner enough votes to win an election. Over time, however, this policy paradigm may fail to deliver for its supporters, whether as a result of its own internal contradictions and blind spots, or because of changing external circumstances (economic shocks, international crises, long-term social and political transformations). This weakens the growth regime, creating space for outsiders to propose new ideas and policies and to assemble rival coalitions.

   The electoral coalition that formed around the idea of knowledge-based growth in the 1990s and 2000s was impressive in its breadth. It consisted of economically successful entrepreneurs and professionals engaged in knowledge work, who were promised public investment in their industries and a light-touch approach to taxation of their income, profits and wealth; the young people who hoped to follow in their footsteps, in whose name the state invested in education from early-years provision through to university-level degrees; people in lower-skilled employment, who were to be offered opportunities to upskill, and thereby make their work more knowledge-intensive, more valuable and thus better paid; denizens of thriving multicultural cities, who were assured that investment and jobs would continue to flow and that government would provide them with a platform from which they could access global markets; as well as residents of regions undergoing relative economic decline, who were promised knowledge work as a replacement for the industrial jobs that had been lost to lower-wage parts of the world. Public officials, as well as the academics, media commentators and think tanks that feed into the policy-making process, adopted the nostrums of knowledge-driven growth, emphasizing supply-side interventions such as investment in skills and infrastructure as key to productivity, prosperity and social inclusion. International institutions such as the EU and OECD championed the knowledge economy agenda, incorporating these ideas into their best-practice recommendations and compiling comparative data on the spread of high-tech industries and knowledge work across advanced economies. Theories of endogenous technological change were reflected in the economic models of finance ministries and in the logic of international agreements.

Yet, as we saw in Part II, the realities of knowledge-based growth have increasingly sidelined many parts of the coalition that originally supported it. Consider young people, for example. Although some have benefited from investments in their education and opportunities to do well-paid work within knowledge-intensive parts of the economy, many of their peers have struggled. According to a 2018 study by the Resolution Foundation, in countries as diverse as Denmark, Germany, the USA, Italy and Spain, young people born between 1981 and 2000 enjoyed lower income levels than the preceding generation did when they were at a similar stage in their careers, despite the productivity growth of the intervening years. Even in countries that bucked this trend – such as the UK and Finland – generation-on-generation income growth for this cohort has slowed dramatically.[1] Clearly, the global financial crisis wreaked havoc on this generation's economic prospects. The pandemic, too, looks set to disproportionately disadvantage younger people, as they struggle to start their careers at a time of rising unemployment, without the support and training provided by the conventional work environment. But it is also evident that, even before the crises of recent years, the knowledge economy has not proved to be bountiful enough to offer these cohorts a clear pathway to prosperity. Education alone has not been sufficient to provide them with access to opportunities. Access to social networks, access to affordable housing in reach of thriving urban centres, access to real-world experience (often gained while working low-paid entry-level positions) all have an enduringly important part to play in ensuring young people are equipped for knowledge work. And even if they are so equipped, there may not be that much demand for their labour anyway: as knowledge-intensive tasks are increasingly performed for free (or for costless access to online platforms), as semi-skilled and even highly skilled work is increasingly automated and/or offshored, and as superstar effects and winner-take-all market dynamics funnel rewards to a limited number of individuals and businesses. Finally, those young people fortunate enough to find a foothold in a knowledge-intensive business often discover that their bargaining power is weaker than a previous generation of policy-makers anticipated. Far from businesses being dependent on the skills and know-how of their young knowledge workers, salary levels and working conditions often suggest that employers hold the upper hand in these negotiations. This is unsurprising, given the liberalization of labour markets mandated by both neoliberalism and the knowledge-driven growth agenda, as well as the ongoing reliance of young people on their employers' capital (physical and intangible) in order to turn their skills into something saleable. (Younger people are also beholden to other capital owners, in the form of landlords renting out residential property in conurbations where knowledge jobs are clustered.) Some businesses face a surfeit of suitably qualified candidates, putting further downward pressure on salaries, and even where there are skills shortages, it is not clear whether addressing these will increase the salaries of the young or reduce the amount of income that owners of capital need to relinquish to their employees.[2]

Lower-skilled workers have faced a very similar predicament to young people. Indeed, their situation is generally worse: while investment in young people's education was more modest than the political rhetoric of the 1990s and early 2000s implied, it was still relatively generous compared to the level of investment most governments made in adult education and lifelong learning. Added to this, the "knowledgification" of lower-skilled work – which was to allow low-skilled workers to add more value, thereby improving their pay and living standards, within their existing roles and industries – has been limited and piecemeal. Indeed, in some roles, the opposite has happened, with lower-paid jobs becoming increasingly routinized by advances in managerial technology, a trend epitomized by the Amazon warehouse worker, whose optimal path around the site is dictated by algorithm and whose every move (or failure to move) is automatically logged and monitored. Even where tasks themselves do not invite routinization – such as in the field of social care – the time frames and conditions under which this non-routine work is performed are increasingly rationalized and prescribed. Not only has knowledgification failed to emerge but traditional options for progression out of lower-skilled work have been eroded. The further routinization of lower-paid work has facilitated the removal of mid-tier managerial roles: as decision-making autonomy is removed, so is the need for management and review of those decisions in all but the most formulaic way. Platforms can substitute for management in taxi companies, cleaning agencies, home maintenance services, childcare providers and much more besides. Other traditional mid-skilled jobs – clerical workers, trained machinists and the like – have been offshored or automated (or both). This is not to deny that some lower-paid workers have progressed into some of the expanding number of higher-skilled, higher-paid roles; but for those who have not, opportunities for progression appear to be narrowing rather than expanding.

Admittedly, some workers in lower-skilled roles, who are based in thriving cities specializing in internationally marketable goods and services, will have seen their productivity rise, reflecting the fact that highly paid knowledge workers can afford higher-cost in-person services. To the extent that these gains are not eroded by higher housing costs (for instance, because these workers purchased their home many years back, because they inherited property in a thriving city region or because they are protected by rent controls) or by higher outgoings for goods and services that they themselves consume locally, then these people too might be seen as net beneficiaries of knowledge-based growth.

The corollary of this, however, is that people who are based outside these thriving urban centres have seen little benefit from the last three decades of knowledge-based growth. In towns and cities that have not specialized in knowledge-intensive goods and services – including many places that were historically involved in heavy industry and resource extraction – highly trained individuals have struggled to access job opportunities that make the most of their skill set. The remote working revolution and the virtual office have not emerged, or at least not in ways that have extended knowledge work to more remote towns and rural areas, although the Covid-19 pandemic may yet see this shift, a point we will take up again in Chapter 10. Because salaries and house prices in thriving and stagnating areas have steadily diverged, relocating to where the opportunities are is at best a significant financial risk, at worst outright unaffordable, even for skilled individuals; to say nothing of the emotional costs involved in moving away from places where you have built a life for yourself. In the absence of highly paid workers and highly profitable businesses that face outward to national and international markets, these areas suffer from a persistent lack of demand, which dampens the wages of other workers too: restaurateurs, personal trainers and the whole panoply of in-person service providers that form an important part of the success of thriving city regions. Local amenities close down, rendering areas less attractive, destroying jobs and further widening the gap that separates declining places from their more affluent counterparts. The kinds of compensating investment advocated by the knowledge-driven growth regime – spending on skills and infrastructure – have generally not been sufficient to transform lagging areas into magnets for knowledge-intensive investment, a point often tacitly acknowledged by local policy-makers, who focus such funds on the skills needs of local employers rather than attempting to attract global frontier companies.

In summary, the knowledge-driven growth regime has failed to deliver for three groups who might once have been expected to support it: young people, lower-skilled people and people in places that have been bypassed by knowledge-driven growth. We would thus expect these groups to be particularly disillusioned with those mainstream parties and politicians who have championed the knowledge economy over recent decades. To be sure, these are generalizations. Some young people, some lower-skilled people and some people in "left-behind" regions will buck these trends, either benefiting from knowledge-driven growth directly themselves or championing it in spite of their own personal economic experiences. But, by and large, we would expect support for knowledge-driven growth – and its political champions – to diminish within these demographics.

Three further implications of the growth regimes analysis are worth flagging. First, political discontent does not move in lockstep with economic disappointment. People who subscribe to a particular vision of growth, or place their trust in politicians, policy-makers and other elites who appear to have such a vision, will not immediately interpret downturns in their personal economic circumstances (or aggregate regional or national economic performance) as evidence that their earlier judgement was wrong. They will, in general, accept that it may take time for economic benefits to be realized; that the hoped-for benefits might from time to time be thwarted by circumstance. Occasional anomalies will not necessarily be interpreted as reasons for rejecting an approach to growth: they may be nothing more than noise. Nevertheless, over time mismatches between the reality of a growth regime and its theoretical benefits will mount up, ultimately translating into apathy and disengagement, protest votes or active support for outsiders who offer condemnation of (and alternatives to) the prevailing growth regime.

Added to this, growth regimes may work tolerably well for particular demographics for a period, before ceasing to do so. In the case of the knowledge-driven growth regime, for example, the balance of benefits and costs for younger people has shifted over time. "Generation-Xers" born between the early 1960s and the end of the 1970s enjoyed an increase in knowledge jobs, for which they were often better equipped than their elders, having come of age in the early days of the IT revolution: before opportunities in knowledge-intensive industries were eroded by platforms, automation and market concentration; before entry costs to labour markets (residential property) and product markets (start-up capital) became prohibitively high; when there were more unclaimed fields of endeavour emerging in which people could establish themselves as "superstars". As knowledge-intensive sectors of the economy have matured, as dominant technologies have changed, as the long-term distributive implications of global economic trends, power shifts and policy choices have become ever more tangible, knowledge-driven growth has come to seem like a less attractive proposition to subsequent generations of young people. For other groups on whose support the knowledge-based growth regime depended, the extent to which the knowledge economy ever really worked in their favour is debatable. Some older lower-paid workers will have made the transition to higher-skilled employment as these roles expanded in number, and some lower-paid workers in cities will have seen a trickle-down effect from the growth of higher-value-added industries in their vicinity (particularly lower-paid workers who were insulated from rising housing costs, for instance through private home ownership). These effects will generally have been small and short-lived, however. For people in regions experiencing relative decline – the American Rust Belt, the former industrial heartlands of the north of England – the knowledge economy offered more hope than substance, albeit cushioned by readily available credit, at least until the financial crisis.

Finally, the growth regimes framework highlights that there is no necessary reason why groups that have become disenchanted with the dominant approach to economic growth should necessarily converge on the same alternative. Indeed, there is no necessary reason why they should be attracted to any alternative at all: this is primarily a story about the decline of the centre rather than the strength of the alternatives. That decline may make different social and economic groups more open to alternatives, or it may simply foster apathy and disengagement. Either way, support for centrists erodes, lowering the electoral hurdle that outsiders championing alternatives must clear if they want to challenge mainstream parties and politicians. In the case of the knowledge economy, knowledge-driven growth has disappointed parts of its support base in different, albeit potentially overlapping and complementary, ways. For each of these groups, there are multiple causes for grievance that will be ranked differently by different people, leading them towards different political alternatives.

The decline of the centre

How have patterns of support for knowledge-driven growth – and the parties and politicians who have championed it – changed in the wake of the global financial crisis? Figure 9.1 shows the changing electoral fortunes of the two largest parties (pre-financial crisis) in four different developed democracies: the two most populous EU countries (Germany and France) and the liberal market economies of the USA and UK.[3] The data cover what might be termed the "inter-crisis" period, from the first rumblings of financial meltdown in early 2007 through to the advent of the Covid-19 pandemic at the end of 2019. In the more proportional electoral systems of Germany and France, the story is unambiguous: the old establishment parties commanded a smaller share of the popular vote by the end of the inter-crisis period than they did at the beginning, substantially so in France. The same pattern is observable in the USA, albeit from a much higher base; and the UK appears to buck the trend, with Labour and the Conservatives enjoying more support at the end of the decade than they did at the beginning.

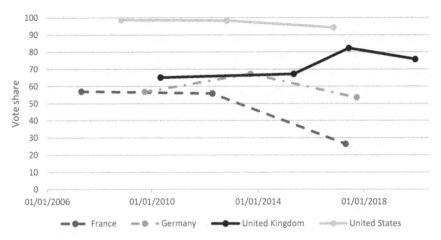

Figure 9.1 Vote share of two largest mainstream parties in major elections, 2007–19

Sources: Conseil Constitutionnel (France), Bundeswahlleiter (Germany), Electoral Commission (UK), Federal Election Commission (USA).

Note: National elections with highest turnout levels: US presidential elections, French first-round presidential elections, UK parliamentary elections, German federal elections (*Zweitstimme* or party choice). German sister parties CDU (Christlich Demokratische Union) and CSU (Christlich-Soziale Union) treated as one entity.

As with any cross-country political comparison, these high-level data conceal country-level nuances. Several of these elections featured mainstream centrist parties that positioned themselves between their larger counterparts on the centre-right and the centre-left: for example, the Liberal Democrats in the UK or the Union for French Democracy (latterly the Democratic Movement) in France. Factoring these parties into the analysis does not dramatically alter the diagnosis of a declining centre, however, as many of these centrist parties also saw their vote share decline over the inter-crisis period.[4] The major exception to this rule in the four countries shown was Emmanuel Macron's En Marche! in France, a new party that promoted an explicitly centrist agenda. Yet, even if these votes are combined with those for the dominant pre-crisis centrist parties, they still do not reverse the downward trend in electoral support for the centre. Similarly, other parties might be considered part of the political establishment, even though they fall to the left and right of the mainstream parties: the Greens and the FDP (Freie Demokratische Partei) in Germany, for example, who have a record of forming coalition governments with the SPD (Sozialdemokratische Partei Deutschlands) and the CDU/CSU. Again, however, including these parties in the total only serves to emphasize the decline of support for the erstwhile establishment (see Figure 9.2).

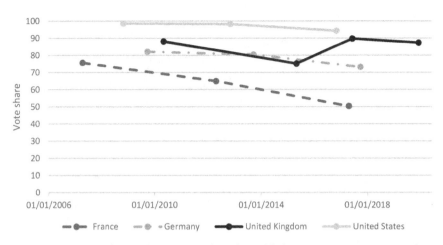

Figure 9.2 Vote share of centrist/political establishment parties in major elections, 2007–19

Sources: Conseil Constitutionnel (France), Bundeswahlleiter (Germany), Electoral Commission (UK), Federal Election Commission (USA).

Perhaps the most misleading aspect of the foregoing analysis, however, is its failure to capture ideological shifts within mainstream parties. This is particularly true in the USA and the UK, where the last five years of the inter-crisis period saw leaders of major parties explicitly renounce their predecessors and make significant moves away from the policy consensus of the knowledge economy era: away from openness to international trade, investment and migration, and away from limited state intervention in market outcomes. In the USA, Donald Trump's election campaign excoriated his rivals in both the Democratic and Republican Parties for their complicity in the economic status quo, portraying himself as the leader of "a worker's party", a "party of people that haven't had a real wage increase in eighteen years, that are angry".[5] Threaded through this economic narrative was a critique of the cultural dimension of liberal internationalism and a hostility to immigrants who he condemned as "bringing drugs, they're bringing crime, they're rapists".[6] In the UK, 2015 saw Jeremy Corbyn – from the Labour Party's old militant left-wing – installed as leader of the opposition, promising a more interventionist and redistributive economic policy agenda. Meanwhile, the 2016 Brexit referendum prompted the Conservative Party to turn its back on the European single market and the unobstructed movement of goods, services, capital and people across borders that it implied. In quick succession, two new Conservative leaders (Theresa May in 2016 and Boris Johnson in 2019) condemned the neglect of "left-behind" regions of the country by previous policy-makers of all political persuasions and explicitly renounced the austerity agenda of the Cameron–Osborne years. Were we to reclassify these

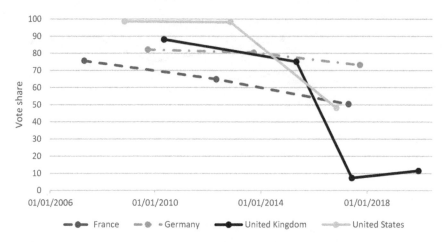

Figure 9.3 Vote share of centrist/political establishment parties in major elections, adjusting for party realignment in UK and USA, 2007–19

Sources: Conseil Constitutionnel (France), Bundeswahlleiter (Germany), Electoral Commission (UK), Federal Election Commission (USA).

parties in light of these changes in leadership, then UK and US election results would imply an even more pronounced shift away from the pre-crisis status quo (see Figure 9.3).

The voting patterns cited above provide a clear indication of the declining electoral fortunes of parties and politicians associated with the erstwhile political mainstream. But do those patterns match the shifts we would expect in light of the unravelling of knowledge-driven growth? In the remainder of this section, we examine data from opinion polls and other sources, to help us to describe the composition (and decomposition) of the political centre.

Younger voters

Younger voters were once a crucial part of the electoral coalition that supported knowledge-driven growth, particularly as championed by centre-left social democratic parties. However, the global financial crisis had a disproportionate impact on younger people, with high levels of youth unemployment across the developed democracies and, in many countries, lower salary levels than the previous generation had enjoyed at a comparable point in their careers.[7] Post-crisis attempts by the political centre to double down on the knowledge-driven growth agenda in a climate of fiscal austerity have done little to win back the youth vote. Generally speaking, the reaction of young voters against the centre has translated into support for left-leaning outsiders – politicians such as Bernie

Sanders in the USA or Jean-Luc Mélenchon in France. This is hardly surprising, given that younger voters tend on average to be more socially liberal than their elders and more supportive of LGBTQ+ rights, cultural diversity and environmental causes. Consequently, the nativist and traditionalist policy platforms of right-leaning outsiders have held comparatively little appeal to this demographic.[8] Nevertheless, right-leaning outsiders have also profited to some degree from younger voters' drift from the centre.

In France, the left-leaning outsider Jean-Luc Mélenchon was the main beneficiary of younger voters' rejection of centrist candidates in the first round of the 2017 presidential election. Comparing data from 2017 to 2007, 18–24 year olds registered the lowest level of support for the three main centrist candidates (Hamon of the Parti Socialiste, Fillon of Les Républicains and the eventual winner Emmanuel Macron). These mainstream candidates enjoyed a mere 37 per cent of the vote share within this demographic, whereas the three main centrist candidates in 2007 (Sarkozy, Royal and Bayrou) had polled double that amount. By contrast, Mélenchon received 30 per cent of the vote among 18–24 year olds, an increase of 21 percentage points on the vote share received by Olivier Besancenot, the main left-outsider candidate at the 2007 election. Interestingly, Mélenchon performed strongly across all age categories in comparison to Besancenot, although the increase in vote share was largest among 18–24 year olds and 25–34 year olds, demographics that were already more likely to vote for a left-leaning outsider back in 2007. Nevertheless, support for the far-right Front National also increased among these age groups, albeit less dramatically: in 2017, Marine Le Pen enjoyed the support of 21 per cent of 18–24 year olds and 24 per cent of 25–34 year olds, gains of 14 points and 8 points respectively when compared to the performance of her father in the first round of the 2007 election.[9]

The trajectory of the youth vote in post-financial crisis Germany is more complex. The collapse of the centre-left SPD vote was already obvious in 2009, the first election following the financial crisis – down 11.2 percentage points on its 2005 performance – and this collapse was particularly pronounced among younger voters, historically among the party's core supporters. Support for the SPD more than halved among 18–24 year olds between 2005 and 2009, falling 18.7 points to 18.2 per cent, and the party fared little better among 25–34 year olds (down 15.7 points to 17.0 per cent). The loss of the youth vote proved long-lasting, with the SPD performing little better in these age groups come the 2017 election. The fall in support for the CDU/CSU among younger voters was less dramatic – more a process of steady erosion than sudden collapse – but still amounted to declines of 6.5 points among 18–24 year olds and 8.8 points among 25–34 year olds over little more than a decade, with the latter constituting the sharpest fall among any age group. However, there was no single clear beneficiary of this shift in voting patterns: the left-leaning Greens and the radical left Die Linke both saw their share of the youth vote increase between 2005 and 2017, and the radical right Alternative für Deutschland (AfD) – only formed in 2013, a few months before the Bundestag elections in September of that year – also succeeded in making inroads among younger voters.[10]

The UK and the USA offer contrasting examples of the transformation of the youth vote under first-past-the-post electoral systems. In the primaries prior to the 2016 US presidential election, young Democrat supporters overwhelmingly opted for the left-leaning outsider Bernie Sanders rather than Hillary Clinton, the candidate of the party establishment. A survey conducted by the Pew Research Center in March 2016 estimated that Sanders enjoyed three and a half times more support from 18–29-year-old Democratic-leaning voters than Clinton – 74 per cent as opposed to 21 per cent of the age group. This can be compared to the 2008 Democratic primary, in which Obama – who had positioned himself outside the Democratic establishment, notably by his opposition to the Iraq War, but whose economic policy was predicated on knowledge-driven growth – enjoyed a more modest lead over Clinton among younger voters: as of 5 February 2008, the *NBC News* primary exit polls gave him a lead of around 20 percentage points over Clinton among the under-30s.[11] Of course, Clinton went on to win the 2016 nomination, but lack of enthusiasm for her candidacy among younger voters contributed to the ultimate failure of her campaign. Whereas in 2008, exit polls saw Obama leading McCain by more than two to one among the youngest voter groups, the 2016 result was far closer: with 18–24 year olds favouring Clinton over Trump by 56 per cent to 35 per cent and 25–29 year olds by 53 per cent to 39 per cent.[12]

By contrast, the selection of Jeremy Corbyn as leader of the UK Labour Party saw a surge in turnout among younger voters, who opted overwhelmingly for the left-leaning outsider. Early estimates suggested double-digit increases in turnout among 18–24 year olds in the 2017 general election, prompting diagnoses of a "youthquake" sending tremors through the political establishment.[13] While these findings were later challenged with data collected using (generally more reliable) face-to-face surveys, even these data found a pronounced increase in turnout among under-45s as a whole.[14] Moreover, younger people voted overwhelmingly in favour of Corbyn's party. Ipsos MORI estimated that 62 per cent of 18–24-year-old voters opted for Labour in 2017 (compared to 27 per cent who voted Conservative) and that Labour led the Conservatives by sizeable margins among 25–34 and 35–44 year olds too (by 39 points and 16 points respectively). This pattern became even more acute in 2019, with Labour leading by 43 percentage points among 18–24-year-old voters while retaining the support of older "young" voters too, albeit by diminishing majorities: among 35–44 year olds, the Labour lead was only three points. This marked a dramatic shift in the youth vote in less than a decade: in 2010, 18–24 year olds were al-most evenly split between the Conservatives (30 per cent), Labour (31 per cent) and the Liberal Democrats (30 per cent). Although the Conservatives enjoyed a majority in all the older voter categories in 2010, age was far less polarizing than it would become by the end of the decade: the Conservative lead among over-65s would extend from 13 points in 2010 to 47 points in 2019.

Does this shift away from the centre, towards outsider parties, indicate that support for liberal democracy itself is in decline among the young? In a widely cited article published in 2016 in *The Journal of Democracy*, the political scientists Roberto Foa and Yascha Mounk argued that disillusionment with democratic in-stitutions was on the rise across the world, including in developed democracies such as the UK, USA and Sweden, and that this disillusionment was particularly acute among younger people. Using data from the World Values Survey, Foa and Mounk claim that each successive generation appears to be less inclined to view living in a democracy as "essential".[15] Mounk conjectures that this trend can be attributed to the fact that "a lot of young people ... have little conception of what it would mean to live in a different political system".[16] New generations of voters are ever more distanced from the experience of twentieth-century po-litical horror – civil war, world war, police states and concentration camps, the foundations of what the political theorist Judith Shklar described as the "liber-alism of fear" – which produced a consensus in favour of limited representative government, motivated by the memory of what its absence looks like.[17]

This generational effect is, however, somewhat overstated. As Pippa Norris points out, the downward trend in support for democratic institutions by age cohort is largely confined to the Anglo-American democracies: the UK, USA, Canada, Australia and New Zealand.[18] Moreover, Foa and Mounk interpret the World Values Survey data such that only respondents who, on a scale of 1 to 10, score a 10 for the prompt "how important is it for you to live in a country that is governed democratically?" are deemed to believe it is "essential" to live in a democracy. Different interpretations of the data produce less dramatic de-clines in the democratic proclivities of millennials.[19] What is clear, however, is that younger voters in developed democracies are deeply dissatisfied with the political status quo and highly likely to support outsiders, although to date they have tended to support outsiders with strong liberal and democratic credentials.

Lower-skilled and lower-paid workers

The rise of the knowledge economy privileges the highly educated, highly skilled workers on whom knowledge-intensive businesses depend. By con-trast, lower-skilled workers (and workers who find themselves in lower-skilled occupations) have tended to see a decline in their wages, at least in relative terms. Although advocates of the knowledge economy espoused a doctrine of inclusive prosperity, driven by increased investment in the education of the young and lifelong learning for existing members of the workforce, the scale of these investments rarely matched this rhetoric. In any event, given the changing shape of labour markets in the knowledge economy era – the disappearance of mid-skilled roles that lower-skilled workers might historically have moved into, the tendency for lower-skilled work to become increasingly proceduralized rather than increasingly knowledge-intensive – it is not clear whether increased investment would necessarily have enabled many more people to join the ranks of the better paid. At the same time, labour market liberalization has seen this group stripped of protections it might otherwise have enjoyed, such as legally enforceable employment rights and strong trade union representation, and forced to be flexible, without the security of employability in well-paid roles that the knowledge economy was supposed to supply in return.

In many countries, voters working in lower-skilled occupations and/or with lower levels of education have gravitated towards outsider parties, particularly right-leaning outsiders that express hostility towards immigrants and scepticism towards liberal values more broadly. In their study of the UK Independence Party (UKIP), Robert Ford and Matthew Goodwin draw on survey data from 2004 to 2013 to suggest that the average UKIP supporter was more likely than the average Conservative or Labour supporter to have left school aged 16 or younger and to either be unemployed or perform routine manual work.[20] During UKIP's surge in popularity between the 2010 and 2015 general elections, when it moved from registering just 3.1 per cent of the overall vote to a more influential 12.6 per cent (simultaneously securing a commitment from the Conservatives to hold a referendum on EU membership), these groups were responsible for some of the largest increases in UKIP support in absolute terms. This should not be overstated: UKIP support increased across the board, in a manner broadly proportionate to prior levels of support in particular demographic divisions (see Table 9.1). Moreover, support for UKIP was still a minority pursuit, even in these demographics, suggesting that the rise of UKIP was consistent with the decline of the knowledge-driven growth regime: with the erosion of support for the erstwhile centre rather than the establishment of a rival political consensus.

A similar pattern of growing support for outsider politics in lower-skilled occupational categories and less educated parts of society can be observed in France. The Front National had long drawn a substantial proportion of its (historically limited) support from less educated and/or lower-earning members of society. As it increased in electoral strength following the financial crisis, it made further inroads into these economically marginalized groups.[21] In the first round of the 2007 presidential election, while polling data indicates the Front

Table 9.1 Changing demographics of UKIP supporters.

	Percentage of group 2007–10	Percentage of group 2012–13	Percentage point change	Proportional change
Socioeconomic class				
Working class	3.8	12.3	8.5	×3.2
Middle class	2.5	8.9	6.4	×3.6
Education				
Left school at 16 or younger	4.3	15.4	11.1	×3.6
Continued education after 16	2.1	7.2	5.1	×3.4
Age				
Over 55	4.4	15.8	11.4	×3.6
Under 55	2.0	6.2	4.2	×3.1

Source: Ford and Goodwin, *Revolt on the Right*, based on British Election Study Continuous Monitoring data.

National was the most popular party among manual workers (with 23 per cent of the vote), the centre-left and centre-right candidates were only just behind (on 21 per cent each). By 2017, this gap had widened dramatically: support for the traditional parties of the centre-left and centre-right among manual workers had collapsed to 5 per cent each, and even the centrist Macron only won 16 per cent of their votes. By contrast, the Front National's Marine Le Pen enjoyed the backing of 37 per cent of this demographic. Similarly, in 2007, Le Pen's father won over 22 per cent of voters with no high school diploma and 13 per cent of those with vocational secondary qualifications; in 2017, the Front National's support among those who had not completed the *Baccalauréat* (encompassing both of the 2007 categories) stood at 30 per cent.

It is important to note, however, that the Front National was not the only beneficiary of disenchantment with the political mainstream among lower-skilled voters. The left-wing outsider Jean-Luc Mélenchon also performed strongly among these groups. He secured 17 per cent of the votes of those who had not completed the *Baccalauréat*, registering an even greater gain in relative terms among this group than the Front National: Besancenot's far-left candidacy in 2007 had won over a mere 8 per cent of voters with no high school diploma and 4 per cent of those with vocational secondary qualifications only. Indeed, in absolute terms, it was the left-wing outsider that made the greatest gains among the manual working classes in comparison to 2007: Mélenchon secured the support of 24 per cent of this demographic in 2017 compared to Besancenot's 8 per cent, a gain of 16 percentage points compared to Marine Le Pen's 14-point improvement on her father's performance. Discontent among lower-skilled, lower-paid voters does not automatically translate into support for the anti-immigrant radical right: many economically precarious voters are themselves immigrants, and many members of the white working class would never countenance voting for parties that they perceive as racist.[22] Consequently, these political developments are best understood in terms of the disintegration of the political coalition that had formed around the erstwhile centre rather than the magnetic attraction of a particular alternative.

The withdrawal of working-class support for mainstream political parties, and a concomitant increase in support for outsiders of both right-wing and left-wing persuasions, can be seen in developed democracies across Europe.[23] Analysis of survey data from 2016 in Germany suggests that people with incomes below 70 per cent of the median were somewhat more likely to express a preference for the AfD than people in higher income brackets, as were those in working-class roles, self-employment or unemployment.[24] (This is not to say that these economic factors are necessarily the primary driver of voter preferences for the AfD; as with any large political party, their platform appeals to a range of voters on a range of economic, cultural and normative grounds.)[25]

In the USA, where the electoral system presents voters with a more limited choice of viable candidates, the 2016 election saw less educated voters come out in support of the right-wing outsider Trump, in preference to the mainstream Clinton. According to the exit polls, among voters who left the education system with a high school diploma or no qualifications at all, Trump held a six-point lead over his rival. This marked a striking shift in less than a decade: in 2008, Obama won the support of this group by almost a two-to-one majority (63 per cent to McCain's 35 per cent). Admittedly, households with annual incomes below $50,000 continued on average to support the Democratic candidate in 2016, but even here the margins of victory fell sharply in comparison to 2008.

"Left-behind" regions

One of the most striking features of the outsider insurgency has been its electoral geography: the tendency for economically marginalized regions to vote in favour of political outsiders. This pattern was particularly pronounced in the twin electoral shocks of 2016: the UK's vote to leave the European Union and the election of Donald Trump in the USA. In the former case, economically thriving cities and their more prosperous commuter hinterlands generally voted "Remain", whereas smaller towns, less economically prosperous city regions and rural areas tended to vote for "Leave". Measures of the relative affluence of local authority areas – for example, by median wages or by regional contributions to GDP – were correlated with higher vote shares for the Remain status quo.[26] To be sure, part of this effect is compositional, with economically marginalized regions tending to have higher proportions of older and less educated voters.[27] But people and places are not independent variables. Economic factors influence demographics, as younger people (particularly those with more readily marketable skills) will seek to move from areas of low economic opportunity to places where they can secure higher wages and better career prospects, if they can afford to do so. In subsequent analyses of the Brexit vote, localized economic decline – expressed in the form of pub closures, shuttered high streets, loss of public facilities and crime – often emerged as an important factor in people's decision to reject the status quo.[28]

In the USA, the 2016 presidential election saw several of the former industrial heartland states of the American Midwest – states such as Michigan and Pennsylvania – come out in favour of Donald Trump. These working-class areas had been a reliable source of Democratic votes from 1992 through to 2012. Trump's campaign attributed the relative economic decline of places such as these to the trade policies of previous governments, who had forced American industry into an unwinnable competition with cheaper overseas labour, particularly from China. This message appears to have cut through – the five Rust Belt states of Iowa, Michigan, Ohio, Pennsylvania and Wisconsin saw some of the largest swings towards the Republicans in 2016 when compared to the 2012 election. Iowa saw the largest swing; and only Maine and Rhode Island (much smaller than the Rust Belt states in terms of population and electoral college votes) saw larger swings than Ohio, Michigan and Wisconsin. Importantly, this victory was not necessarily a matter of converting working-class Democratic voters to enthusiastic Trump supporters. Extrapolation of polling data in Iowa, Michigan, Ohio, Pennsylvania and Wisconsin suggests that in 2016 Trump gained an additional 335,000 votes among poorer segments of the electorate (with income less than $50,000), but that Democrats *lost* 1.17 million votes from the same demographics, in comparison to 2012.[29] Such a pattern is consistent with the decline of a growth regime: a loss of support for the status quo which might manifest itself as disengagement as well as support for a range of outsider alternatives. It suggests that we focus our analytical efforts on what repels voters from the centre rather than what attracts them to the fringes. To underscore the point, analysis of voting patterns for the House of Representatives suggests that Congressional districts where the local economy was disproportionately exposed to competition with Chinese-produced goods tend to become more polarized, often voting in greater numbers for more radically right-wing Republican candidates but also (in some areas in which Democrats were originally in the ascendant) for more radically left-wing Democrats too.[30]

Similar patterns can be observed in Germany, where support for the radical right AfD is comparatively high in economically disadvantaged areas of the former West, as well as across the less prosperous former East.[31] A 2015 study suggested that German districts (*Landkreise*) that experience import competition from China and eastern Europe see the vote share of the extreme-right increase, whereas the opposite applies to areas that benefit from the export opportunities created by global economic integration.[32] However, there are exceptions to this geographic rule: it is worth noting that support for left-leaning outsiders often takes on a different pattern, concentrated in affluent city regions with higher proportions of younger voters.[33] Nevertheless, the point remains that voters in left-behind regions – who formed an important part of the political coalition undergirding the knowledge-driven growth agenda – have become increasingly disillusioned with the dominant growth regime of the last three decades, facilitating (if not necessarily directly supporting) the rise of outsider parties.

Reappraising the outsider insurgency

The decline of the centre has spawned mountains of academic scholarship and media commentary on political outsiders, often disparagingly referred to as "populists", a term of abuse that encompasses such unlikely bedfellows as Bernie Sanders and Donald Trump in the USA, Jeremy Corbyn, Nigel Farage and Boris Johnson in the UK, or Jean-Luc Mélenchon and Marine Le Pen in France. Explanations of the outsider insurgency have tended to focus on some combination of economic discontent and cultural anxiety, with voters motivated on the one hand by the experience of economic hardship, a lack of adequately paid and secure employment opportunities or the relative economic decline of their home regions, and on the other hand by concerns about loss of status in open multicultural societies, hostility towards women's liberation and LGBTQ+ rights or impatience with the compromises required to govern complex and globally interconnected societies. Some commentators even portray these outsider politicians and parties as an existential threat to liberal democracies, attacking core institutions and principles including the rule of law, the democratic process and freedom of expression.[34]

Portraying the outsider insurgency in terms of the decline of knowledge-driven growth is complementary to many of these analyses. The majority of the economic problems identified in the literature – widening divergences between the richest and the rest, between wealth holders and wage earners, between thriving city regions and declining rust belts, between skilled and unskilled – can be seen as products of the knowledge-driven growth strategies that governments have pursued over the last 30 years. True, many proponents of this economic explanation seek to extend their historical accounts further, back to the market liberalization of the 1980s. Yet, while many of the trends in inequality and insecurity can indeed be traced back this far, such accounts do not adequately explain why economically marginalized voters and regions did not vote for anti-system parties in the 1990s, when many of the social and economic problems arising from the neoliberal agenda were already apparent. Recognizing the interposition of knowledge-driven growth enables us to add nuance to this historical account and better explain the timing of the outsider insurgency. As we have seen, in the 1990s policy elites presented knowledge-driven growth as a solution to the centrifugal forces of the neoliberal era, alleviating the economic exclusion of particular demographic groups and regions while simultaneously securing broad-based economic prosperity. And – for some people and places – knowledge-driven growth worked, at least for a time, or at least it appeared to do so.[35]

Similarly, the cultural backlash that commentators such as Pippa Norris and Ronald Inglehart view as key to the outsider insurgency can also be interpreted as a rejection of knowledge-based growth.[36] Advocates of knowledge-driven growth often accompanied their economic policies with a moral message, championing a particular set of cultural and political values. Openness, tolerance and diversity were depicted as drivers of creativity and invention; consequently, individuals, organizations and political institutions that embraced those values would excel in the knowledge economy era. In practice, accepting such norms does not appear to have borne fruit for all communities equally, while the logic of this link between prosperity and values permits an unpleasant form of victim-blaming: you are not intolerant because you are economically marginalized, rather you are economically marginalized because you are intolerant.[37] As Hillary Clinton observed in Mumbai in 2018, "I won the places that are optimistic, diverse, dynamic, moving forward", whereas Trump's campaign was "looking backwards".[38] Under these circumstances, it would be unsurprising if the backlash against liberal norms was not – at least in part – a backlash against the disappointments of knowledge-driven growth (as well as against the shame-driven narrative that some liberals adopt towards the poor).[39]

Focusing on the decline of the knowledge-driven growth regime also helps to explain the radical heterogeneity of the outsider insurgency. Any attempt to reduce this multifaceted phenomenon to a reaction against neoliberal market policies, liberal values and/or democratic norms founder on the rocks of obvious counter-examples. While left-leaning outsiders have made their opposition to neoliberalism explicit, the same is not necessarily true of right-leaning outsiders, many of whom were historically linked with extreme libertarian ideas propounded by anti-tax campaign movements.[40] True, some of these parties – such as France's Front National, particularly under the leadership of Marine Le

Pen – have sought to court working-class votes with a programme of economic nationalism, pledging substantial state intervention in the market (on behalf of indigenous citizens, at least). Yet, many remain wedded to a neoliberal agenda of slashing welfare entitlements for poorer households and reducing taxes on richer members of society, and some espouse a deepening of global trading relationships rather than protectionism.[41] Conversely, while hostility to immigration, women's reproductive rights and LGBTQ+ minorities is a feature of many right-outsider political platforms (and often reflected in the values of their voters), this is not the case for left-leaning outsiders, many of whom advocate more radical forms of liberal inclusivity than mainstream parties have hitherto adopted.[42] Finally, although there is undoubtedly a strain of intolerance towards democratic norms such as freedom of speech on the radical left as well as the radical right, not to mention an impatience with democratic procedures, these sentiments have largely remained on the fringes of electorally successful left-leaning outsider movements. Whereas right-leaning populists often style themselves as tribunes of "the people" – implicitly or on occasion explicitly denying the legitimacy of political alternatives – left-outsiders such as Bernie Sanders in the USA or Jeremy Corbyn in the UK have tended to portray themselves as leaders of "a movement" instead, the indefinite article and the non-totalizing noun implying that they offer one among a plurality of options.[43] Moreover, where left-leaning outsiders have participated in government, they have tended to act as conventional parties in a procedural sense rather than seeking to dismantle the guardrails of democracy, albeit championing a very different economic agenda to their mainstream peers.[44]

What these diverse outsiders have in common is not, therefore, some populist "essence", let alone a shared substantive policy agenda, but rather a repudiation of the orthodoxies that have defined mainstream politics over the last three decades, orthodoxies which have become increasingly untenable in the post-financial crisis world. These orthodoxies, this book has argued, are neatly captured by the concept of knowledge-driven growth.[45] Erstwhile supporters of the status quo have a diverse range of grievances. They may find themselves supporting a correspondingly diverse range of outsider positions or disengaging from politics altogether. The diversity of outsider politics indicates that the search for alternatives to the status quo is ongoing and that no single alternative has yet become embedded.[46] To be sure, some of these alternatives are highly unpalatable, and the desire to cling to old certainties for fear of worse is eminently understandable. However, the search for alternatives per se is both legitimate and necessary. Dismissing all outsiders as "populist" or somehow "deplorable" is not simply inaccurate: it risks stymying that search. Admittedly, some outsiders do pose an existential threat to liberal norms and democratic institutions and need to be treated as such. However, the best way to frustrate these groups may be to let go of the centre that cannot hold and allow a new growth regime to emerge in its place, a process that requires us to recognize the limitations of the knowledge-driven growth agenda of the last 30 years and to treat the search for alternatives as not merely legitimate but imperative. The next and final chapter of this book explores some of the ways in which developed democracies might redeem the promises of the knowledge economy, both by rebooting the knowledge-driven growth agenda, and also by reaching beyond it.

10
PARADIGM SHIFT

Can the knowledge economy redeem its promise of inclusive prosperity? Or is an alternative needed if policy-makers are to achieve equitable growth? Certainly, the belief that knowledge-driven growth strategies might yet succeed seems to underpin existing plans to "build back better" in developed democracies following the Covid-19 pandemic.[1] After the savage cuts of the austerity years, social investments in skills, infrastructure and research are once again on the agenda. The OECD has argued that governments need to engage in "high-quality public investment", with a particular focus on "active labour market programmes and enhanced vocational education and training ... to create opportunities for all".[2] The UK chancellor of the exchequer professed the same creed in his 2021 Autumn Budget speech, declaring that, "as well as investing in infrastructure and innovation, there is one further part of our plan for growth that is crucial: providing a world-class education to all our people", which would "lead to higher regional productivity [which] leads to higher wages".[3] In Germany, the SPD's 2021 plurality-winning election manifesto committed to the creation of "sustainable, good jobs" by using the power of the state "to encourage innovations, to promote science and research, to embark on large ongoing investments in modern infrastructure".[4]

It is far from clear, however, whether such knowledge-driven growth strategies will prove effective. As we saw in Part II, over the last 30 years, both the tempo and the inclusivity of growth in the knowledge economy era have disappointed. Labour-saving innovation continues apace, but it is by no means certain that knowledge-intensive industries will generate enough new tasks to redeploy the labour that they displace, at least not in the short or even medium term. The rewards of knowledge-driven growth to date have been highly concentrated geographically, with unfavoured regions trapped in a self-reinforcing cycle of depressed demand, inadequate investment and economic stagnation. These rewards have also been highly concentrated socially, with the benefits accruing to the already wealthy and those with a capital stake in cutting-edge firms, as well as to the comparatively small workforces these high-tech businesses need in order to develop and exploit high-value knowledge assets such as intellectual property rights and data from proprietary platforms. High barriers to entry constrain entrepreneurial dynamism while simultaneously curtailing social mobility.

Yet, perhaps these problems can be attributed to the inadequate ways in which developed democracies have pursued knowledge-driven growth to date. This chapter evaluates whether the knowledge-driven growth agenda can be rebooted or whether inclusive prosperity requires a more radical policy shift. It begins by considering whether a more radical social investment programme might yet offer a solution to economic stagnation and rising inequality or whether more proactive forms of stimulus and redistribution are required. We then turn to the geography of opportunity, exploring whether the remote working revolution precipitated by the pandemic might help to rebalance high-value knowledge work across regions, and if not, what alternatives policy-makers will need to consider in order to "level up" the "left behind". The penultimate section discusses the relationship between the state and the market in developed democracies and how developed democracies relate to the global economy as a whole. Can countries recreate the competitive dynamism of the early knowledge economy era? Are international openness and macroeconomic stability, as they were understood in the 1990s, still essential to prosperity? Or do we need to reimagine the relationship between the state, the market and the wider world altogether? Finally, the chapter examines the green growth agenda, assessing whether it is merely another permutation of knowledge-driven growth or whether it constitutes a more radical departure from the policy consensus of the last three decades.

Social investment, inequality and inclusion

Although "education, education, education" was the professed priority of earlier advocates of knowledge-driven growth, truly transformative levels of social investment were often precluded by other considerations: concerns about the destabilizing effects of government borrowing, the drag on competitive dynamism caused by higher tax rates (as well as the political challenges of raising taxes) and the risk of capital flight in a world of open borders. Yet, this cautious approach to knowledge-driven growth did not go uncontested: for example, prominent figures in both the Blair government and the Clinton administration advocated higher levels of social investment, as did opponents of austerity in the wake of the global financial crisis. Moreover, some developed democracies bucked this trend, and instead made the transition to the knowledge economy era on the basis of a high-tax, high-spending economic model. Nordic countries such as Sweden, Finland and Denmark invested more public money in education (measured as a proportion of GDP) than many of their European neighbours; they also tended to spend more on active labour market policies (job creation and matching initiatives, targeted retraining for the unemployed) and social safety nets. These countries generally enjoyed higher rates of growth during the heyday of the knowledge economy as well as greater resilience in the face of the financial crisis. On top of this, labour's share of national income also tended to hold up better in the Nordic countries than in many of their peers, limiting the growth of inequality.

Reviewing this historical record, it is tempting to conclude that what developed democracies need, in order to deliver inclusive prosperity for their citizens, is not an alternative to knowledge-driven growth strategies but rather a different *form* of knowledge-driven growth strategy: one that prioritizes social investment over lower taxes and lower borrowing and lives up to the transformative levels of spending implied by its own political rhetoric. Higher levels of public investment in primary education could improve baseline literacy and numeracy, increasing the adaptability and productivity of tomorrow's workers. Although participation in higher education increased massively in many developed democracies over the knowledge economy era, the quality of provision has been variable, and courses could be better matched to the skills needs of high-productivity knowledge-intensive businesses. More money for retraining initiatives could help the unemployed back into higher-value work. And governments could do more to instil a culture of lifelong learning: recognizing that the public benefits of adult education exceed the private returns enjoyed by individuals and firms and addressing the opportunity costs that workers face when taking time off to study mid-career through better subsidies and incentives.

Higher levels of social investment, then, could improve productivity, prosperity and social inclusion, just as earlier advocates of knowledge-driven growth claimed. Nevertheless, it is also worth noting that even Nordic countries have experienced some of the socially divisive downsides of knowledge-driven growth. In most Nordic countries, young people have still seen generation-on-generation growth in income stall and sometimes even go into reverse.[5] Nor do Nordic countries necessarily achieve high levels of social mobility (although the more compressed nature of their income distributions renders this less socially divisive than in many other countries).[6] While the labour share of national income expanded in countries such as Finland, Sweden and Denmark between the mid-1990s and the mid-2010s, wage inequality also grew (albeit less dramatically than in liberal market economies such as the UK and USA).[7] Even with higher levels of social investment, then, countries are not immune to the centrifugal forces unleashed by the rise of the knowledge economy.

On the one hand, this might be taken as evidence of the need for greater levels of social investment than even Nordic countries have achieved thus far.

On the other hand, it is also possible for state-sponsored social investment to overshoot, leading to overreliance on particular industries or businesses and a misallocation of resources.[8] Beyond a certain point, perhaps social investment is better complemented by other policy measures if inclusive prosperity is the goal.

In order to appreciate the rationale for going beyond social investment, and the kind of policies that this might require, it is worth revisiting the various mechanisms driving inequality in the knowledge economy era. The most prominent of these mechanisms in mainstream policy circles is skill-biased technological change, whereby new technologies complement high-skilled workers but substitute for lower-skilled workers. This dynamic leads to increasing wage inequality between in-demand higher-skilled workers and their lower-skilled counterparts. It also has the potential to skew the distribution of national income in favour of capital. Although new capital investments will increase the relative productivity of higher-skilled workers, who can use these new technologies to generate more and more valuable output (and thereby increase their share of national income relative to both capital and lower-skilled labour), these investments will have the opposite effect on lower-skilled workers, who must either accept lower wages or find themselves replaced by machines. The labour share falls if the latter effect outweighs the former.[9] On this account, the solution to both widening wage inequality and larger capital shares of national income is social investment in education. This will increase the proportion of higher-skilled workers in the workforce, reducing the wage premiums they can command relative to their lower-skilled counterparts (reducing wage inequality) while simultaneously increasing the average productivity of labour (which, in a perfect market where workers are compensated in line with their marginal productivity, should result in labour receiving a higher share of national income).[10]

Now consider an alternative scenario, in which high wage inequality and increased capital shares are not a product of skills-biased technological change but are instead a product of rents, earned by businesses monopolizing scarce resources that their rivals struggle to replicate: perhaps intellectual property rights to particular brands, microchip designs or chemical formulae, perhaps a popular digital platform and the data it generates, perhaps some essential piece of physical or digital infrastructure. In order to extract value from said resources, these businesses still need highly skilled workers to update algorithms, refine and improve product designs, streamline manufacturing processes and so forth. Under these circumstances, we would expect high returns to capital as well as high wages for the highly skilled employees of these businesses – a pattern that can be observed in many of the largest knowledge-intensive firms operating in advanced democracies today.[11] However, under these conditions, social investment in education would not have the same equality-promoting effects as it would in the skill-biased technological change scenario. True, increasing the supply of skilled workers should increase competition between skilled workers, reducing the premiums that they can command relative to their lower-skilled counterparts and thereby reducing wage inequality. But this competition between workers will also reduce the premium that owners of capital need to pay to their highly skilled workers, reducing the costs of generating value from the scarce, difficult-to-replicate resources that they monopolize. As a result, workers receive a smaller share of the income that those scarce resources generate. Replicated across the economy as a whole, such dynamics would skew national income away from labour and towards capital. In order to generate a more egalitarian outcome, policy-makers would instead need to tackle the source of economic rents (perhaps by limiting the scope or duration of intellectual property rights, or by forcing operators of digital platforms to make their users and data accessible to competitors) or else minimize the amount of rent that can be extracted (perhaps through regulation of the prices that can be charged and the conditions imposed on users of infrastructure, perhaps through increased taxation of monopoly rents).[12]

Inequality arising from superstar effects, too, is not readily remedied by means of greater social investment. As discussed in Chapter 7, these effects arise when demand is concentrated on the top performers in a particular market: novelists, sportspeople and rock stars, but potentially also developers of digital platforms, pharmaceutical researchers, CEOs, lawyers and more besides. Here, increasing the supply of wannabe superstars through social investment in their training will have a minimal effect on the structure of rewards: the top performers can still command astronomical amounts because of a lack of demand for the also-rans. One solution to such inequalities would be to introduce more progressive taxation rates, redistributing income from the highest earners to wider society. (Quite how much superstars could be taxed depends on how sensitive superstars' efforts are to changes in financial incentives and whether there is really any discernible difference between their performance and that of the next-best would-be superstar who is not put off by higher tax rates.)[13] Alternatively, where superstars depend on the labour of others in their organizations and supply chains, pushing up the earnings of those others (through minimum wage hikes, collective bargaining agreements, more extensive forms of trade union representation and so forth) would reduce the amount available for superstars to claim.[14]

Finally, the skills-biased technological change account outlined above is predicated on the assumption that new technologies substitute for lower-skilled workers and complement higher-skilled workers. Yet there is a risk that new technological advances, particularly in artificial intelligence, may substitute for the labour of higher-skilled workers too. Absent the invention of new goods and services that generate new tasks for labour to perform, labour-displacing inventions will tend to shrink labour's share of overall output (although workers might still benefit in absolute terms from the rising societal productivity and prosperity created by these technological advances). Under these circumstances, social investment in education is unlikely to reduce inequality, as capital rather than labour serves as the main source of future wealth. Instead, governments will need to move beyond providing workers with human capital and consider endowing them with other forms of capital as well.[15] For example, Mark Blyth and Eric Lonergan propose creating national wealth funds, using the fact that governments of developed democracies can presently borrow at historically low rates to build up a portfolio of publicly owned global equities, the returns from which could be paid out to citizens in the future.[16] Higher taxes on wealth and business profits (which have often been treated favourably by the tax systems of the knowledge economy era, as policy-makers sought to encourage start-up activity by increasing entrepreneurial incentives) could also help to limit the growth of inequalities that originate in escalating returns to capital.[17]

The point here is not that social investment is unnecessary or unimportant, only that it is insufficient. In the knowledge economy era, inequality is fed by a range of different mechanisms, including not just skills-biased technological change but also insider rents, superstar effects and unbiased forms of technological change that threaten to displace skilled and unskilled labour alike. Each of these mechanisms requires different policy responses in order to combat the inequalities to which it gives rise. The policy agenda advanced by earlier advocates of knowledge-driven growth only offered a partial solution, focusing on social investments designed to increase the supply of skilled workers (and, in some cases, on competition policies designed to prevent large firms from abusing their market power). If policy-makers are serious about reducing inequality, then they may have little choice but to consider more radical interventions to alter the structure of opportunities that the knowledge economy creates.

Some opportunities are more equal than others

To some policy-makers of the knowledge economy era, the idea of altering the structure of opportunities, to rebalance the rewards on offer, was anathema: "it's not a burning ambition for me to make sure that David Beckham earns less money", as Tony Blair once observed to an interviewer.[18] But reducing inequality between different opportunities does matter, both politically and economically. Politically, as we saw in Chapter 2, the appeal of knowledge-driven growth explicitly rested not just on equal access to whatever opportunities the knowledge economy threw up but also on the idea that there would be an abundance of *good* opportunities. This claim was based on the assumption that developed democracies would, through social investment, attract a disproportionate share of global knowledge work; that barriers to entry in the knowledge economy were low, and thus that a plethora of knowledge-intensive businesses would create a plethora of knowledge jobs; that the proceeds of growth would flow primarily to skilled workers rather than to capital; that all kinds of job could become more knowledge-intensive and thus more rewarding. If the policy agenda of the knowledge economy fails to produce an adequate range of good opportunities, then it would be unsurprising if its erstwhile supporters were to investigate alternatives.

More equality between opportunities matters, too, for economic growth. To the extent that the productivity gains from the rise of the knowledge economy accrue primarily to the upper echelons of the income distribution and to the already wealthy, the result will be a shortfall of demand in the economy as a whole. The very richest on average save or invest a greater proportion of their income (whether this income comes from salaries, dividends or capital appreciation) than their poorer peers. As a consequence, all else being equal, greater inequality either leads to a shortfall in consumer spending (depressing demand, lowering incentives for businesses to invest and suppressing growth in the economy as a whole) or else sees household spending funded by debt rather than earnings (increasing financial volatility and decreasing the financial resilience of families during economic downturns).[19] It is thus unsurprising that rising income inequality is associated with declining levels of growth.[20]

Finally, more equality between opportunities is a precondition for greater equality of opportunity. Where inequality is high and the number of good opportunities is limited, the cost of failing to secure one of the good opportunities on offer increases. Under these circumstances, well-resourced parents are tempted to invest more and more to ensure that their offspring succeed. There is already extensive evidence that more affluent households in developed democracies engage in "opportunity hoarding".[21] Through hiring private tutors, paying private school fees, moving to areas with good publicly funded schools (and correspondingly unaffordable house prices), arranging work experience through their social networks and so forth, richer families increase the odds that their children will secure a more cognitively and financially rewarding job than their poorer peers. Moreover, such families might resist social investments that could extend opportunity to other children, fearing that doing so will increase competition for the limited number of good opportunities on offer. (They might also argue that such investments are an inefficient use of public resources and that it is wasteful for society to train millions of graduates if there are not millions of graduate jobs.)[22]

Altering the structure of outcomes that has emerged from the knowledge economy era is key to addressing these economic and political problems.

Compressing the income distribution, such that more of the proceeds of growth flow to lower- and middle-income households, will produce a more sustainable basis for demand (and thus growth) in developed democracies. It will also produce a more sustainable political settlement, one in which social investment enjoys widespread popular support and the appeal of outsiders diminishes.

Geography and opportunity

So far, we have focused on the structure of opportunities and outcomes within developed democracies considered as a whole. But, as we saw in Chapter 7, the structure of opportunities in the knowledge economy era has a distinctive geographical pattern, clustered around thriving, international-facing cities: the world is not flat but spiky. Knowledge-driven growth, far from presenting regions ravaged by globalization and deindustrialization with new opportunities, appears to have contributed yet further to their economic marginalization. Can rebooting the knowledge-driven growth agenda "level up" the people and places that have been "left behind", or is a more radical policy agenda required?

The ability of social investment to address regional inequality appears at first somewhat limited. The idea that government spending on skills, infrastructure and research will suffice to attract knowledge-intensive investment and jobs to particular places looks quixotic: it is difficult to see the attractions of such social investments outweighing the benefits of deep labour markets, social networks and ecosystems of complementary firms that already exist elsewhere. Nevertheless, social investment can still help to improve the productivity of local businesses up to a point, addressing particular place-specific skills shortages. New clusters of knowledge-intensive work do emerge from time to time, and they are unlikely to form in places where an educated workforce is lacking. Moreover, through improving transport infrastructure, lagging areas can be connected up to more knowledge-intensive local economies, allowing residents of poorer regions to access opportunities in comparatively buoyant labour markets. Social investment in digital infrastructure remains important too. Even in developed democracies, high-speed internet access is far from universal: providing this infrastructure to underserviced communities would help to increase their productivity and make it viable for workers in these locations to work remotely (at least, in roles where that option exists).

By contrast, the idea that digital infrastructure will enable residents of lagging regions to participate en masse in the knowledge economy, by telecommuting to the virtual offices of knowledge-intensive businesses, seems somewhat less plausible. To date, remote working has tended to act as a supplement to, rather than a substitute for, face-to-face working. Knowledge work tends to require at least some face-to-face interaction, in order to build trust, exchange ideas, mentor new employees and be mentored in turn. While remote working loosens geographical ties, in most cases it does not sever them: workers still need to physically commute into central locations from time to time, although the fact they need to do so less often extends the horizon of tolerable commutes.

Early indications are that this will remain the case following the pandemic. True, firms and employees – having invested in new remote working technologies, having learned new working practices – are unlikely to revert back to pre-pandemic working patterns outright, in light of the time and money they can save by scaling back on expensive city-centre office space and unproductive travel. Nevertheless, evidence from surveys of workers and firms, and data on commercial property rentals, suggests that the legacy of the pandemic will be more extensive adoption of hybrid working patterns rather than a shift to virtual offices staffed by workers working exclusively from home.[23] In other words, the pandemic will accelerate the stretching of geography that was already taking place, enabling workers to live (and, more frequently, work) further away from their home office locations, but will not result in the wholesale disembedding of knowledge work from geography.

This stretching of geography could certainly help to reduce the regional disparities that have characterized the rise of the knowledge economy thus far. Freed from the obligation to commute every day, more distant towns and rural areas will become increasingly attractive to knowledge workers, offering more space at a lower price, which is invaluable for home offices as well as for lifestyle reasons. The demand that these knowledge workers generate for in-person services such as restaurants, gyms and nightclubs might thus disperse away from city centres, allowing a broader range of local economies to support a wider variety of businesses and jobs than was previously the case, revitalizing town centres. Even if knowledge workers do not move directly to left-behind places, individuals and firms based in economically marginalized areas may still have better access to these affluent potential customers than was hitherto the case, as these knowledge workers (and their consumer spending) move further away from the city regions in which knowledge-intensive work was previously concentrated.

Nevertheless, there will be some places that remain disconnected from growth, even as social investments in physical and digital infrastructure connect more and more places up to major cities, and even as the adoption of hybrid working patterns expands their commuter hinterlands. In these instances, policy-makers may need to look beyond the standard playbook of knowledge-driven growth if they intend national prosperity to be genuinely geographically inclusive. Rather than focusing on supply-side improvements to infrastructure and local skills, governments might look at how public spending can shape demand for skills in particular localities. By relocating large publicly funded knowledge-intensive organizations (universities, government departments, public broadcasting companies and so forth) to economically marginalized areas, governments might succeed in stimulating knowledge-intensive growth locally, with these organizations acting as "anchor tenants" that crowd in skilled workers and other knowledge-intensive businesses, as well as additional firms looking to supply these organizations and their employees. Local-level policy-makers might seek to coordinate procurement by large public and private sector organizations, to ensure that more money is spent locally on local businesses that employ local workers and benefit local owners, and thus drive up local demand.[24] Admittedly, these strategies may be more a case of moving prosperity around a country rather than creating additional prosperity, and such moves risk diminishing the positive network effects created by concentrating pools of knowledge workers and knowledge industries in the same physical locations. Nevertheless, policy-makers might reasonably conclude that such trade-offs are worthwhile; and, over the longer term, providing a wider range of opportunities in a wider range of localities might deepen the pool of experienced knowledge workers available nationally.

At the end of the day, however, such strategies may not be viable for all places at all times. This may be for reasons of population density or geography – more remote towns and rural areas may lack the population size necessary to support viable clusters of knowledge industries and may be difficult to reach from areas where such jobs might conceivably cluster. Ultimately, it may be desirable to concentrate knowledge workers in a smaller number of places to reap the benefits of larger agglomeration effects; demand for knowledge workers may simply not be growing fast enough to provide good knowledge jobs everywhere, for reasons including international competition, limited potential for the knowledgification of existing jobs, obstacles to market entry (such as high capital investment requirements or incumbents presiding over proprietary platforms, data and intellectual property) or the labour-displacing effects of artificial intelligence. Consequently, if policy-makers are serious about making prosperity inclusive, they must think seriously about how to extend prosperity in the absence of knowledge work.

One option is to transfer resources directly, in the form of redistributive taxes and benefit payments. Yet, such handouts are rarely popular; not just among those who fund them but also those who receive them. The other option is to change how traditionally lower-paid kinds of work are valued, both economically and culturally. The pandemic might provide an opening for such a conversation, highlighting the importance of workers in what has been described as the "foundational economy".[25] The foundational economy encompasses economic activities that are essential to everyday life, and thus activities that needed to carry on in spite of lockdowns and the circulation of a deadly virus: activities such as health and social care, food production and distribution, energy provision and waste management services. Because these activities must be performed wherever people live, they are widely distributed geographically, making them an ideal channel for tackling regional inequality. Many of them involve public sector employees, or at least public sector procurement, meaning policy-makers can stipulate higher salaries and better working conditions directly. Where activities are carried out in the private sector, policy tools such as increased minimum wage levels, or sector-wide collective wage bargaining agreements, might produce similar results.

In so doing, the price of foundational services may well increase, at the expense of taxpayers and household budgets. To ensure these transitional costs are fairly distributed, increased rewards for foundational economy workers should be accompanied by reforms to tax and benefit systems, to ensure that any accompanying tax rises and inflationary pressures fall on those with the greatest ability to pay. In the short term at least, levelling up poorer regions and lower-paid households may require transferring resources from other people and places. Over the longer term, however, reduced inequality has the potential to help "grow the pie" as well. The redistribution of resources geographically means a redistribution of resources to households with a higher marginal propensity to consume, encouraging higher levels of economic activity. Higher levels of local demand can stimulate higher levels of aspiration and innovation among individuals and businesses located in economically marginalized places. Lower levels of regional inequality might even be beneficial for knowledge-intensive industries based in more affluent places: smaller regional disparities in prosperity and wealth should mean lower barriers to workers relocating from poorer areas to more expensive city regions, allowing knowledge-intensive industries in those city regions to draw on a deeper pool of talent taken from across the entirety of society.

The state, the market and the world

To date, champions of knowledge-driven growth have been reluctant to intervene in markets beyond the requirements of social investment in skills, infrastructure and research. This broadly laissez-faire approach, coupled with openness to the global economy, was supposed to increase the competitive dynamism of developed democracies, attracting investment and incentivizing entrepreneurship while making it easier for businesses to respond flexibly to ever-changing market conditions and customer demands.

This overall trend admitted of some important variations, however. So far as labour market liberalization was concerned, while almost all developed democracies tried to make it easier for businesses to hire and fire workers, and to offer part-time and/or fixed-term contracts in addition to full-time permanent vacancies, some countries (such as the UK, USA and Germany) adopted a more "workfarist" approach that sought to coerce the unemployed into work through a threadbare social safety net, whereas others (such as the Nordic countries) offered higher levels of out-of-work benefits, arguing that this approach was more likely to provide workers with the security necessary to make labour markets truly dynamic. Interestingly, data on job-to-job transitions bear out the Nordic strategy. Between 2011 and 2020, working-age people in Denmark, Finland and Sweden were more likely to change jobs than in other European countries, suggesting that stronger safety nets do indeed support workers in moving jobs, whereas less generous unemployment benefits (and less well-funded active labour market policies) are associated with lower levels of job-to-job mobility.[26] Under the workfarist model, people are likely to cling to their existing employer, which might inhibit them from taking up new opportunities that would increase their productivity and that of society as a whole.

These patterns make psychological sense. If policy-makers' goal is to incentivize productivity-maximizing labour market decisions (moving to a new high-productivity firm, launching your own start-up) then they can either do this by increasing the rewards of success (increasing inequality through low tax rates and low out-of-work benefits) or by reducing the costs of failure (reducing inequality through higher tax rates and more comprehensive out-of-work benefits). Over the last 40 years, behavioural economists have amassed a raft of data that suggests that human beings are in general risk-averse, placing greater weight on losses than on gains.[27] It follows that policy-makers interested in encouraging dynamic labour markets should obsess less about maximizing the rewards on offer and instead focus on minimizing potential penalties. In a more compressed income distribution, with stronger safety nets, entrepreneurial activity may be more rather than less likely; a point that appears to be borne out by the experience of Nordic countries.

Different choices could also be made with respect to the regulation of competition between firms, in order to promote more dynamic markets. Market concentration in knowledge-intensive industries can stifle innovation, thus undermining prosperity-enhancing productivity growth. The problem is particularly noticeable in the digital sector, where a handful of companies dominate the essential infrastructure of the modern economy, but it is also observable more broadly: in retail, telecoms, finance and many other fields besides.[28] A more proactive approach to curbing abuses of dominant market positions – as advocated by earlier analysts of knowledge-driven growth such as Joseph Stiglitz, Paul Romer and Brian Arthur – thus appears to be justified. In the tech sector, this might involve regulating platforms to prevent them from privileging their own goods and services ahead of those offered by competitors; monitoring uses of personal data and the algorithms that determine what content and products are promoted to different users; prohibiting future mergers and acquisitions that would increase market concentration, and unwinding previous transactions; insisting upon data sharing across platforms; or requiring greater interoperability, such that users of one platform can connect with users of another (be these social connections or connections between customers and vendors for various goods and services).[29] To be sure, there is no one-size-fits-all solution. Regulators must be alert to the fact that competition may not always be feasible or desirable, as breaking up networks can also diminish the positive network effects enjoyed by their users, while insisting upon interoperability and data sharing might violate user privacy and data security.[30] Government intervention could promote competition in other sectors too: for example, preventing mergers that increase market concentration in particular industries and/or locations, insisting that service providers make it easy for consumers to switch to rival firms, reappraising the protections offered by intellectual property rights such as patents and copyrights, and scrutinizing the actions of dominant companies more closely for anticompetitive practices such as predatory pricing or exclusionary contracts.

Rethinking international openness

Clearly, there are resources available within the ambit of knowledge-driven growth strategies to rethink the relationship between state and market and to explore alternative ways of unlocking productivity-enhancing market dynamism. But it may be desirable to go beyond a reboot and to rethink some of the more fundamental features of those strategies.

One such feature is the unqualified embrace of international openness characteristic of many knowledge-driven growth strategies. Both on the centre-left and the centre-right, openness to trade, investment and immigration were widely held to be straightforwardly beneficial, giving rise to such sizeable societal gains that it would be an easy matter for governments to "deal with the losers", as per Obama's rather infelicitous phrase. Today, however, free trade stands accused of robbing indigenous workers of their livelihoods, by forcing them to compete with lower-cost overseas labour; migration stands accused of bringing these competitive pressures to bear on the wages of those who provide in-person services in sectors such as construction or hospitality. Hopefully it is clear by now that such analyses are incomplete: many of these pressures are also (if not more so) the product of automation, of competition against machines as well as overseas workers. Nevertheless, champions of knowledge-based growth advocated both for technological change and for international openness, and international openness has still contributed somewhat to the relative economic decline of regions formerly dependent on traditional industries and to the hollowing out of the middle class more broadly. Discontent with a policy agenda in which international openness played an integral part is thus understandable. Restructuring opportunity along the lines set out earlier in this chapter, to ensure that there are good options available to people outside the upper echelons of knowledge-intensive industries and outside the cities in which such industries tend to cluster, might go a long way towards addressing this discontent.[31] In so doing, these reforms have the potential to rehabilitate international openness, by making the benefits of immigration and international trade tangible in the lives of the overwhelming majority of people, not just in aggregate GDP figures: figures which mask how the lion's share of growth has accrued to the very highest earners and to the wealthiest households.

At the same time, disabusing ourselves of the assumptions of the knowledge economy era may lead to a more nuanced policy approach to international borders. In the past, developed democracies too often treated trade as an unalloyed good, without ensuring that the natural environment, human rights and intellectual property were adequately protected by trading partners. Shifts in international trade policy – such as the growing schism between the USA and China, or the EU's proposals for a Carbon Border Adjustment Mechanism (a new charge pegged to the carbon emissions embodied in goods that enter the single market) – may reshape the landscape of cross-border commerce, emphasizing regional trade between countries with similar standards in the place of unbridled globalization. As the economist and *Financial Times* columnist Martin Sandbu argues, it is perfectly legitimate, and in keeping with free trade principles, for developed democracies to insist that any products entering their internal markets have been manufactured in accordance with the same environmental and labour standards that their electorates have chosen to impose domestically.[32]

Similarly, it is legitimate for developed democracies to demand that immigrant labour is not used as a device to undermine domestic rules around working standards, employee rights, collective bargaining arrangements and trade unions, as has unfortunately sometimes been the case under EU freedom of movement rules.[33] If that makes immigrant labour less attractive to would-be employers (and correspondingly reduces levels of migration), so be it. Even beyond these economic arguments, however, immigration can make psychological demands both on immigrants and the indigenous communities into which they migrate, as they adjust and adapt to each other. Inflows of immigrants can exacerbate pressure on housing and public services, as well as on wages. Even for communities that experience low levels of migration, the ready availability of migrant labour elsewhere might still have a negative impact on opportunities to move to more prosperous regions that promise better career prospects and on incentives for businesses and better-off taxpayers to fund the education of less affluent indigenous workers. To be sure, there are counterbalancing benefits to immigration too, but costs and benefits are not evenly distributed to the same individuals, and those who bear the highest costs are often those who have barely shared in the productivity growth of recent decades. The trade-offs are complex, and champions of liberal immigration rules need to make the ethical and prudential case for freer movement to their fellow citizens – not just in their arguments but also in their policy decisions – rather than dismiss these concerns out of hand.

The benefits of international openness are particularly ambiguous with regard to certain parts of the digital economy, where user-generated network effects and data form a substantial part of the business model. As we have seen, these platform markets display a marked tendency towards concentration, as would-be challengers do not just need to replicate (and improve upon) the basic functionality of incumbents but also mimic the networks of connections that they offer: the array of goods, services and content offered by other users. These platforms generate monopoly rents: the excess earnings related to the near impossibility of competition in the particular niches in which they are established. We have already discussed how governments might seek to reduce these rents, either by regulatory interventions designed to promote competition or regulatory interventions designed to limit abuses of monopoly power; they might also seek to capture a share of them via targeted tax measures. However, a further option would be to encourage the emergence of domestic providers in fields characterized by strong network effects, by erecting regulatory and other obstacles to foreign tech giants. By either delaying the entry of overseas tech companies into particular markets, or encouraging them to abandon markets in which they already operate (admittedly a far more challenging proposition), countries and regional trading blocs might create space for the emergence of domestic monopolists in place of foreign-based monopolists. This would mean that the geographic location of these businesses' headquarters, as well as of their founders, investors and employees, would more closely correspond to the geographic location of their value-generating user base. In turn, this would potentially render it easier for countries to capture the economic benefits of these platforms (job creation here and now, and also strategic access to data and users upon which future innovation in fields such as artificial intelligence depends) and their fiscal proceeds (from taxes on sales, salaries, profits and investment returns), and potentially also make these businesses easier for countries to regulate (by dint of data centres physically located within their territories and of entrepreneurs and executives residing within reach of domestic legal systems). Chinese tech giants such as Alibaba, Baidu and Tencent have benefited from obstacles that the

Chinese government placed in the path of US rivals; their commercial success, as well as the data and users they have at their disposal, have contributed to the development of China's tech industries more broadly, including the country's burgeoning artificial intelligence sector. Parts of the EU's digital decade strategy – in particular, its aspirations towards "digital sovereignty", overcoming reliance on (frequently foreign-owned) proprietary systems – seem to signal similar ambitions.[34] Of course, this strategy is only viable for markets that are sufficiently large in their own right to reap substantial benefits from network effects and economies of scale: digital sovereignty may make sense for the EU, China and India, but the arguments are weaker for the UK or Australia, for example.

For all of the above qualifications, in one important respect, international openness is *less* problematic today than advocates of knowledge-driven growth once assumed. To a previous generation of policy-makers, open borders meant exposing countries to the risk that capital and highly skilled workers would respond to more onerous regulations and higher taxes by simply relocating elsewhere. They believed that the shift to knowledge-intensive production exacerbated this risk, as knowledge-intensive firms do not need to worry about relocating expensive physical capital: plant, machinery or entire factories. However, knowledge work and knowledge-intensive industries have proved to be far less footloose than this earlier generation of policy-makers assumed.[35] Knowledge-intensive firms and their workers enjoy place-specific agglomeration effects: the benefits that arise from locating your firm or your labour in a region that offers a deep pool of would-be employees and employers, coupled with a supportive ecosystem of potential collaborators, investors, customers, suppliers and professional advisers. Although knowledge-intensive businesses may be comparatively weightless, much of their value is still bound up in the skills and relationships of their staff, and these staff are if anything harder to relocate en masse across borders than physical capital, bound as they are to particular locations (generally economically prosperous city regions) by ties of family and friendship, property investments, local amenities and career opportunities. Suitably educated knowledge workers in another location might be able to substitute for existing staff in the long term, but this will still require the relocation of many existing staff to the new location, potentially for a period of several years, in order to transfer firm-specific and location-specific skills to the new workforce.[36]

True, geographical stickiness alone does not guarantee higher tax revenues. Multinational corporations and high-net-worth individuals have long deployed elaborate schemes of transactions and holding companies, designed to shift profits and wealth away from jurisdictions where they operate and reside to countries where they pay lower rates of tax. However, as we saw in Chapter 8, developed democracies have made significant strides in combating such practices over the last decade.[37] An array of unilateral and multilateral initiatives have sought to force disclosure of foreign-based bank accounts, mandate country-by-country reporting of taxes and profits, and introduce surcharges on artificial tax arrangements. These efforts look set to continue, in light of current proposals for a global minimum tax rate on corporate profits and moves to apportion the profits of the world's largest companies by a single internationally agreed formula rather than through the interaction of competing and sometimes contradictory national-level tax rules. Even if these particular proposals falter, even though they do not go as far as tax justice campaigners would like, momentum nevertheless appears to be on the side of international coordination rather than a competitive race to the bottom.

One note of caution, however. Sharp-eyed readers may have spotted that the "stickiness" that makes knowledge-intensive firms and knowledge workers easier to tax is the same stickiness that has made it difficult to spread prosperity from thriving city regions to economically marginalized towns and countryside. Consequently, the changes in working patterns induced by the pandemic, which could help to combat regional economic imbalances, might also dissolve the glue that binds workers and firms to particular places, which makes them easier to tax and regulate. In an extreme scenario, we might yet find ourselves inhabiting Thomas Friedman's flat earth, where organizations based anywhere in the world could access labour based anywhere in the world, and where there are no place-specific clusters of specialized skills as people can acquire, develop and deploy those abilities in online communities dispersed across the entire globe. Nevertheless, at present this outcome seems unlikely. Assuming the pandemic and its aftermath results in a loosening rather than a severing of geographic ties, policy-makers may yet find themselves in a "Goldilocks zone" where knowledge workers (and the wealth they generate) are more widely dispersed but not so widely dispersed that they slip beyond the reach of national-level laws and tax rules.

Rethinking macroeconomic stability

The final pillar of conventional knowledge-driven growth strategies was macroeconomic stability, characterized by low interest rates and low levels of public borrowing. Macroeconomic stability was supposed to reassure knowledge-intensive industries that they could undertake risky long-term R&D projects, without needing to factor volatile interest rates and inflation into their decision-making. As we have seen, this stance constrained governments from embarking on more ambitious programmes of social investment. Even in the heyday of knowledge-driven growth, central bankers such as Alan Greenspan threatened to hike interest rates (thereby stymying investment) if elected politicians failed to slash deficits. Following the global financial crisis, this emphasis on macroeconomic "prudence" was used to justify swingeing cuts to public spending, sending social investment into reverse.

In retrospect, the austerity agenda of the last decade was clearly counter-productive.[38] (Indeed, the counterproductive nature of austerity was evident in prospect, too, to many sensible voices in the economics profession and the wider economic policy community.)[39] The claim that government spending crowds out private investment, and thus that the rolling back of the state would unleash a wave of private enterprise, was not borne out by events. Instead, private sector investment languished, as businesses responded to a lack of demand from both consumers and the public sector (and from similarly austere overseas markets) by reining in their spending plans. Growth stalled, paving the way for political upheavals that have proved far more destabilizing than modest budget deficits. To a certain extent, monetary policy-makers sought to compensate for the lack of fiscal stimulus through interest rate reductions and quantitative easing, al-though such measures were often tentative rather than wholehearted, reactive rather than timely.[40]

The experience of the last decade has emphasized the vital role that gov-ernments play in supporting demand and the capacity of public spending to "crowd in" rather than "crowd out" private sector investment. The massive fiscal response to the Covid-19 pandemic – involving a dramatic expansion of the welfare state to support households and businesses through lengthy periods of lockdown, as well as huge public investments in healthcare and medical re-search – has underscored the fact that developed democracies do not operate under the same financial constraints as normal households. A more expansion-ary macroeconomic policy stance, using the state to boost aggregate demand, can be used to support a higher level of social investment, as well as other forms of public spending that might help to extend prosperity to economically margin-alized people and places.

There are two risks associated with a more expansionary approach. First, conventional forms of monetary stimulus (namely, quantitative easing and lower interest rates) tend to push up the value of existing assets such as property or shares. Stimulus therefore risks exacerbating inequality by increasing the wealth of the already wealthy. In addition to creating problems for social cohesion, greater inequality risks reducing aggregate demand by concentrating resources in the hands of more affluent households with a lower marginal propensity to con-sume. These problems might be mitigated by altering the mechanisms through which central bank money enters the wider economy. For example, rather than injecting new money into the economy through the purchase of assets from financial markets, as under quantitative easing, central banks could transfer money directly to households, a policy known in the economics literature as "helicopter money". Alternatively, rather than financing government spending indirectly, by purchasing government debt from financial institutions, central banks could transfer funds directly to governments, as proponents of "modern monetary theory" advocate.[41] To be sure, such novel policy measures carry risks: even if they are perfectly coherent in and of themselves, if they cut against the received wisdom of financial markets, investors may respond unfavourably. A more conventional approach would be to use fiscal policy to complement monetary stimulus, using the tax system to offset the windfall gains that would otherwise accrue to the already wealthy. Perhaps the most straightforward option would be to remove the various tax loopholes that apply to wealth as opposed to income: in many developed democracies, gains on capital are taxed at lower rates than regular income, meaning millionaires can end up paying proportionately less than middle-class households.[42] More radically, a recurring annual tax on individuals' net assets might help to curb extreme forms of wealth inequality.[43] For policy-makers that favour wealth taxes but are put off by the complexity, a surcharge on ordinary taxes on income (salaries, dividends, trading profits, capital gains and potentially inheritance and other wealth transfers too) after a particular lifetime threshold has been passed (for example, an additional 5 per cent tax on lifetime income over a million dollars) would replicate many of the distributive effects of a wealth tax.[44]

Aside from inequality, the other risk associated with a looser approach to macroeconomic policy is inflation. When inflation is high, prices rise quickly, and the real purchasing power of people's income and savings falls. Injecting more money into the economy without increasing the quantity of goods and services produced will squeeze the living standards of average households. However, when economies are depressed, when businesses choose not to invest and hire because they do not see future demand that will justify those outlays, when individuals do not see jobs worth training for and working towards, stimulus will encourage individuals and businesses to deploy unused and underused resources more productively. This increases the quantity of goods and services produced in aggregate, increasing output rather than triggering inflation (over the medium term, at least). For much of the lost decade that followed the global financial crisis, inflation in developed democracies languished below levels targeted by central banks, suggesting that macroeconomic policy could have done far more to stimulate growth.[45]

Whether governments have the same capacity for stimulus in the aftermath of the Covid-19 pandemic, without lasting inflationary effects, is not yet clear. Some of the money created by governments since the pandemic hit has ended up in the hands of households, in the form of government handouts to locked-down workers. As economies reopen, creating new opportunities for consumption, some of these pent-up savings will be spent, acting as a temporary stimulus in its own right. Quite how much scope governments have for further non-inflationary stimulus on top of that remains to be seen. What is abundantly clear, however, is that erring on the side of caution did lasting damage to economic growth in developed democracies over the last ten years, and governments had much more fiscal firepower at their disposal than advocates of austerity argued.

A green solution?

Many proposals for "building back better" in the wake of the pandemic closely resemble the rhetoric and reasoning of the knowledge economy era: for example, the idea that improved education and training can lead to a "high-skill, high-wage" equilibrium, or the emphasis on public support for science and research to encourage the creation of well-paid knowledge jobs. In many respects, the green growth agenda appears to fit this template too. Emphasizing the importance of new technologies in reducing carbon emissions, governments claim that strategic social investments in education and innovation can help to position their countries at the forefront of high-growth green industries, securing a disproportionate share of the jobs and profits that these industries will create.[46]

The experience of knowledge-driven growth should make us wary about how many well-paid high-skilled knowledge jobs this green industrial revolution will actually produce, given that developed democracies and emerging markets all seem to be competing in similar ways for the same global market, and given the relatively limited numbers of knowledge workers high-tech firms have tended to employ to date. This is not to say that social investments in innovation and skills are not essential to the development of new green technologies, which are in turn essential to the future of the planet. It is only to point out that the quantity and quality of "green jobs" that result may prove disappointing, and that it would be unwise to rely exclusively on the growth of green industries to solve wider problems of social exclusion and inequality.

However, the parallels between green growth strategies and the policy agenda of the knowledge economy should not be overstated. Some advocates of a "green industrial revolution" or "green new deal" argue that governments need to do more than simply ensure a supply of suitably skilled individuals who are capable of inventing the new technologies that are essential to limiting global heating. They also insist that the state has a vital role to play on the demand side, whether by funding new inventions and infrastructure directly itself or by taxing and regulating unsustainable practices out of existence.[47] Furthermore, many proponents of green growth envisage the creation of jobs beyond the design and development of new technologies, beyond the creation of knowledge. Such is the scale of the climate challenge, there is substantial work to be done rolling out new technologies: fitting heat pumps, insulating buildings, installing charge points for electric vehicles, upgrading the electricity grid, creating new public transport infrastructure, setting up solar panels and erecting wind turbines. While skilled and specialist, many of these jobs would not necessarily require college degrees;[48] many of them would be dispersed over a wide geographic area too. In this respect, the green industrial revolution can be seen as a potential boost to the foundational economy. After all, energy production and distribution are among the core components of the foundational economy, economic tasks that must be performed wherever people live. As with other foundational sectors, these jobs may not be "good jobs" by default: institutions such as trade unions, as well as government procurement and policy, may be needed to ensure adequate pay and working conditions, and this may impose costs on other people, in the form of higher prices and taxes. As with other foundational sectors, whether it is well-paid or not, this work is not optional: it is foundational to our future survival.

A more profound challenge to green growth strategies is the question of whether green growth is possible at all, or whether ever-expanding economic output is fundamentally incompatible with the ecological constraints of the planet. Interestingly, back in the 1990s, the shift to the knowledge economy was widely held to be a way of greening growth. As workers and consumers in advanced economies increasingly make and consume immaterial, weightless things – computer games, novels and TV shows, all reduced to nothing more than a signal passed down a cable – the resource intensity of economic activity should decline, effectively decoupling growth from environmental destruction.[49] Similarly, advances in telecommunications would supposedly cut the carbon intensity of modern life by rendering travel increasingly unnecessary, whether to work, shop or socialize.

As with so many optimistic predictions from the heyday of the knowledge economy concept, this greening of the economy has not come to pass. Although the resource intensity of developed democracies appears to have declined, a substantial proportion of this decline can be attributed to the offshoring of resource-intensive production.[50] While there is evidence of the ecological efficiency of growth increasing in some contexts, overall the outlook for growth that is not only decoupled from global resource usage but actively sees resource usage declining to a sustainable level is not altogether promising.[51]

In short, there is no guarantee that green growth is possible; even if it is, it may look very different to the growth of the last century. Nevertheless, economic strategies that explicitly steer public and private research and investment towards the invention, improvement and installation of green technologies will enhance the prospects of sustainability (and ultimately survival), growth or no growth. Furthermore, developed democracies that address the socioeconomic divisions of the recent past (in particular, the marginalization of the young, the lower skilled and residents of "left-behind" areas) will be better equipped to make the sacrifices and compromises that a sustainable future requires. Redeeming the promises of the knowledge economy era remains imperative, on ecological as well as economic grounds.

Living in the future

Despite the faltering and uneven growth that developed democracies have experienced over the last three decades, knowledge-driven growth remains the default economic strategy for many policy experts and mainstream politicians in the post-pandemic era. However, even a return to the pre-austerity policy agenda of the late 1990s and early 2000s is unlikely to close the economic and political rifts that divide developed democracies today. Indeed, as we have seen, that policy agenda has actively contributed to those divisions, accelerating the hollowing out of the middle class, the growth of income and wealth inequalities, the economic polarization between internationally oriented cities and regions that have been "left behind", and the collapse in support for politicians and parties of the erstwhile centre ground. Nevertheless, there are promising signs that the post-pandemic reboot of knowledge-driven growth may overcome some of the hesitancy that typified a previous generation of policy-makers. Certainly, there appears to be an emerging consensus that a higher level of social investment is needed in education, research and infrastructure, in order to increase the pace, inclusivity and ecological sustainability of growth, and that the state must play a key role in financing and directing those investments: a vision shared by international institutions such as the IMF, OECD and the EU, as well as national-level leaders from across the political spectrum.

Yet, even if developed democracies do succeed in rebooting the knowledge-driven growth agenda with a transformative level of social investment, questions remain as to whether that alone will deliver a genuinely inclusive form of growth. A supply-side emphasis on education, skills, R&D and infrastructure may have only limited impacts on the overall structure of opportunity. In particular, it is difficult to see how these policy interventions will address the limited number of well-paid knowledge jobs available in developed democracies (a product of factors such as superstar effects, automation, job polarization and competition from emerging economies) and the knowledge economy's tendency towards wealth concentration (with national income skewing towards capital rather than labour, reflecting the ongoing importance of capital to knowledge work, in the form of finance, intellectual property rights, proprietorial networks and data, R&D investment, commercial and residential property in places where knowledge work clusters and so forth). To date, both work and wealth in the knowledge economy era have been distributed in a highly uneven fashion, resulting in large differences in opportunity and outcome between different regions and different demographics.

A highly unequal structure of opportunity might be tolerable at times when growth is rapid and the benefits of growth are widely diffused. But growth in developed democracies in the knowledge economy era has been slow by postwar standards, and so unevenly distributed that many households have seen only modest improvements in their circumstances while others still have experienced outright stagnation or decline. In fact, inequality may be actively harming economic growth. It risks encouraging rent-seeking anticompetitive behaviours among elite workers and firms, dampening risk-taking and innovation among economically insecure households worried about making ends meet, and suppressing demand across the economy as a whole.

In order to achieve the inclusive prosperity once promised by knowledge-driven growth, policy-makers today thus need to look beyond the knowledge economy. While knowledge-intensive industries will play an important role in any future economic strategy, a transformative agenda for the wider economy is essential if growth is to be made truly inclusive. Driving up working conditions and wages in the foundational economy would provide a basis for better opportunities that are also more broadly distributed. This could be achieved through higher minimum wage floors and strengthened employee rights, through using the public sector and public procurement to set higher standards in socially vital but traditionally lower-paid industries and through investments in new technologies and new skills to improve productivity among foundational workers. In so doing, this would help demand return to local and regional economies that have thus far failed to benefit from the geographically concentrated growth of the last three decades, supporting the development of a greater diversity of private sector businesses and jobs in these areas. Such investments must be linked to the transition to a greener economy, as foundational sectors such as housing, transport, energy generation and agriculture are among the largest producers of carbon emissions in developed democracies today.

Revaluing and revitalizing realms of social and economic endeavour far from the technological frontier will not be entirely cost-free. Governments have a responsibility to ensure that those costs fall primarily upon households that are better able to bear them. Fortunately, governments have the ability to reallocate burdens, too, up to a point. The individuals and firms who have reaped the lion's share of growth over the knowledge economy era are not as footloose as they might initially have seemed, and there is scope for raising taxes on the most affluent members of society. Moreover, there is more that policy-makers can do to stimulate growth, which should soften the impact of rising costs.

Knowledge-intensive industries can be made more dynamic by tackling the market dominance of incumbents; social investments in skills can still deliver productivity gains, both at the technological frontier and also in the long tail of lower productivity firms; active labour market policies can assist in reallocating workers to more productive roles; and governments can encourage the more efficient use of society's resources by maintaining high levels of aggregate demand.

The outsider insurgency has rocked the political establishment in many developed democracies. The weakness of centre-ground politics leaves countries vulnerable to power grabs by anti-democratic outsiders. The old centre can no longer command the support of a sufficiently broad coalition to face down such threats. If an inclusive new growth regime is to replace it, politicians must recognize the failings of the old policy paradigm and set out an agenda that addresses the legitimate grievances of today's outsiders (which is not, of course, to imply that all outsiders' grievances are legitimate). Creating a new political coalition to underwrite a new agenda of inclusive growth will not be easy: it will require sacrifices on the part of some, particularly those who have benefited most from the policy consensus of the last three decades. Nevertheless, it is far from impossible. The ongoing disintegration of the knowledge-driven growth regime – the shortcomings of its policies, the unravelling of the coalition that once supported it – creates political instability and volatility. At the same time, however, it also creates a window of opportunity for positive change.

NOTES

Introduction

1. Poll of polls; https://www.realclearpolitics.com/epolls/2016/president/us/2016_democratic_presidential_nomination-3824.html.
2. Bill Clinton, remarks at HFA Fundraiser in Potomac MD, 19 October 2015.
3. Bill Clinton, "Fighting for the Forgotten Middle Class", 1992, http://www.4president.org/brochures/billclinton1992brochure.htm.
4. Hillary Clinton, campaign launch speech, 13 June 2015, https://time.com/3920332/transcript-full-text-hillary-clinton-campaign-launch/.
5. Barack Obama, remarks at the America's Promise Alliance Education Event, 1 March 2010, https://obamawhitehouse.archives.gov/photos-and-video/video/helping-america-become-a-grad-nation#transcript.
6. European Commission, *Europe 2020: A European Strategy for Smart, Sustainable and Inclusive Growth* (Brussels: European Commission, 2010).
7. OECD, *The Future of Productivity* (Paris: OECD, 2015).
8. HM Government, *Industrial Strategy: Building a Britain Fit for the Future* (London: HM Government, 2017).
9. En Marche!, "Notre projet économique: efficace, juste et credible", 28 February 2017, https://en-marche.fr/articles/actualites/emmanuel-macron-notre-projet-economique-efficace-juste-et-credible.
10. CDU, *Regierungsprogramm 2017–2021* (Berlin: CDU/CSU, 2017).
11. High Level Group chaired by Wim Kok, *Facing the Challenge: The Lisbon Strategy for Growth and Employment* (Luxembourg: Office for Official Publications of the European Communities, 2004): 9.
12. The concept is also enjoying a resurgence in the academic analysis of recent political and economic developments in developed democracies; see e.g. Torben Iversen & David Soskice, *Democracy and Prosperity* (Princeton, NJ: Princeton University Press, 2019); Roberto Unger, *The Knowledge Economy* (London: Verso, 2019); Kathleen Thelen, "Transitions to the knowledge economy in Germany, Sweden, and the Netherlands", *Comparative Politics* 51:2 (2019), 295–315; David Hope & Angelo Martelli, "The transition to the knowledge economy, labor market institutions, and income inequality in advanced democracies", *World Politics* 71:2 (2019), 236–88; Peter Hall, "The electoral politics of growth regimes", *Perspectives on Politics* 18:1 (2020), 185–99.

13. See e.g. White House, "President Biden announces the Build Back Better Framework", 28 October 2021, https://www.whitehouse.gov/briefing-room/statements-releases/2021/10/28/president-biden-announces-the-build-back-better-framework/; Boris Johnson, speech to Conservative Party conference, 6 October 2021, https://www.conservatives.com/news/2021/boris-johnson-s-keynote-speech---we-re-getting-on-with-the-job.
14. Mario Draghi, speech at Rimini meeting, 18 August 2020, https://www.meetingrimini.org/en/draghis-speech-at-rimini-meeting/.
15. Boris Johnson, remarks ahead of Queen's Speech, 11 May 2021. Reported at: https://www.bbc.co.uk/news/uk-politics-57060588.
16. Rishi Sunak, budget speech to the House of Commons, 27 October 2021, https://www.gov.uk/government/speeches/autumn-budget-and-spending-review-2021-speech.
17. On the fairness of these charges, see in particular Jan-Werner Müller, *What Is Populism?* (London: Penguin, 2017).
18. See e.g. Iversen & Soskice, *Democracy and Prosperity*; Jonathan Hopkin, *Anti-System Politics: The Crisis of Market Liberalism in Rich Democracies* (Oxford: Oxford University Press, 2020); Eric Lonergan & Mark Blyth, *Angrynomics* (Newcastle upon Tyne: Agenda Publishing, 2020); Martin Sandbu, *The Economics of Belonging* (Princeton, NJ: Princeton University Press, 2020).
19. See e.g. Pippa Norris & Ronald Inglehart, *Cultural Backlash: Trump, Brexit, and Authoritarian Populism* (Cambridge: Cambridge University Press, 2019); Diana Mutz, "Status threat, not economic hardship, explains the 2016 presidential vote", *Proceedings of the National Academy of Sciences* 115:19 (2018), E4330–39. For examples of analyses that fuse cultural and economic narratives, see John Judis, *The Populist Explosion* (New York: Columbia Global Reports, 2016); Yascha Mounk, *The People vs. Democracy* (Cambridge, MA: Harvard University Press, 2018); Noam Gidron & Peter A. Hall, "Populism as a problem of social integration", *Comparative Political Studies* 53:7 (2020), 1027–59. For a valuable survey of the populism literature as a whole, see Sheri Berman, "The causes of populism in the West", *Annual Review of Political Science* 24 (2021), 71–88.

Chapter 1

1. See https://www.theguardian.com/culture/charlottehigginsblog/2010/may/10/economics-gordon-brown.
2. Peter Drucker, *The Effective Executive* (New York: Harper & Row, 1967); Daniel Bell, *The Coming of Post-industrial Society* (London: Heinemann Educational, 1974).
3. Gary Loveman, "An assessment of the productivity impact of information technologies" in Thomas Allen and Michael Morton (eds), *Information Technology and the Corporation of the 1990s* (Oxford: Oxford University Press, 1994), 84–110.
4. Robert Solow, "Book review of *Manufacturing Matters: The Myth of the Post-industrial Economy* by Cohen, SS and Zysman, J." *New York Times Book Review*, 12 July 1987, 36.

5. Danny Quah, "Increasingly weightless economies", *Bank of England Quarterly Bulletin* 37:1 (1997), 49–56.

6. Martin Baily & Robert Lawrence, "Do we have a new e-conomy?", *American Economic Review* 91:2 (2001), 308–12.

7. Debra Howcroft, "After the goldrush: deconstructing the myths of the dot.com market", *Journal of Information Technology* 16:4 (2001), 195–204.

8. Peter Drucker, *Post-Capitalist Society* (London: Routledge, 1994).

9. W. Brian Arthur, "Increasing returns and the new world of business", *Harvard Business Review* 74:4 (1996), 100–9.

10. Walter Powell & Kaisa Snellman, "The knowledge economy", *Annual Review of Sociology* 30 (2004), 199–220.

11. Anthony Giddens, *The Third Way and Its Critics* (Cambridge: Polity, 2000).

12. David Autor, Lawrence Katz & Alan Krueger, "Computing inequality: have computers changed the labor market?", *Quarterly Journal of Economics* 113:4 (1998), 1169–213; Eli Berman, John Bound & Stephen Machin, "Implications of skill-biased technological change: international evidence", *Quarterly Journal of Economics* 113:4 (1998), 1245–79.

13. Thomas Piketty, *Capital in the Twenty-First Century*, trans. Arthur Goldhammer (Cambridge, MA: Belknap Press, 2014).

14. David Audretsch & A. Roy Thurik, "Capitalism and democracy in the 21st century: from the managed to the entrepreneurial economy", *Journal of Evolutionary Economics* 10:1–2 (2000), 17–34.

15. Richard Rosecrance, "The rise of the virtual state", *Foreign Affairs* 75:4 (1996), 45–61.

16. Charles Leadbeater, *Living on Thin Air: The New Economy* (London: Penguin, 2000), 32.

17. Diane Coyle, *The Weightless World: Strategies for Managing the Digital Economy* (Cambridge, MA: MIT Press, 1999); Thomas Friedman, *The World Is Flat: A Brief History of the Twenty-First Century* (London: Macmillan, 2006).

18. Accounts that fall into this category include: Colin Crouch, *The Strange Non-death of Neo-liberalism* (Cambridge: Polity, 2011); Andrew Gamble, *Crisis without End? The Unravelling of Western Prosperity* (London: Macmillan, 2014); Wolfgang Streeck, *Buying Time: The Delayed Crisis of Democratic Capitalism* (London: Verso, 2014); Martin Carstensen & Matthias Matthijs, "Of paradigms and power: British economic policy making since Thatcher", *Governance* 31:3 (2018), 431–47.

19. Stephanie Mudge, "What is neo-liberalism?", *Socio-Economic Review* 6:4 (2008), 703–31.

20. Paul Pierson, "The new politics of the welfare state", *World Politics* 48:2 (1996), 143–79.

21. Paul Cammack, "Giddens's way with words", in Sarah Hale, Will Leggett & Luke Martell (eds), *The Third Way and Beyond: Criticisms, Futures and Alternatives* (Manchester: Manchester University Press, 2004).

22. Giddens, *The Third Way*.

23. Gordon Brown, *My Life, Our Times* (London: Random House, 2017), 23.

24. Robert Reich, *Locked in the Cabinet* (London: Vintage, 1998).

25. In light of these implementation failures, a number of scholars have argued that developed democracies' "real" growth strategies over the last two decades have differed markedly from the approaches to growth put forward in politicians' public statements. In the UK and the USA, what was previously celebrated as knowledge-driven growth looks in retrospect more like an attempt to encourage household borrowing in order to sustain demand in the absence of robust, broad-based wage increases. See e.g. Colin Crouch, "Privatised Keynesianism: an unacknowledged policy regime", *British Journal of Politics and International Relations* 11:3 (2009), 382–99; Colin Hay, "Pathology without crisis? The strange demise of the Anglo-liberal growth model", *Government and Opposition* 46:1 (2011), 1–31. Other developed democracies opted for different strategies, which nevertheless existed in symbiosis with this approach: for instance, the export-driven economies of northern Europe depended to a degree on demand from countries that were willing to engage in finance-led, debt-fuelled growth. See Marc Lavoie & Engelbert Stockhammer, "Wage-led growth: concept, theories and policies" in Marc Lavoie & Engelbert Stockhammer (eds), *Wage-Led Growth* (Basingstoke: Palgrave Macmillan, 2013), 13–39; Lucio Baccaro & Jonas Pontusson, "Rethinking comparative political economy: the growth model perspective", *Politics & Society* 44:2 (2016), 175–207.

26. For an insightful recent account of developments in macroeconomic policy that emphasizes changes in the economy and the state of the art of economics as drivers of policy change, see David Vines & Samuel Wills, "The rebuilding macroeconomic theory project: an analytical assessment", *Oxford Review of Economic Policy* 34:1–2 (2018), 1–42.

27. James Buchanan & Gordon Tullock, *The Calculus of Consent* (Ann Arbor, MI: University of Michigan Press, 1962); George Stigler, "The theory of economic regulation", *Bell Journal of Economics and Management Science* 2:1 (1971), 3–21.

28. Hugh Heclo, *Modern Social Politics in Britain and Sweden* (New Haven, CT: Yale University Press, 1974).

29. Alexander Rosenberg, "If economics isn't science, what is it?", *Philosophical Forum* 14:3–4 (1983), 296–314.

30. Peter A. Hall, "How growth regimes evolve in the developed democracies", 22nd International Conference of Europeanists, Paris, 8–10 July 2015.

31. An almost identical typology can be found in Anton Hemerijck's "Social investment as a policy paradigm", *Journal of European Public Policy* 25:6 (2018), 810–27.

32. Peter A. Hall, "Policy paradigms, social learning, and the state: the case of economic policymaking in Britain", *Comparative Politics* 25:3 (1993), 275–96.

33. Cited in Alex Sundby, "Bank execs offer head-scratching answers", *CBS News*, 13 January 2010, https://www.cbsnews.com/news/bank-execs-offer-head-scratching-answers/.

34. In this respect, political scientists have noted that shifts in economic ideas resemble paradigm shifts in the physical sciences, as documented in Thomas Kuhn's work, *The Structure of Scientific Revolutions* (see Peter A. Hall, "Policy paradigms"). As Kuhn pointed out, established scientific theories are not abandoned the instant that some contradictory evidence comes to light. For example, astronomers had been aware that the orbit of Mercury did not perfectly fit the predictions of Newtonian

mechanics for many years before Einstein's theory of general relativity explained the anomaly, yet they continued to use Newton's framework until the explanatory power of Einstein's alternative was widely understood and accepted. On the limitations of the analogy between policy change and scientific revolutions, see e.g. Vivien Schmidt, *The Futures of European Capitalism* (Oxford: Oxford University Press, 2002), 217–25.

35. See Anand Menon, "2016: a review", the UK in a Changing Europe, https://ukandeu.ac.uk/2016-a-review/. For a detailed treatment of the fetishization of GDP growth, see Diane Coyle, *GDP: A Brief but Affectionate History* (Princeton, NJ: Princeton University Press, 2015).

36. Sheri Berman, "Ideational theorizing in the social sciences since 'Policy paradigms, social learning, and the state'", *Governance* 26:2 (2013), 217–37; Colin Hay & Ben Rosamond, "Globalization, European integration and the discursive construction of economic imperatives", *Journal of European Public Policy* 9:2 (2002), 147–67

37. Peter A. Hall, *Governing the Economy: The Politics of State Intervention in Britain and France* (Cambridge: Polity, 1986).

38. Antonio Gramsci, *Prison Notebooks*, Vol. 2, trans. Joseph Buttigieg (New York: Columbia University Press, 1992), 32–3 (Third Notebook, §34).

39. Paul Douglas & Charles Cobb, "A theory of production", *American Economic Review* 18:1 (1928), 139–65.

40. Paul Krugman, *The Age of Diminished Expectations* (Cambridge, MA: MIT Press, 1997), 11. For an earlier statement of the economic significance of technological progress, see Robert Solow, "Technical change and the aggregate production function", *Review of Economics and Statistics* 39:3 (1957), 312–20.

41. Robert Solow, "A contribution to the theory of economic growth", *Quarterly Journal of Economics* 70:1 (1956), 65–94. A similar model was published by Trevor Swan the same year, hence the model is sometimes referred to as the Solow–Swan growth model. See Trevor Swan, "Economic growth and capital accumulation", *Economic Record*, 32:2 (1956), 334–61. However, for our purposes, it is noteworthy that Solow's was the more influential on subsequent theorists, and that Swan's contribution also contained a more nuanced approach to productivity growth, betokening a reluctance to conceive of it as entirely exogenous. See Robert Dimand & Barbara Spencer, "Trevor Swan and the neoclassical growth model", *History of Political Economy* 41:Suppl. 1 (2009), 107–26.

42. Solow, "Theory of economic growth".

43. On the "convergence controversy", see Paul Romer, "The origins of endogenous growth", *Journal of Economic Perspectives* 8:1 (1994), 3–22. See also Robert Lucas' critique of the Solow model in "On the mechanics of economic development", *Journal of Monetary Economics* 22:1 (1988), 3–42. (Lucas was on Romer's PhD dissertation committee and credited his student with the ideas in question.)

44. Kenneth Arrow attempted to account for productivity gains by operationalizing knowledge as a function of capital investment, as firms and workers engaged in "learning by doing" from the introduction of new machines into new contexts; see "The economic implications of learning by doing", *Review of Economic Studies* 29:3 (1962), 155–73. Influenced by Arrow, other theorists such as Karl Shell and Hirofumi

Uzawa constructed models purporting to explain how policy might influence the growth trajectories of different countries; see Karl Shell (ed.), *Essays on the Theory of Optimal Economic Growth* (Cambridge, MA: MIT Press, 1967).

45. David Warsh, *Knowledge and the Wealth of Nations: A Story of Economic Discovery* (New York: Norton, 2006), 156–7.

46. Paul Romer, "Increasing returns and long-run growth", *Journal of Political Economy* 94:5 (1986), 1002–37.

47. Paul Romer, "Endogenous technological change", *Journal of Political Economy* 98:5 Part 2 (1990), S71–S102: S84.

48. *Ibid.*, S73.

49. AnnaLee Saxenian, "Regional networks and the resurgence of Silicon Valley", *California Management Review* 33:1 (1990), 89–112.

50. AnnaLee Saxenian, "The origins and dynamics of production networks in Silicon Valley", *Research Policy* 20:5 (1991), 423–37.

51. See the essays collected in Martin Kenney (ed.), *Understanding Silicon Valley: The Anatomy of an Entrepreneurial Region* (Stanford, CA: Stanford University Press, 2000).

52. Dixit and Stiglitz's model of "monopolistic competition" described a world of unique (but potentially rather similar and thus substitutable) products, each of which would exhibit potentially ever-increasing returns to scale: e.g. competition between subtly different brands of breakfast cereal. See Avinash Dixit & Joseph Stiglitz, "Monopolistic competition and optimum product diversity", *American Economic Review* 67:3 (1977), 297–308. Stiglitz also discussed high-tech firms specifically; see Joseph Stiglitz, "Technological change, sunk costs, and competition", *Brookings Papers on Economic Activity* 3 (1987), 883–937.

    Paul Krugman adapted the Dixit–Stiglitz model to explain patterns of cross-border commerce between advanced capitalist economies. Consumer preferences for differentiated products (e.g. different makes and models of car), coupled with economies of scale in production (per-unit costs are lower when producing more cars for a global market than they are when producing a smaller number of cars exclusively for domestic consumers), meant that trade between developed countries often resulted in broadly similar products (in this case, cars) being exchanged across borders. This contradicted earlier theories in which trade flows were dictated by countries' comparative advantages in the production of categorically different kinds of products (for instance, wine production in Portugal and cloth production in England); see Paul Krugman, "Increasing returns, monopolistic competition, and international trade", *Journal of International Economics* 9:4 (1979), 469–79.

53. W. Brian Arthur, *Increasing Returns and Path Dependence in the Economy* (Ann Arbor, MI: University of Michigan Press, 1994), 3.

54. W. Brian Arthur, "Increasing returns and the new world of business", *Harvard Business Review* 74:4 (1996), 100–9: 104.

55. Arthur, *Increasing Returns*, 112. See also Michael Katz & Carl Shapiro, "Network externalities, competition, and compatibility", *American Economic Review* 75:3 (1985), 424–40. Katz and Shapiro are widely credited with popularizing the concept within the economics profession; however, their focus is on incentives for businesses

to move towards shared standards (or not), whereas Arthur focuses on the process by which market structure emerges in these industries. For a survey of recent literature, see Paul Belleflamme & Martin Peitz, "Platforms and network effects" in Luis C. Corchón & Marco A. Marini (eds), *Handbook of Game Theory and Industrial Organization*, Vol. 2, *Applications* (Cheltenham: Elgar, 2018).

56. Timothy Bresnahan & Shane Greenstein. "Technological competition and the structure of the computer industry", *Journal of Industrial Economics* 47:1 (1999), 1–40.
57. Arthur, *Increasing Returns*, 49–67; Paul Krugman, "Increasing returns and economic geography", *Journal of Political Economy* 99:3 (1991), 483–99.
58. To be sure, a number of critics have contested this view, arguing that a superior alternative should attract investment even if the benefits only become apparent in the long term. See e.g. Stan Liebowitz & Stephen Margolis, "Path dependence, lock-in, and history", *Journal of Law, Economics, & Organization* 11:1 (1995), 205–26.
59. For the canonical account of this view of price signals, see Friedrich Hayek, "The use of knowledge in society", *American Economic Review* 35:4 (1945), 519–30.
60. Stiglitz, "Technological change, sunk costs".
61. Arthur, *Increasing Returns*, 28.
62. *Ibid.*, 9–10.
63. More empirically minded economists, whose work on questions of innovation and growth had continued uninterrupted throughout the latter half of the twentieth century, viewed the "discovery" of endogenous growth by their theoretician counterparts with a degree of bemusement. Zvi Griliches of the National Bureau of Economic Research bemoaned "the rather limited acquaintance of ['new growth theory'] practitioners with the previous empirical literature". See Zvi Griliches, *R&D and Productivity: The Econometric Evidence* (Chicago, IL: University of Chicago Press, 1998), 7. Early examples of this literature included Raymond Ewell, "The role of research in economic growth", *Chemical and Engineering News* 33 (1955), 298–304; Zvi Griliches, "Research costs and social returns: hybrid corn and related innovations", *Journal of Political Economy* 66:5 (1958), 419–31; Fritz Machlup, *The Production and Distribution of Knowledge in the United States* (Princeton, NJ: Princeton University Press, 1962).
64. Warsh, *Knowledge and the Wealth of Nations*, 212.
65. In Mitterrand's case, this involved economic policies such as committing to exchange rate stability under the European Monetary System and opening the French economy up to international investment, forcing businesses to become more competitive in order to secure funding. See Hall, *Governing the Economy*.
66. Joan Ramón Rosés & Nikolaus Wolf, *The Economic Development of Europe's Regions: A Quantitative History since 1900* (Abingdon: Routledge, 2018), 16, 37.
67. Ivor Crewe, "Values: the crusade that failed", in Denis Kavanagh & Anthony Seldon (eds), *The Thatcher Effect* (Oxford: Oxford University Press, 1989).
68. Terry Nichols Clark, Seymour Martin Lipset & Michael Rempel, "The declining political significance of social class", *International Sociology* 8:3 (1993), 293–316; Jane Gingrich & Silja Häusermann, "The decline of the working-class vote, the

reconfiguration of the welfare support coalition and consequences for the welfare state", *Journal of European Social Policy* 25:1 (2015), 50–75.

69. Ronald Inglehart, *The Silent Revolution: Changing Values and Political Styles Among Western Publics* (Princeton, NJ: Princeton University Press, 1977).

70. Ronald Inglehart & Pippa Norris, "Trump and the populist authoritarian parties: the silent revolution in reverse", *Perspectives on Politics* 15:2 (2017), 443–54.

71. Herbert Kitschelt with Anthony J. McGann, *The Radical Right in Western Europe: A Comparative Analysis* (Ann Arbor, MI: University of Michigan Press, 1997).

Chapter 2

1. Tony Blair, Knowledge 2000 conference speech, 7 March 2000, https://webarchive. nationalarchives.gov.uk/20040426081744/http://www.pm.gov.uk/output/Page1521. asp.

2. Stiglitz, "Technological change, sunk costs"; Partha Dasgupta & Joseph Stiglitz, "Potential competition, actual competition, and economic welfare", *European Economic Review* 32:2–3 (1988), 569–77.

3. Reported in Warsh, *Knowledge and the Wealth of Nations*, 289, 298.

4. Jonathan Orszag, Peter Orszag & Laura Tyson, "The process of economic policy-making during the Clinton administration", Conference on American Economic Policy in the 1990s, June 2001.

5. Reich was nevertheless familiar with developments in academic economics too; although his *Work of Nations* does not cite the new growth theory pioneered by Romer, it does reference Brian Arthur's work on "increasing returns". See Robert Reich, *The Work of Nations* (New York: Vintage, 1992), 109.

6. Ed Balls, *Speaking Out: Lessons in Life and Politics* (London: Random House, 2016), 206.

7. Peter Mandelson, *The Third Man: Life at the Heart of New Labour* (London: HarperPress, 2010), 151.

8. Balls, *Speaking Out*, 111–12.

9. *The Economist*, "New Labour's gurus: the American connection", 6 November 1997.

10. OECD, *The Knowledge-Based Economy* (Paris: OECD Publishing, 1996); for a comprehensive overview of the OECD's role in promoting the concept, see Benoit Godin, "The new economy: what the concept owes to the OECD", *Research policy* 33:5 (2004), 679–90.

11. Giddens, *The Third Way*, 4–7.

12. European Commission, *Growth, Competitiveness, Employment* (Luxembourg: Office for Official Publications of the European Communities, 1993): 22.

13. European Commission, *Europe and the global information society* (1994): 8.

14. Council of the European Union (2000) *Presidency Conclusions*, Lisbon European Council, 23–24 March 2000, https://www.consilium.europa.eu/uedocs/cms_data/docs/pressdata/en/ec/00100-r1.en0.htm.

15. Bill Clinton & Al Gore, *Putting People First: How We Can All Change America* (New York: Times Books, 1992): 6.

16. Tony Blair, Labour Party conference leader's speech, 1 October 1996, http://www.britishpoliticalspeech.org/speech-archive.htm?speech=202.

17. Department for Education and Skills, *14–19: Extending Opportunities, Raising Standards* (London: Department for Education and Skills, 2002), 5.

18. European Council, *Lisbon Strategy*.

19. See e.g. European Commission, *The Lisbon European Council: An Agenda of Economic and Social Renewal for Europe* (Brussels: European Commission, 2000), 28.

20. See e.g. Reich, *Locked in the Cabinet*, 316; Giddens, *The Third Way*, 103; Bill Clinton as quoted by Alan Greenspan (and Alan Greenspan himself) in *The Age of Turbulence: Adventures in a New World* (New York: Penguin, 2008), 162.

21. Sherwin Rosen, "The economics of superstars", *American Economic Review* 71:5 (1981), 845–58; Robert Frank & Philip Cook, *The Winner-Take-All Society: Why the Few at the Top Get So Much More than the Rest of Us* (London: Random House, 1995); Alan Krueger, "The economics of real superstars: the market for rock concerts in the material world", *Journal of Labor Economics* 23:1 (2005), 1–30. With respect to the knowledge economy specifically, see Coyle, *Weightless World*, 13.

22. HM Treasury, *Productivity in the UK* (London: The Stationery Office, 2000): 28.

23. Clinton and Gore, *Putting People First*, 17.

24. Giddens, *The Third Way*, 117.

25. European Commission, *Lisbon European Council*, 11. See also Giddens, *The Third Way*, 117.

26. Peter Mandelson, *The Blair Revolution Revisited* (London: Politico's, 2002), 89.

27. Reich, *Work of Nations*, 248. Reich himself used the phrase "symbolic analysts" to describe knowledge workers.

28. Department of Commerce, *The Emerging Digital Economy* (Washington, DC: US Department of Commerce, 1998), 47.

29. Blair, Knowledge 2000 speech.

30. Tony Blair, Role of Work speech, 30 March 2007, https://webarchive.national archives.gov.uk/ukgwa/20100505202725/http://www.number10.gov.uk/archive/2007/03/our-nations-future-the-role-of-work-11405.

31. Coyle, *Weightless World*, 117.

32. As economics editor of the *Independent*, her chief correspondent was Yvette Cooper (who would be elected as a Labour MP in the 1997 election). Gordon Brown's adviser Ed Balls was also credited in the book's acknowledgements.

33. See e.g. Mandelson, *Blair Revolution*, 93.

34. James Bloodworth, *The Myth of Meritocracy: Why Working-Class Kids Still Get Working-Class Jobs* (London: Biteback, 2016); Michael Sandel, *The Tyranny of Merit: What's Become of the Common Good?* (London: Penguin, 2020); Jon Cruddas, *The Dignity of Labour* (Cambridge: Polity, 2021).

35. Geoff Mulgan, *Connexity: Responsibility, Freedom, Business and Power in the New Century* (London: Vintage, 1997), 214.

36. Reich, *Work of Nations*, 105.

37. Leadbeater, *Living on Thin Air*, 33.

38. Coyle, *Weightless World*, 13.

39. European Commission, *Growth, Competitiveness, Employment*, 23.

40. Danny Quah, *The Invisible Hand and the Weightless Economy* (London: LSE, 1996).
41. Reich, *Work of Nations*, 273.
42. European Commission, "Lisbon European Council", 8.
43. Friedman, *The World is Flat*, 7, emphasis added.
44. European Commission, *Growth, Competitiveness, Employment*, 22.
45. Blair, Role of Work speech.
46. Coyle, *Weightless World*, xvii; Reich, *Work of Nations*, 234–5.

Chapter 3

1. HM Treasury, *Productivity*, 21.
2. Mandelson, *Third Man*, 265–6.
3. European Council, *Lisbon Strategy*.
4. Department of Trade and Industry, *Our Competitive Future: Building the Knowledge Driven Economy* (London: Department of Trade and Industry, 1998): 15.
5. HM Treasury, *Productivity*, 24.
6. James Browne & David Phillips, *Tax and Benefit Reforms under Labour* (London: Institute for Fiscal Studies, 2010).
7. European Council, *Lisbon Strategy*.
8. Tony Blair and Gerhard Schröder, *Europe: The Third Way/die Neue Mitte* (1998).
9. Blair and Schröder, *Third Way*.
10. On the history, assumptions and blind spots of the concept of a "European Social Model", see Colin Hay & Daniel Wincott, *The Political Economy of European Welfare Capitalism* (London: Macmillan, 2012).
11. Blair and Schröder, *Third Way*.
12. Department of Social Security, *New Ambitions for Our Country: A New Contract for Welfare* (London: Department of Social Security, 1998), 43.
13. Cited in Coyle, *Weightless World*, 108.
14. Blair, Role of Work speech.
15. European Commission, *Towards Common Principles of Flexicurity* (Luxembourg: Office for Official Publications of the European Communities, 2007), 10, 12, 8, 14.
16. See Marco Simoni & Tim Vlandas, "Labour market liberalization and the rise of dualism in Europe as the interplay between governments, trade unions and the economy", *Social Policy & Administration* 55:4 (2021), 637–58. Within the EU, France was the most notable outlier in maintaining similarly rigid labour markets from the mid-1980s to the cusp of the global financial crisis. For useful descriptions of labour market reforms in Italy, see Maurizio Ferrera & Elisabetta Gualmini, *Rescued by Europe? Social and Labour Market Reforms in Italy from Maastricht to Berlusconi* (Amsterdam: Amsterdam University Press, 2004); in the Netherlands, see Jelle Visser, "The first part-time economy in the world: a model to be followed?", *Journal of European Social Policy* 12:1 (2002), 23–42; in Germany, see Achim Kemmerling & Oliver Bruttel, "'New politics' in German labour market policy? The implications of the recent Hartz reforms for the German welfare state", *West European Politics* 29:1 (2006), 90–112.

17. European Commission, *Flexicurity*, 7. See also Sandbu, *Economics of Belonging*, 105–10.

18. Note that a similar ranking of countries occurs if spending is standardized relative to unemployment levels, although the gap between Sweden and Germany increases and that between Germany and the UK/USA narrows.

19. Note that this is a summary statistic, averaging across different personal and family circumstances. After 2005, the OECD ceased collecting the data for this statistic, preferring net replacement rates that incorporated tax effects and disaggregated different benefit recipient circumstances.

20. European Commission, *Global Information Society*, 8.

21. Mandelson, *Blair Revolution*.

22. Leadbeater, *Living on Thin Air*, 115.

23. Lawrence Summers, The New Wealth of Nations speech, 10 May 2000, https://www.treasury.gov/press-center/press-releases/Pages/ls617.aspx.

24. The anti-trust case against Microsoft described this as "the applications barrier to entry". See *US* vs. *Microsoft*, Findings of Fact, 28 July 1999, paragraphs 36–52, https://www.justice.gov/atr/us-v-microsoft-courts-findings-fact.

25. By 1996, Netscape was estimated to account for around 80 per cent of the browser market: GVU WWW User Survey, October 1996, https://www.cc.gatech.edu/gvu/user_surveys/survey-10–1996/graphs/use/Browser_You_Expect_To_Use_In_12_Months.html.

26. *US* vs. *Microsoft*, Findings of Fact, paragraph 72.

27. *US* vs. *Microsoft*, Findings of Fact, paragraph 160.

28. Joseph Stiglitz, "Public policy for a knowledge economy", address to UK Department of Trade and Industry, 27 January 1999.

29. Warsh, *Knowledge and the Wealth of Nations*, 356–7.

30. Paul Kedrosky, "The more you sell, the more you sell", *Wired*, 1 October 1995, https://www.wired.com/1995/10/arthur/.

31. Paul Romer, *US* vs. *Microsoft*, Testimony, 27 April 2000: paragraphs 5, 71, https://archive.nytimes.com/www.nytimes.com/library/tech/00/04/biztech/articles/29soft-romer.html.

32. George Bittlingmayer & Thomas Hazlett, "DOS Kapital: has antitrust action against Microsoft created value in the computer industry?", *Journal of Financial Economics* 55:3 (2000), 329–59.

33. Summers, *New Wealth of Nations*.

34. *CBS News*, "Justice: we won't break up Microsoft", 6 September 2001, https://www.cbsnews.com/news/justice-we-wont-break-up-microsoft/.

35. Shoshana Zuboff, *Surveillance Capitalism* (London: Profile, 2019): 112–21.

36. See e.g. Department of Trade and Industry, *Knowledge Driven Economy*, 51.

37. Summers, *New Wealth of Nations*.

38. Department of Trade and Industry, *Knowledge Driven Economy*, 45.

39. *BBC News*, "Call for immigration rethink", 12 September 2000, http://news.bbc.co.uk/1/hi/uk_politics/920182.stm.

40. Tony Blair, *New Britain: My Vision of a Young Country* (London: Fourth Estate, 1996), 112, 123.

41. Department of Trade and Industry, *Knowledge Driven Economy*, 6.
42. Reich, *Work of Nations*, 247.
43. Not all contemporary commentators agreed: see e.g. Coyle, *Weightless World*, 56.
44. Leadbeater, *Living on Thin Air*, 15.
45. Stiglitz, "Public policy".
46. The urban studies scholar Richard Florida extended the argument to individual cities; see *The Rise of the Creative Class* (New York: Basic Books, 2002).
47. Department of Trade and Industry, *Knowledge Driven Economy*, 12.
48. European Council, *Lisbon Strategy*.
49. For example, on taxation, compare Gordon Brown, *My Life, Our Times*, 101, 149, to Tony Blair, *A Journey* (London: Vintage, 2010), 116.
50. Reich, *Locked in the Cabinet*, 65.
51. Greenspan, *Age of Turbulence*, 143–4.
52. Summers, New Wealth of Nations.
53. Greenspan, *Age of Turbulence*, 160.
54. *Ibid.*, 208, 160.
55. Darius Ornston, *When Small States Make Big Leaps* (Ithaca, NY: Cornell University Press, 2012); Kees Van Kersbergen & Anton Hemerijck, "Two decades of change in Europe: the emergence of the social investment state", *Journal of Social Policy* 41:3 (2012), 475–92.
56. Ornston, *When Small States Make Big Leaps*.

Chapter 4

1. George W. Bush, speech on economy and training, 2 April 2004, https://georgewbush-whitehouse.archives.gov/news/releases/2004/04/20040402-4.html.
2. George W. Bush, *Blueprint for New Beginnings*, 28 February 2001, https://georgewbush-whitehouse.archives.gov/news/usbudget/blueprint/budi.html.
3. George W. Bush, state of the economy speech, 31 January 2007, https://georgewbush-whitehouse.archives.gov/news/releases/2007/01/20070131-1.html.
4. Ben Bernanke, remarks to Greater Omaha Chamber of Commerce, 6 February 2007, https://www.bis.org/review/r070207a.pdf.
5. European Council, Presidency Conclusions, 22–23 March 2005: 7, 2.
6. Kok, *Facing the Challenge*, 9.
7. *Ibid.*, 12.
8. *Ibid.*
9. Friedman, *The World Is Flat*, 266–7, emphasis in original.
10. Barack Obama, inaugural address, 21 January 2009.
11. Mandelson, *Third Man*, 445.
12. HM Treasury, *Science and Innovation*, 82, emphasis added.
13. Mandelson, *Third Man*, 457.
14. Cited in Adam Tooze, *Crashed: How a Decade of Financial Crises Changed the World* (London: Penguin, 2018): 26–7. Full transcript available at: https://www.

nakedcapitalism.com/2013/04/obama-at-the-hamilton-project-2006-this-is-not-a-bloodless-process.html.

15. *Ibid.*

16. White House, "US-Mexico High Level Economic Dialogue, 6 January 2015", https://obamawhitehouse.archives.gov/the-press-office/2015/01/06/joint-statement-united-states-mexico-high-level-economic-dialogue-1.

17. White House, "Sunshine Week: Increasing Access to Publicly Funded Research", 15 March 2013, https://obamawhitehouse.archives.gov/blog/2013/03/15/sunshine-week-increasing-access-publicly-funded-research.

18. Barack Obama, remarks at Business and Entrepreneurship event, 24 May 2016, https://obamawhitehouse.archives.gov/the-press-office/2016/05/24/remarks-president-discussion-business-and-entrepreneurship-event.

19. Barack Obama, remarks at America's Promise Alliance event, 1 March 2010, https://obamawhitehouse.archives.gov/photos-and-video/video/helping-america-become-a-grad-nation.

20. Barack Obama, remarks on Investing in America's Future, 25 October 2013, https://obamawhitehouse.archives.gov/the-press-office/2013/10/25/remarks-president-investing-americas-future.

21. European Commission, *Europe 2020: A European Strategy for Smart, Sustainable and Inclusive growth* (Brussels: European Commission, 2010), preface.

22. *Ibid.*, 5.

23. *Ibid.*, 5–6.

24. *Ibid.*, 3.

25. *Ibid.*, 9.

26. Josh Bivens, *Why Is Recovery Taking So Long – and Who's to Blame?* (Washington, DC: Economic Policy Institute, 2016).

27. Mark Blyth, *Austerity: The History of a Dangerous Idea* (Oxford: Oxford University Press, 2013).

28. European Commission, *Europe 2020*, 24.

29. Michael Gove, speech on state education, 6 November 2009, https://conservative-speeches.sayit.mysociety.org/speech/601248.

30. Conservative Party, *Raising the Bar, Closing the Gap* (London: Conservative Party, 2007), 12.

31. Notably, many of the centre-left policy-makers who had advocated fiscal prudence in the boom years of the 1990s and early 2000s advocated for stimulus when confronted with the largest financial crisis for almost a century. See e.g. Lawrence Summers, "Why America must have a fiscal stimulus", *Financial Times*, 7 January 2008; Ed Balls, Bloomberg Speech (August 2010), https://www.edballs.co.uk/bloomberg-speech.

32. Labour Party, *Manifesto* (London: Labour Party, 2015): 20, 25, 27, 33.

33. Hillary Clinton, plan to win the global competition for advanced manufacturing jobs, 7 December 2015, https://web.archive.org/web/20160204093918/https://www.hillaryclinton.com/briefing/factsheets/2015/12/07/winning-competition-for-global-manufacturing-jobs/.

34. En Marche!, "Notre projet économique: efficace, juste et credible", 28 February 2017, https://en-marche.fr/articles/actualites/emmanuel-macron-notre-projet-economique-efficace-juste-et-credible.

Chapter 5

1. James Bloodworth, *Hired: Six Months Undercover in Low-Wage Britain* (London: Atlantic, 2018).
2. James Stock & Mark Watson, "Has the business cycle changed and why?", *NBER Macroeconomics Annual* 17 (2002), 159–218; Ben Bernanke, remarks made at meeting of the Eastern Economic Association, 20 February 2004; Peter Summers, "What caused the Great Moderation? Some cross-country evidence", *Federal Reserve Bank of Kansas City Economic Review* 90:3 (2005), 5–32.
3. On Brown's diverse uses of this claim over the course of his time as Chancellor, see *Channel 4 News*, "Factcheck: no more boom and bust", 17 October 2008, http://www.channel4.com/news/articles/politics/domestic_politics/factcheck+no+more+boom+and+bust/2564157.html.
4. Lawrence Summers, "US economic prospects: secular stagnation, hysteresis, and the zero lower bound", *Business Economics* 49:2 (2014), 65–73: 66–7, 69.
5. Crouch, "Privatised Keynesianism".
6. Marc Lavoie & Engelbert Stockhammer, "Wage-led growth: concept, theories and policies" in Marc Lavoie & Engelbert Stockhammer (eds), *Wage-Led Growth* (Basingstoke: Palgrave Macmillan, 2013), 13–29; Lucio Baccaro & Jonas Pontusson, "Rethinking comparative political economy: the growth model perspective", *Politics & Society* 44:2 (2016), 175–207.
7. PwC, *Global Innovation 1000* (2018), https://www.strategyand.pwc.com/gx/en/insights/innovation1000.html.
8. Jean-Charles Rochet & Jean Tirole, "Platform competition in two-sided markets", *Journal of the European Economic Association* 1:4 (2003), 990–1029.
9. Fabrizio Silvestri, "Mining query logs: turning search usage data into knowledge", *Foundations and Trends in Information Retrieval* 4:1–2 (2010), 1–174.
10. Admittedly, for some functionality, what matters is not the number of users *currently* on the platform (the network effect) but the amount of data the business has harvested in the past (either from past users or by other means). In the latter circumstances, we might instead refer to what the UK's Digital Competition Expert Panel termed "the data advantage for incumbents". See Furman *et al.*, *Unlocking Digital Competition*.
11. For a broader discussion of these differences, and their implications for market concentration, see Nick O'Donovan, "Personal data and collective value: data-driven personalisation as network effect" in Uta Kohl & Jacob Eisler (eds), *Data-Driven Personalisation in Markets, Politics and Law* (Cambridge: Cambridge University Press, 2021).
12. Tim O'Reilly, "What is Web 2.0?", *Communications and Strategies* 65:1 (2007), 17–37.

13. Reid Hoffman & Chris Yeh, *Blitzscaling: The Lightning-Fast Path to Building Massively Valuable Businesses* (New York: Broadway Business, 2018).
14. Stanley M. Besen & Joseph Farrell, "Choosing how to compete: strategies and tactics in standardization", *Journal of Economic Perspectives* 8:2 (1994), 117–31. It follows that the claim that a given sector is competitive because competition occurred earlier in the sector's lifecycle – found e.g. in Robert Bork & J. Gregory Sidak, "What does the Chicago School teach about internet search and the antitrust treatment of Google?", *Journal of Competition Law and Economics* 8:4 (2012), 663–700 – is not credible.
15. Such practices are increasingly subject to antitrust scrutiny; see Jonathan Baker & Fiona Scott Morton, "Antitrust enforcement against platform MFNs", *Yale Law Journal* 127 (2017): 2176–202.
16. This advantage is not just restricted to new digital services. Lina Khan argues that Amazon's ability to monitor product innovations on its Marketplace platform enables it to ape successful products as part of its own offering; its wealth of consumer data coupled with control over the sales platform itself then allows it to target its in-house products towards would-be consumers, driving the competitor from the market. See "Amazon's antitrust paradox", *Yale Law Journal* 126:3 (2017), 710–805.
17. See K. Sabeel Rahman, "The new utilities: private power, social infrastructure, and the revival of the public utility concept", *Cardozo Law Review* 39:5 (2017), 1621–92; José Van Dijck, Thomas Poell & Martijn De Waal, *The Platform Society: Public Values in a Connective World* (Oxford: Oxford University Press, 2018).
18. Council of Economic Advisers, "Benefits of competition and indicators of market power", Council of Economic Advisers Issue Brief April 2016, https://obamawhitehouse.archives.gov/sites/default/files/page/files/20160414_cea_competition_issue_brief.pdf; Gustavo Grullon, Yelena Larkin & Roni Michaely, "Are US industries becoming more concentrated?", *Review of Finance* 23:4 (2019), 697–743.
19. Federico Diez, Daniel Leigh & Suchanan Tambunlertchai, *Global Market Power and Its Macroeconomic Implications* (Washington, DC: International Monetary Fund, 2018); Sara Calligaris, Chiara Criscuolo & Luca Marcolin, *Mark-Ups in the Digital Era* (Paris: OECD, 2018).
20. David Autor *et al.*, "The fall of the labor share and the rise of superstar firms", *Quarterly Journal of Economics* 135:2 (2020), 645–709; Tommaso Bighelli *et al.*, "European firm concentration and aggregate productivity", IWH-CompNet Discussion Papers, 2021.
21. Mario Draghi, welcome address to conference on fostering innovation and entrepreneurship in the euro area, 13 March 2017, https://www.ecb.europa.eu/press/key/date/2017/html/sp170313_1.en.html.
22. Ryan Decker *et al.*, "Where has all the skewness gone? The decline in high-growth (young) firms in the US", *European Economic Review* 86 (2016): 4–23.
23. Chiara Criscuolo, Peter Gal & Carlo Menon, *The Dynamics of Employment Growth: New Evidence from 18 Countries* (Paris: OECD, 2014).

24. Dan Andrews, Chiara Criscuolo & Peter Gal, *The Best versus the Rest* (Paris: OECD, 2016).

25. Müge Adalet McGowan, Dan Andrews & Valentine Millot, "The walking dead? Zombie firms and productivity performance in OECD countries", *Economic Policy* 33:96 (2018), 685–736.

26. Paul Romer, expert testimony in Microsoft antitrust case, 27 April 2000, https://archive.nytimes.com/www.nytimes.com/library/tech/00/04/biztech/articles/29soft-romer.html.

27. Plausibly, this behaviour might also be explained by a lack of investable opportunities, although this is difficult to reconcile with techno-optimistic accounts affirming an ever-expanding horizon of lucrative possibilities; accounts often put forward by the leaders of large businesses themselves.

28. Herman Mark Schwartz, "Wealth and secular stagnation: the role of industrial organization and intellectual property rights", *Russell Sage Foundation Journal of the Social Sciences* 2:6 (2016), 226–49; Herman Mark Schwartz, "Global secular stagnation and the rise of intellectual property monopoly", *Review of International Political Economy* (2021): 1–26.

29. Jonathan Haskel & Stian Westlake, *Capitalism without Capital: The Rise of the Intangible Economy* (Princeton, NJ: Princeton University Press, 2018), 107.

Chapter 6

1. Maarten Goos, Alan Manning & Anna Salomons, "Explaining job polarization: routine-biased technological change and offshoring", *American Economic Review* 104:8 (2014), 2509–26.

2. OECD, *Employment Outlook* (Paris: OECD Publishing, 2017), chapter 3.

3. Daniel Oesch & Giorgio Piccitto, "The polarization myth: occupational upgrading in Germany, Spain, Sweden, and the UK, 1992–2015", *Work and Occupations* 46:4 (2019), 441–69.

4. Several commentators point out that the slowdown might also be attributed to flawed measures of growth: the fact that economic statistics are poorly equipped to register qualitative improvements in technologies, such as faster computers, higher-resolution television screens or longer-lasting batteries; or free-to-use products such as platforms hosting user-generated content. See e.g. Martin Feldstein, "Underestimating the real growth of GDP, personal income, and productivity", *Journal of Economic Perspectives* 31:2 (2017), 145–64.

5. Josh Bivens & Lawrence Mishel, *Understanding the Historic Divergence between Productivity and a Typical Worker's Pay: Why It Matters and Why It's Real* (Washington, DC: Economic Policy Institute, 2015); Cyrille Schwellnus, Andreas Kappeler & Pierre-Alain Pionnier, *Decoupling of Wages from Productivity: Macro-Level Facts* (Paris: OECD, 2017).

6. See e.g. David Autor, Lawrence Katz & Melissa Kearney, "The polarization of the US labor market", *American Economic Review* 96:2 (2006), 189–94.

7. Note that the classifications of jobs as "high-paying" in Goos *et al.*, "Explaining job polarization" depends on the relative *mean* salaries of different occupational categories, so it would not detect changes in the distribution of wages *within* a particular job type.

8. For example, on intra-occupational wage inequality, see ChangHwan Kim & Arthur Sakamoto, "The rise of intra-occupational wage inequality in the United States, 1983 to 2002", *American Sociological Review* 73:1 (2008), 129–57; Mark Williams, "Occupations and British wage inequality, 1970s–2000s", *European Sociological Review* 29:4 (2013), 841–57.

9. Haskel & Westlake, *Capitalism without Capital*, 188–200.

10. Caroline Lloyd & Ken Mayhew, "Skill: the solution to low wage work?", *Industrial Relations Journal* 41:5 (2010), 429–45. See also Caroline Lloyd & Jonathan Payne, "Flat whites: who gets progression in the UK café sector?", *Industrial Relations Journal* 43:1 (2012), 38–52.

11. Department of Commerce, *The Emerging Digital Economy* (Washington, DC: US Department of Commerce, 1998): 47.

12. See the discussion in Van Dijck *et al.*, *The Platform Society*, particularly 49–72.

13. High Fliers Research, *The Graduate Market in 2020* (2020), https://www.highfliers.co.uk/download/2020/graduate_market/GM20Report.pdf.

14. Tiziana Terranova, "Free labor: producing culture for the digital economy", *Social Text* 18:2 (2000), 33–58.

15. Lisa Margonelli, "Inside AOL's 'cyber-sweatshop'", *Wired*, 1 October 1999; Lauren Kirchner, "AOL settled with unpaid 'volunteers' for $15m", *Columbia Journalism Review*, 10 February 2011.

16. Adrian Johns, *Piracy: The Intellectual Property Wars from Gutenberg to Gates* (Chicago: University of Chicago Press, 2010).

17. Mark Bender & Yongsheng Wang, "The impact of digital piracy on music sales: a cross-country analysis", *International Social Science Review* 84:3–4 (2009), 157–70.

18. Coyle, *Weightless World*, 117.

19. Nick Srnicek, *Platform Capitalism* (Chichester: Wiley, 2017), 33–4.

20. Adrian Wood, "Variation in structural change around the world, 1985–2015: patterns, causes and implications", WIDER working paper 34 (2017).

21. Michael Hicks & Srikant Devaraj, "The myth and the reality of manufacturing in America", Center for Business and Economic Research, Ball State University (2015); PwC, *The Future of UK Manufacturing* (2009), https://www.pwc.co.uk/assets/pdf/ukmanufacturing-300309.pdf.

22. IMF, *World Economic Outlook* (Washington, DC: IMF, October 2019), chapter 2.

23. Mario Aloisio, "The calculation of Easter Day, and the origin and use of the word computer", *IEEE Annals of the History of Computing* 26:3 (2004), 42–9.

24. David Autor, "Why are there still so many jobs? The history and future of workplace automation", *Journal of Economic Perspectives* 29:3 (2015), 3–30.

25. See Daron Acemoglu & Pascual Restrepo, "Artificial intelligence, automation and work", National Bureau of Economic Research No. w24196 (2018).

26. See e.g. John Maynard Keynes, "Relative movements of real wages and output", *Economic Journal* 49:93 (1939), 34–51; Nicholas Kaldor, "A model of economic

growth", *Economic Journal* 67:268 (1957), 591–624. Robert Solow was famously sceptical of these claims: see "A skeptical note on the constancy of relative shares", *American Economic Review* 48:4 (1958): 618–31.

27. European Commission, *Employment in Europe* (Luxembourg: Office for Official Publications of the European Communities, 2007), 237–72; IMF, *World Economic Outlook* (Washington, DC: IMF, April 2007), 161–92.

28. IMF, *World Economic Outlook* (Washington, DC: IMF, April 2017), chapter 3; Schwellnus *et al.*, *Decoupling of Wages.*

29. João Paulo Pessoa & John Van Reenen, *Decoupling of Wage Growth and Productivity Growth? Myth and Reality* (London: Resolution Foundation, 2012); Bivens &Mishel, *Understanding the Divergence*; Taehyoung Cho, Soobin Hwang & Paul Schreyer "Has the labour share declined? It depends", OECD Statistics Working Papers (2017).

30. Schwellnus *et al.*, *Decoupling of Wages.*

31. The pattern (or lack thereof) does not change markedly if average education spending is lagged by a decade and/or if developed democracies in North America and Oceania are included to the analysis, although the availability of strictly comparable data decreases.

32. Blair, Role of Work speech.

33. Tali Kristal, "Good times, bad times: postwar labor's share of national income in capitalist democracies", *American Sociological Review* 75:5 (2010), 729–63; Engelbert Stockhammer, "Determinants of the wage share: a panel analysis of advanced and developing economies", *British Journal of Industrial Relations* 55:1 (2017), 3–33.

34. Acemoglu & Restrepo, "Artificial intelligence".

35. Autor, "So many jobs".

36. Carl Benedikt Frey, *The Technology Trap: Capital, Labor, and Power in the Age of Automation* (Princeton, NJ: Princeton University Press, 2019).

37. See Robert Gordon, "Does the 'new economy' measure up to the great inventions of the past?", *Journal of Economic Perspectives* 14:4 (2000), 49–74; Robert Gordon, *The Rise and Fall of American Growth: The US Standard of Living Since the Civil War* (Princeton, NJ: Princeton University Press, 2017). Gordon's emphasis is on productivity gains from technology, arguing that new technologies associated with the digital revolution appear unlikely to yield returns as large as previous technological revolutions. In light of advances in automation and artificial intelligence, this seems debatable; but what is interesting for our purposes is the prospect that the range of *labour-generating* productive innovations created over this period might have been a historical one-off.

38. Moreover, from a GDP perspective, these technologies were unambiguously labour-generating, as salaries for workers involved in (e.g.) designing and manufacturing washing machines counted towards economic output, whereas the unpaid domestic labour these washing machines replaced did not.

39. Erik Brynjolfsson & Andrew McAfee, *The Second Machine Age: Work, Progress, and Prosperity in a Time of Brilliant Technologies* (New York: Norton, 2014).

40. Joe Keohane, "What news-writing bots mean for the future of journalism", *Wired*, 16 February 2017; Jane Croft, "Law firms programmed for more technological

disruption", *Financial Times*, 2 June 2017; Xiaoxuan Liu *et al.*, "A comparison of deep learning performance against health-care professionals in detecting diseases from medical imaging: a systematic review and meta-analysis", *The Lancet Digital Health* 1:6 (2019): e271–97.

41. James Manyika *et al.*, *Disruptive Technologies: Advances that Will Transform Life, Business, and the Global Economy* (Washington, DC: McKinsey Global Institute, 2013).

42. For a detailed discussion of how the technologies of the digital revolution appear to be primarily labour-replacing, see Frey, *Technology Trap*.

43. *Ibid.*

Chapter 7

1. OECD, *A Broken Social Elevator? How to Promote Social Mobility* (Paris: OECD Publishing, 2018).

2. Elisa Giannone, "Skilled-biased technical change and regional convergence", unpublished manuscript, University of Chicago (2017).

3. Rosés & Wolf, *Economic Development of Europe's Regions*.

4. OECD, *Regions and Cities at a Glance* (Paris: OECD Publishing, 2018).

5. Edward Glaeser, Jed Kolko & Albert Saiz, "Consumer city", *Journal of Economic Geography* 1:1 (2001), 27–50.

6. Ed Pemberton, "A question of value: raising productivity by lowering inequality" in Craig Berry (ed.), *What We Really Mean When We Talk about Industrial Strategy* (Manchester: Future Economies Research Centre, 2018).

7. Data available at: https://www.destatis.de/DE/Themen/Wirtschaft/Preise/Baupreise-Immobilienpreisindex/Tabellen/haeuserpreisindex-kreistypen.html.

8. Data available at: https://www.ons.gov.uk/economy/inflationandpriceindices/bulletins/housepriceindex/december2019#regional-house-prices-including-london.

9. Data available at: https://www.economist.com/graphic-detail/2019/03/11/american-cities-house-price-index?date=1993–03&index=real_price&places=DAL&places=LAN.

10. Stephen Clarke, *Get a Move On? The Decline in Regional Job-to-Job Moves and Its Impact on Productivity and Pay* (London: Resolution Foundation, 2017).

11. Ben Ansell, "The politics of housing", *Annual Review of Political Science* 22 (2019), 165–85.

12. Data available at: https://www.ons.gov.uk/employmentandlabourmarket/peoplein work/employmentandemployeetypes/articles/coronavirusandhome workingintheuklabourmarket/2019. For a useful discussion of these trends, see Alan Felstead & Golo Henseke, "Assessing the growth of remote working and its consequences for effort, well-being and work-life balance", *New Technology, Work and Employment* 32:3 (2017), 195–212.

13. The data for 2005 covered EU member states and (then) candidate countries; 2015 data covered the EU28, Norway, Switzerland, Albania, the Former Yugoslav Republic of Macedonia, Montenegro, Serbia and Turkey.

14. Data available at: https://www.bls.gov/opub/ted/2019/29-percent-of-wage-and-salary-workers-could-work-at-home-in-their-primary-job-in-2017–18.htm.

15. Data available at: https://www.ons.gov.uk/employmentandlabourmarket/peoplein work/employmentandemployeetypes/articles/coronavirusandhome workingintheuklabourmarket/2019.

16. AnnaLee Saxenian, *Regional Advantage* (Cambridge, MA: Harvard University Press, 1996); Martin Kenney, *Understanding Silicon Valley: The Anatomy of an Entrepreneurial Region* (Stanford, CA: Stanford University Press, 2000); Jane Jacobs, *The Economy of Cities* (London: Random House, 1969); Edward Glaeser *et al.*, "Growth in cities", *Journal of Political Economy* 100:6 (1992), 1126–52.

17. Schwellnus *et al.*, *Decoupling of Wages*, 18.

18. Claudia Goldin & Lawrence Katz, *The Race between Education and Technology* (Cambridge, MA: Harvard University Press, 2009).

19. *Ibid.*, 303.

20. Greenspan, *Age of Turbulence*, 397–8.

21. Daron Acemoglu & David Autor, "Skills, tasks and technologies: implications for employment and earnings", in *Handbook of Labor Economics*, Vol. 4 (Amsterdam: Elsevier, 2011), 1043–71. See also Frey, *Technology Trap*, 224.

22. Ian Walker & Yu Zhu, "The college wage premium and the expansion of higher education in the UK", *Scandinavian Journal of Economics* 110:4 (2008), 695–709.

23. Alison Kershaw, "More than half of young people now going to university", *The Independent*, 27 September 2019.

24. Pedro Martins & Pedro T. Pereira, "Does education reduce wage inequality? Quantile regression evidence from 16 countries", *Labour Economics* 11:3 (2004), 355–71.

25. Antoni Calvo-Armengol & Matthew Jackson, "The effects of social networks on employment and inequality", *American Economic Review* 94:3 (2004), 426–54; Matthew Jackson, Brian Rogers & Yves Zenou, "The economic consequences of social-network structure", *Journal of Economic Literature* 55:1 (2017), 49–95.

26. Alice Sullivan, "Cultural capital and educational attainment", *Sociology* 35:4 (2001), 893–912; Annette Lareau & Elliot Weininger, "Cultural capital in educational research: a critical assessment", *Theory and Society* 32:5–6 (2003), 567–606; David Throsby, "Cultural capital", *Journal of Cultural Economics* 23:1–2 (1999): 3–12. For a more critical take, see Paul Kingston, "The unfulfilled promise of cultural capital theory", *Sociology of Education* (2001), 88–99.

27. Jessica Curiale, "America's new glass ceiling: unpaid internships, the Fair Labor Standards Act, and the urgent need for change", *Hastings Law Journal* 61:6 (2009): 1531–60; Leslie Regan Shade & Jenna Jacobson, "Hungry for the job: gender, unpaid internships, and the creative industries", *Sociological Review* 63 (2015): 188–205; Tess Lanning & Katerina Rudiger, *Youth Unemployment in Europe: Lessons for the UK* (London: IPPR, 2012).

28. Early expositions of this analysis can be found in Rosen, "The economics of superstars"; Frank & Cook, *The Winner-Takes-All Society*.

29. Krueger, "Economics of real superstars".

30. Martins & Pereira, "Wage inequality". If this is the case, more emphasis needs to be placed upon improving ability earlier in the education process.

31. Jeff Grogger & Eric Eide, "Changes in college skills and the rise in the college wage premium", *Journal of Human Resources* 30:2 (1995), 280–310; Ian Walker & Yu Zhu, "Differences by degree: evidence of the net financial rates of return to undergraduate study for England and Wales", *Economics of Education Review* 30:6 (2011), 1177–86.

32. Mark Levels, Rolf Van der Velden & Jim Allen, "Educational mismatches and skills: new empirical tests of old hypotheses", *Oxford Economic Papers* 66:4 (2014), 959–82; Rolf Van Der Velden & Ineke Bijlsma, "College wage premiums and skills: a cross-country analysis", *Oxford Review of Economic Policy* 32:4 (2016), 497–513.

33. Reports of the poor working conditions experienced by newly minted knowledge workers in China may offer some indication of what can happen when the supply of graduates is increased but power disparities between employers and employees are not addressed.

Chapter 8

1. Data available at: https://data.worldbank.org/indicator/SE.TER.ENRR?locations= CN-FR-GB-IN

2. Phillip Brown & Hugh Lauder, "Globalisation, knowledge and the myth of the magnet economy", *Globalisation, Societies and Education* 4:1 (2006), 25–57.

3. Leadbeater, *Living on Thin Air*, 15.

4. Francis Fukuyama, *The End of History and the Last Man* (New York: Simon & Schuster, 2006).

5. Mariana Mazzucato, *The Entrepreneurial State: Debunking Public vs. Private Sector Myths* (Washington, DC: Public Affairs, 2015).

6. Overly expansive intellectual property rights might also exert a chilling effect on innovation, precluding competitors from developing similar but superior products or locking down core technologies on which further innovations might be predicated. On some of the definitional issues around intellectual property, see Christopher May, "Thinking, buying, selling: intellectual property rights in political economy", *New Political Economy* 3:1 (1998), 59–78.

7. Sumner La Croix & Denise Eby Konan, "Intellectual property rights in China: the changing political economy of Chinese–American interests", *World Economy* 25:6 (2002), 759–88.

8. Whether this was a deliberate strategy or not is debatable: see Andrew Mertha, *The Politics of Piracy: Intellectual Property in Contemporary China* (Ithaca, NY: Cornell University Press, 2007).

9. Brett Christophers, *Rentier Capitalism: Who Owns the Economy, and Who Pays for It?* (London: Verso, 2020).

10. Ronen Palan, Richard Murphy & Christian Chavagneux, *Tax Havens: How Globalization Really Works* (Ithaca, NY: Cornell University Press, 2013); Ronen Palan, *The Offshore World: Sovereign Markets, Virtual Places, and Nomad Millionaires* (Ithaca, NY: Cornell University Press, 2006).

11. Clearly, some economies of scale would be lost in the process, and there is an argument that some smaller countries might benefit from banding together to create a single digital market within a regional bloc, a point we return to in Chapter 10.

12. Colin Hay & Ben Rosamond, "Globalization, European integration and the discursive construction of economic imperatives", *Journal of European Public Policy* 9:2 (2002), 147–67; David Hope & Julian Limberg, "The knowledge economy and taxes on the rich", *Journal of European Public Policy* (2021), https://doi.org/10.1080/1350 1763.2021.1992483.

13. Iversen & Soskice, *Democracy and Prosperity*, xiii.

14. Simona Iammarino & Philip McCann, *Multinationals and Economic Geography: Location, Technology and Innovation* (Cheltenham: Elgar, 2013), 203.

15. Reich, *Work of Nations*, 235.

16. Rasmus Corlin Christensen & Martin Hearson, "The new politics of global tax governance: taking stock a decade after the financial crisis", *Review of International Political Economy* 26:5 (2019), 1068–88.

17. Both of these initiatives sprang from the OECD's programme to tackle base erosion and profit shifting, commonly known as BEPS. For a critical but sympathetic analysis, see Allison Christians, "BEPS and the new international tax order" *BYU Law Review* 6 (2016), 1603–47.

18. Paul Collier, *Exodus: How Migration is Changing our World* (Oxford: Oxford University Press, 2013).

19. Steve Coulter, "Skill formation, immigration and European integration: the politics of the UK growth model", *New Political Economy* 23:2 (2018), 208–22.

20. See e.g. Florence Jaumotte, Ksenia Koloskova & Sweta Chaman Saxena, *Impact of Migration on Income Levels in Advanced Economies* (Washington, DC: IMF, 2016); Ekrame Boubtane, Jean-Christophe Dumont & Christophe Rault, "Immigration and economic growth in the OECD countries 1986–2006", *Oxford Economic Papers* 68:2 (2016), 340–60; Giovanni Peri, "The effect of immigration on productivity: evidence from US states", *Review of Economics and Statistics* 94:1 (2012), 348–58.

21. Christian Dustmann, Tommaso Frattini & Ian Preston, "The effect of immigration along the distribution of wages", *Review of Economic Studies* 80:1 (2013), 145–73; Stephen Nickell & Jumana Salaheen, "The impact of immigration on occupational wages: evidence from Britain", Bank of England Staff Working Paper No. 574, December 2015.

22. Coulter, "Skill formation".

23. Andrew Leigh, "Trust, inequality and ethnic heterogeneity", *Economic Record* 82:258 (2006), 268–80; Robert Putnam, "*E pluribus unum*: diversity and community in the twenty-first century the 2006 Johan Skytte Prize Lecture", *Scandinavian Political Studies* 30:2 (2007), 137–74.

24. Holger Stichnoth & Karine Van der Straeten, "Ethnic diversity, public spending, and individual support for the welfare state: a review of the empirical literature", *Journal of Economic Surveys* 27:2 (2013), 364–89.

25. Sascha Becker & Thiemo Fetzer, "Has eastern European migration impacted UK-born workers?", University of Warwick CAGE Discussion Paper 376, June 2018.

Chapter 9

1. Fahmida Rahman & Daniel Tomlinson, "Cross countries: international comparisons of intergenerational trends", LIS Working Paper Series No. 732 (2018).

2. On wage-setting more generally, see Jake Rosenfeld, *You're Paid What You're Worth and Other Myths of the Modern Economy* (Cambridge, MA: Harvard University Press, 2021).

3. A similar story could be told about other long-standing EU and European Free Trade Association members, such as Italy, Spain, Austria or Sweden. See e.g. Lluis Orriols & Guillermo Cordero, "The breakdown of the Spanish two-party system: the upsurge of Podemos and Ciudadanos in the 2015 general election", *South European Society and Politics* 21:4 (2016), 469–92; Piergiorgio Corbetta *et al.*, "Lega and Five-Star Movement voters: exploring the role of cultural, economic and political bewilderment", *Contemporary Italian Politics* 10:3 (2018), 279–93; Jürgen Essletzbichler, Franziska Disslbacher & Mathias Moser, "The victims of neoliberal globalisation and the rise of the populist vote: a comparative analysis of three recent electoral decisions", *Cambridge Journal of Regions, Economy and Society* 11:1 (2018), 73–94; Jonathan Hopkin, *Anti-System Politics* (Oxford: Oxford University Press, 2020); Isabel Airas & Carl Truedsson, "Contesting and envisioning 'trygghet': the Sweden Democrats, Social Democrats, and the 2018 Swedish general election", *Area* (2020), https://doi.org/10.1111/area.12689.

4. Note that regionalist parties such as the Scottish National Party in the UK have not been counted as part of the "centrist" vote, nor have parties that were too small to win seats in legislative elections.

5. Donald Trump, interview with *Bloomberg News*, 26 May 2016, https://www.bloomberg.com/features/2016-reince-priebus/

6. He then offered the rather mealy-mouthed qualification that "some, I assume, are good people". Donald Trump, announcement speech, June 2015, https://time.com/3923128/donald-trump-announcement-speech/.

7. Rahman & Tomlinson, *Cross Countries*.

8. On this generational shift in values, see Pippa Norris & Ronald Inglehart, *Cultural Backlash: Trump, Brexit, and Authoritarian Populism* (Cambridge: Cambridge University Press, 2019).

9. Ipsos, *1er Tour Présidentielle*, 23 April 2007, https://www.ipsos.com/fr-fr/1er-tour-presidentielle-2007; *1er Tour Présidentielle*, 22 April 2017, https://www.ipsos.com/sites/default/files/files-fr-fr/doc_associe/ipsos-sopra-steria_sociologie-des-electorats_23-avril-2017-21h.pdf.

10. Data from bundeswahlleiter.de, *Ergebnisse der Repräsentativen Wahlstatistik*.

11. Tom Rosentiel, "Young voters in the 2008 presidential primaries", *Pew Research Center*, 11 February 2008.

12. Data from Edison Research national exit polls.

13. Data from Essex Continuous Monitoring Survey, https://theconversation.com/understanding-labours-youthquake-80333?utm_medium=ampemail&utm_source=email; and IPSOS Mori, https://www.ipsos.com/ipsos-mori/en-uk/how-britain-voted-2017-election. See James Sloam, Rakib Ehsan & Matt Henn,

"'Youthquake': how and why young people reshaped the political landscape in 2017", *Political Insight* 9:1 (2018), 4–8.

14. See British Election Study data and Christopher Prosser *et al.*, "Tremors but no youthquake: measuring changes in the age and turnout gradients at the 2015 and 2017 British general elections", *Electoral Studies* 64 (2020), 102–29.

15. Roberto Stefan Foa & Yascha Mounk, "The democratic disconnect", *Journal of Democracy* 27:3 (2016), 5–17.

16. Yascha Mounk, *The People vs. Democracy: Why Our Freedom Is in Danger and How to Save It* (Cambridge, MA: Harvard University Press, 2018).

17. Judith Shklar, "The liberalism of fear" in Nancy L. Rosenblum (ed.), *Liberalism and the Moral Life* (Cambridge, MA: Harvard University Press, 1989).

18. Pippa Norris, "Is Western democracy backsliding? Diagnosing the risks", *Journal of Democracy* 28(2) (2017).

19. Jeff Guo, "Debunking the myth that millennials are ushering in the end of the Western world", *Washington Post*, 2 December 2016.

20. Robert Ford & Matthew Goodwin, *Revolt on the Right: Explaining Support for the Radical Right in Britain* (Abingdon: Routledge, 2014), 152–75.

21. Nonna Mayer, "From Jean-Marie to Marine Le Pen: electoral change on the far right", *Parliamentary Affairs* 66:1 (2013), 160–78; Daniel Stockemer & Abdelkarim Amengay, "The voters of the FN under Jean-Marie Le Pen and Marine Le Pen: continuity or change?", *French Politics* 13:4 (2015), 370–90.

22. A point made by David Norman Smith & Eric Hanley, "The anger games: who voted for Donald Trump in the 2016 election, and why?", *Critical Sociology* 44:2 (2018): 195–212. See also Scott Blinder, Robert Ford & Elisabeth Ivarsflaten, "The better angels of our nature: how the antiprejudice norm affects policy and party preferences in Great Britain and Germany", *American Journal of Political Science* 57:4 (2013): 841–57.

23. See e.g. Corbetta *et al.*, "Lega and Five-Star Movement"; Essletzbichler *et al.*, "Victims of neoliberal globalisation"; Hopkin, *Anti-system Politics*.

24. Thomas Lux, "Die AfD und die unteren Statuslagen: Eine Forschungsnotiz zu Holger Lengfelds Studie Die 'Alternative für Deutschland': eine Partei für Modernisierungsverlierer?", *Kölner Zeitschrift für Soziologie und Sozialpsychologie* 70:2 (2018), 255–73.

25. There has been an extensive debate about the primacy of various factors in the AfD's emergence: see e.g. Susanne Rippl and Christian Seipel, "Modernisierungsverlierer, cultural backlash, postdemokratie", *Kölner Zeitschrift für Soziologie und Sozialpsychologie* 70:2 (2018), 237–54; Knut Bergmann, Matthias Diermeier & Judith Niehues, "Die AfD: Eine Partei der sich ausgeliefert fühlenden Durchschnittsverdiener?", *Zeitschrift für Parlamentsfragen* (2017): 57–75.

26. Brian Bell & Stephen Machin, "Brexit and wage inequality" in Richard Baldwin (ed.), *Brexit Beckons: Thinking Ahead by Leading Economists* (London: CEPR Press, 2016): 111–14; Sascha Becker, Thiemo Fetzer & Dennis Novy, "Who voted for Brexit? A comprehensive district-level analysis", *Economic Policy* 32:92 (2017), 601–50.

27. Becker *et al.*, "Who voted for Brexit?"; David Manley, Kelvyn Jones & Ron Johnston, "The geography of Brexit – What geography? Modelling and predicting the outcome

across 380 local authorities", *Local Economy* 32:3 (2017), 183–203; Matthew Goodwin & Oliver Heath, "The 2016 referendum, Brexit and the left behind: an aggregate-level analysis of the result", *Political Quarterly* 87:3 (2016), 323–32.

28. UK in a Changing Europe, *Comfortable Leavers* (2021), https://ukandeu.ac.uk/wp-content/uploads/2021/04/Comfortable-Leavers-1.pdf; Diane Bolet, "Drinking alone: local socio-cultural degradation and radical right support – the case of British pub closures", *Comparative Political Studies* 54:9 (2021), 1653–92.

29. Michael McQuarrie, "The revolt of the Rust Belt: place and politics in the age of anger", *British Journal of Sociology* 68 (2017): S120–S152; Konstantin Kilibarda & Daria Roithmayr, "The myth of the rust belt revolt", *Slate*, 1 December 2016.

30. David Autor *et al.*, "Importing political polarization? The electoral consequences of rising trade exposure", National Bureau of Economic Research no. w22637 (2016).

31. Bergmann *et al.*, "Die AfD".

32. Christian Dippel, Robert Gold & Stephan Heblich, "Globalization and its (dis-) content: trade shocks and voting behaviour", National Bureau of Economic Research no. w21812 (2015).

33. For the UK, see Will Jennings & Gerty Stoker, "The divergent dynamics of cities and towns: geographical polarisation after Brexit", *Political Quarterly* 90:S2 (2019), 155–66. For southern European examples, see Jorge Sola & César Rendueles, "Podemos, the upheaval of Spanish politics and the challenge of populism", *Journal of Contemporary European Studies* 26:1 (2018), 99–116; Yiannis Mavris, "Greece's austerity election", *New Left Review* 76 (2012): 95–107; Hopkin, *Anti-system Politics*.

34. For a useful survey, see Sheri Berman, "The causes of populism in the West", *Annual Review of Political Science* 24 (2021), 71–88.

35. There is certainly a case to be made that what actually worked was not knowledge-driven growth but property-based lending (not just in house price boom countries such as the USA, UK, Spain and Ireland, but also in export-driven economies that relied in large part on that boom as an external demand stimulus). However, one of the factors underwriting that lending was the expectation of growth, driven in large part by optimistic projections about the productivity miracle of the new economy. See Nick O'Donovan, "Demand, dysfunction and distribution: the UK growth model from neoliberalism to the knowledge economy", *British Journal of Politics and International Relations* (2021), https://doi.org/10.1177/13691481211058018.

36. Norris & Inglehart, *Cultural Backlash*.

37. Iversen & Soskice, *Democracy and Prosperity*, 205–6, 217. While the liberal may be more likely to migrate to cities, it is not clear that illiberal individuals have migrated away from cities. Liberal values may be decisive to success, but maybe they are just closely correlated with education levels. For analysis of this last point, see Edward Glaeser's "Review of Richard Florida's *The Rise of the Creative Class*", *Regional Science and Urban Economics* 35:5 (2005), 593–6.

38. Hillary Clinton, Mumbai speech, 13 March 2018. Excepts available at: https://www.businessinsider.com/hillary-clinton-says-trump-won-backwards-states-in-2016-2018-3?r=US&IR=T.

39. On this last point, see Michael Sandel, *The Tyranny of Merit: What's Become of the Common Good?* (London: Penguin, 2020).

40. John Judis, *The Populist Explosion: How the Great Recession Transformed American and European Politics* (New York: Columbia Global Reports, 2016): 98–99; Hans-George Betz, "The new politics of resentment: radical right-wing populist parties in Western Europe", *Comparative Politics* (1993): 413–27.

41. Ralf Havertz, "Right-wing populism and neoliberalism in Germany: the AfD's embrace of ordoliberalism", *New Political Economy* 24:3 (2019), 385–403; Hopkin, *Anti-system Politics*, 62.

42. Nuria Font, Paolo Graziano & Myrto Tsakatika, "Varieties of inclusionary populism? SYRIZA, Podemos and the Five Star Movement", *Government and Opposition* 56:1 (2021), 163–83.

43. Jan-Werner Müller has stressed Sanders' pluralism; see *What Is Populism?* (London: Penguin, 2017), 93. On Corbyn, see Luke March, "Left and right populism compared: the British case", *British Journal of Politics and International Relations* 19:2 (2017), 282–303.

44. Davide Vittori, "Party change in anti-establishment parties in government: the case of Five Stars Movement and SYRIZA", *Italian Political Science* 13:2 (2018), 78–91; Valeria Tarditi & Davide Vittori, "What are we gonna be when we grow up? SYRIZA's institutionalisation and its new 'governing party' role", *Communist and Post-Communist Studies* 52:1 (2019), 25–37.

45. A similar point is made by Jonathan Hopkin in *Anti-System Politics*; however, Hopkin sees the outsider insurgency as a reaction against market liberalism rather than knowledge-driven growth.

46. This might also be termed an "interregnum"; see Rune Møller Stahl, "Ruling the interregnum: politics and ideology in nonhegemonic times", *Politics & Society* 47:3 (2019), 333–60.

Chapter 10

1. The alliterative phrase has been extensively deployed in English-language discussions of economic policy post-pandemic. See e.g. White House, "President Biden announces the Build Back Better Framework", 28 October 2021; Boris Johnson, speech to Conservative Party conference, 6 October 2021; Angel Gurría, remarks made at the OECD Competition Committee Round Table, "Competition Policy in Times of COVID-19", 15 June 2020.

2. OECD, *Economic Outlook* (Paris: OECD Publishing, June 2020), 51, 32.

3. Rishi Sunak, Autumn Budget and Spending Review 2021 speech, 27 October 2021, https://www.gov.uk/government/speeches/autumn-budget-and-spending-review-2021-speech.

4. SPD, *Aus Respekt vor deiner Zukunft* (Berlin: SPD, 2021): 4.

5. Fahmida Rahman & Daniel Tomlinson, "Cross countries: international comparisons of intergenerational trends", LIS Working Paper Series no. 732 (2018).

6. OECD, *A Broken Social Elevator? How to Promote Social Mobility* (Paris: OECD Publishing, 2018).

7. Cyrille Schwellnus, Andreas Kappeler & Pierre-Alain Pionnier, *Decoupling of Wages from Productivity: Macro-Level Facts* (Paris: OECD, 2017), 18.

8. See Darius Ornston, *Good Governance Gone Bad: How Nordic Adaptability Leads to Excess* (Ithaca, NY: Cornell University Press, 2018).

9. A complementary dynamic occurs where the liberalization of labour markets exerts downward pressure on the wages of the lower skilled, freeing up more resources which can then be shared by both capital and highly skilled labour. See Sebastian Diessner, Niccolo Durazzi & David Hope, "Skill-biased liberalization: Germany's transition to the knowledge economy", *Politics & Society* (2021), https://doi.org/10.1177/00323292211006563.

10. For a useful summary of the many problems with the assumptions underpinning this account of worker compensation, see Rosenfeld, *Paid What You're Worth.*

11. Herman Mark Schwartz, "Wealth and secular stagnation: the role of industrial organization and intellectual property rights", *Russell Sage Foundation Journal of the Social Sciences* 2:6 (2016), 226–49

12. Nick O'Donovan, "Personal data and collective value: data-driven personalisation as network effect" in Uta Kohl & Jacob Eisler (eds), *Data-Driven Personalisation in Markets, Politics and Law* (Cambridge: Cambridge University Press, 2021).

13. For a more technical discussion, see Florian Scheuer & Joel Slemrod, "Taxation and the Superrich", *Annual Review of Economics* 12 (2020): 189–211. To summarize: the revenue-maximizing top tax rate could well be higher than it currently is in the USA, but how much higher is anyone's guess, as most of our assumptions about the behaviour of the superrich are highly speculative.

14. In effect, this would be a reversal of the skills-biased liberalization process outlined by Diessner *et al.* in "Skill-biased liberalization".

15. Martin O'Neill & Stuart White, "James Meade, public ownership, and the idea of a citizens' trust", *International Journal of Public Policy* 15:1–2 (2019), 21–37.

16. Lonergan & Blyth, *Angrynomics.*

17. Piketty, *Capital.*

18. Tony Blair, interview with Jeremy Paxman, *BBC Newsnight*, 2001, http://news.bbc.co.uk/1/hi/events/newsnight/1372220.stm. Blair updates his footballer references in his 2010 autobiography *A Journey*, asking "should Wayne Rooney earn more than a nurse?" (587).

19. Lucio Baccaro & Jonas Pontusson, "Rethinking comparative political economy: the growth model perspective", *Politics & Society* 44:2 (2016), 175–207; Heather Boushey, *Unbound: How Inequality Constricts Our Economy and What We Can Do about It* (Cambridge, MA: Harvard University Press, 2019).

20. Era Dabla-Norris *et al.*, *Causes and Consequences of Income Inequality: A Global Perspective* (Washington, DC: IMF, 2015).

21. Abigail McKnight, *Downward Mobility, Opportunity Hoarding and the "Glass Floor"* (London: Social Mobility and Child Poverty Commission, 2015); Laura Hamilton, Josipa Roksa & Kelly Nielsen, "Providing a 'leg up': parental involvement and opportunity hoarding in college", *Sociology of Education* 91:2 (2018), 111–31; Sandel, *The Tyranny of Merit*; Adrian Wooldridge, *The Aristocracy of Talent: How Meritocracy Made the Modern World* (London: Penguin, 2021).

22. Of course, there is no inherent reason why efficiency arguments should trump moral arguments in favour of equality of opportunity, as well as in favour of education as valuable in its own right; and there are efficiency arguments to be made for allocating opportunities to the most able, which presumes the most able can access those opportunities.

23. See e.g. Institute of Directors, "Home-working here to stay", 5 October 2020, https://www.iod.com/news/news/articles/Home-working-here-to-stay-new-IoD-figures-suggest; Oliver Stettes & Michael Voigtländer, "Büroflächenabbau bleibt die Ausnahme", IW-Kurzbericht Nr. 6 (5 February 2021); KPMG, *CEO Outlook Pulse Survey*, 23 March 2021, https://home.kpmg/xx/en/home/media/press-releases/2021/03/nearly-half-of-global-ceos-dont-expect-a-return-to-normal-until-2022-ceo-outlook-pulse.html.

24. Martin O'Neill, "The road to socialism is the A59: the Preston model", *Renewal: A Journal of Labour Politics* 24:2 (2016), 69.

25. Justin Bentham *et al.*, *Manifesto for the Foundational Economy* (Manchester; Centre for Research on Socio-Cultural Change, 2013); Teis Hansen, "The foundational economy and regional development", *Regional Studies* (2021), https://doi.org/10.1080/00343404.2021.1939860.

26. Data on job-to-job transitions by sex and age (annual averages of quarterly transitions, estimated probabilities) available from Eurostat.

27. Daniel Kahneman & Amos Tversky, "Prospect theory: an analysis of decision under risk", *Econometrica* 47:2 (1979), 263–92.

28. Boushey, *Unbound*, 114–38; Scott Corfe, Aveek Bhattacharya & Richard Hyde, *Banking and Competition in the UK Economy* (London: Social Market Foundation, 2021).

29. Furman *et al.*, *Unlocking Digital Competition*; K. Sabeel Rahman, "The new utilities: private power, social infrastructure, and the revival of the public utility concept", *Cardozo Law Review* 39:5 (2017), 1621–92.

30. O'Donovan, "Personal data".

31. This point echoes the argument of the economist and *Financial Times* columnist Martin Sandbu in *The Economics of Belonging*, particularly 211–28. However, Sandbu is more optimistic about the potential for generating knowledge work, given the right combination of demand pressure and microeconomic policies such as wage floors and social investment.

32. Sandbu, *Economics of Belonging*.

33. Anne Davies, "One step forward, two steps back? The Viking and Laval cases in the ECJ", *Industrial Law Journal* 37:2 (2008), 126–48.

34. Sean Fleming, "What is digital sovereignty and why is Europe so interested in it?", *World Economic Forum*, 15 March 2021.

35. Simona Iammarino & Philip McCann, *Multinationals and Economic Geography: Location, Technology and Innovation* (Cheltenham: Elgar, 2013).

36. Iversen & Soskice, *Democracy and Prosperity*.

37. Rasmus Corlin Christensen & Martin Hearson, "The new politics of global tax governance: taking stock a decade after the financial crisis", *Review of International Political Economy* 26:5 (2019), 1068–88.

38. IMF, *World Economic Outlook* (Washington, DC: IMF, October 2012).

39. Blyth, *Austerity*; Simon Wren-Lewis, *The Case against Austerity Today* (London: IPPR, 2011); Simon Wren-Lewis, "A general theory of austerity", Blavatnik School of Government Working Paper 14 (2016); Lawrence Summers, "Why America must have a fiscal stimulus", *Financial Times*, 7 January 2008; Ed Balls, Bloomberg Speech (August 2010), https://www.edballs.co.uk/bloomberg-speech.

40. This is particularly true of monetary policy decisions in the eurozone – see Tooze, *Crashed*, 519–21.

41. Stephanie Kelton, *The Deficit Myth: Modern Monetary Theory and How to Build a Better Economy* (London: John Murray, 2020).

42. In the UK context, see Arun Advani & Andy Summers, "Capital gains and UK inequality: new evidence from tax microdata", University of Warwick CAGE Policy Briefing 19 (2020).

43. Emmanuel Saez & Gabriel Zucman, "Progressive wealth taxation", *Brookings Papers on Economic Activity* 2 (2019): 437–533; Arun Advani, Emma Chamberlain & Andy Summers, *A Wealth Tax for the UK* (London: UK Wealth Tax Commission, 2020).

44. See Nick O'Donovan, "A 'lifetime income super-tax' offers a new way to tax wealth and fix inequality", *The Conversation*, 14 December 2018. Such a policy might also circumvent potential legal challenges to a more conventional wealth tax in the USA, as highlighted by Michael Keen & Joel Slemrod in *Rebellions, Rascals and Revenue* (Princeton, NJ: Princeton University Press, 2021): 116–23.

45. Lonergan & Blyth, *Angrynomics*; Sandbu, *Economics of Belonging*.

46. See e.g. SPD, *Deiner Zukunft*, 8–10; HM Treasury, *Build Back Better: Our Plan for Growth* (London: HM Treasury, 2021), 82–91.

47. See e.g. Mariana Mazzucato & Martha McPherson, *The Green New Deal: A Bold Mission-Oriented Approach* (London: UCL Institute for Innovation and Public Purpose, 2018).

48. Anthony Carnevale & Nicole Smith, *15 Million Infrastructure Jobs* (Washington, DC: Georgetown Center on Education and the Workforce, 2021).

49. See e.g. Coyle, *Weightless World*, 229–30.

50. Thomas Wiedmann *et al.*, "The material footprint of nations", *Proceedings of the National Academy of Sciences* 112:20 (2015), 6271–6.

51. Jason Hickel & Giorgos Kallis, "Is green growth possible?", *New Political Economy* 25:4 (2020), 469–86; Helmut Haberl *et al.*, "A systematic review of the evidence on decoupling of GDP, resource use and GHG emissions, part II: synthesizing the insights", *Environmental Research Letters* 15:6 (2020).

INDEX

Acemoglu, Daron   110, 113, 124
active labour market policies   57–8, 166, 168, 177, 189
agglomeration effects, *see* network effects and city regions
d'Alema, Massimo   41
Alesina, Alberto   81
Alphabet, *see* Google
Amazon   87–8, 92–3, 95, 104–6, 108, 148
apathy   150–51, 161
Apple   17, 31, 62, 92, 95, 97, 135
Arthur, W. Brian   31–2, 34, 63, 177
artificial intelligence (AI)   3, 6, 87, 114–7, 132, 135, 141, 170, 175, 180–81
austerity   9, 71, 80–83, 101–2, 138, 153–4, 166–7, 183, 185
automation   6, 88, 108–110, 113–6, 124, 147–8, 150, 178

Bernanke, Ben   74–5
Balls, Ed   40, 48
Beckham, David   171
Blair, Tony   6, 17, 38, 40–41, 45–7, 69, 77, 167, 171
  education policy   42–3, 45–7
  market liberalization 54–6
  remote working   50
  tax policy   53
Blyth, Mark   171
Bretton Woods   89
Brexit   25, 136, 153, 158, 160–1
Bridget Jones' Diary   48
Brown, Gordon   20, 40, 69, 77, 89

Bush, George H. W.   2
Bush, George W.   64, 73–5

Cameron, David   82, 153
capital   16, 27–9, 67, 97, 166, 171, 184
  diminishing importance to knowledge production   5, 17–8, 42–3, 46–8, 56, 91
  international movement of   19, 66, 69, 75, 129, 133–5, 137–8, 153, 167, 181
  ongoing importance to knowledge production   88, 94, 96, 112, 116–7, 120–1, 125–6, 128, 148, 150, 175
  share of national income   18, 110–3, 116–7, 120–1, 128, 169–72, 187
China   67, 76, 80, 84, 87, 130–5, 161–2, 179, 180–1
Christensen, Rasmus Corlin   138
Clinton, Bill   1–3, 6, 17, 21, 42–43, 47, 69–70, 74–5, 89–90, 167
  competition policy   59, 64
  economic advisers   39–41, 56, 123
  economic policy compared to Barack Obama   78
  economic policy compared to George W. Bush   74–5
  tax policy   54
Clinton, Hillary   1–3, 83, 156, 160, 163
Cold War
  aftermath of   9, 34, 132, 141
  impact on innovation   31

competition 11, 20, 39, 52–4, 77, 91–2, 129, 134
  against machines 108–112, 115–6, 124
  and increasing returns 31–4
  between countries 2–3, 5, 18, 31, 44, 65, 67–8, 76, 80, 82, 84, 129–32, 161–2, 175, 185
  competition policy 57–65, 170–1, 177–8
  knowledge economy as highly competitive 18, 47, 56, 176
  knowledge economy as not highly competitive 39, 88, 93–9, 116–7, 121, 136–8, 180
Corbyn, Jeremy 9, 153, 156, 162, 164
Coyle, Diane 45, 47
creative industries 37, 47–8, 68, 87, 106–07, 186
Crouch, Colin 90

debt (household) 90, 172
debt (public) 69–70, 80, 184
deindustrialization 9, 173
  knowledge–driven growth as response to 5–6, 20–1, 35–6
Dixit, Avinash 31
dot-com bubble 17, 38, 41, 73, 84, 89, 99
Draghi, Mario 8

economies of scale
  in knowledge industries 19, 31–3, 42, 59–60, 88, 94–5, 97, 116–7, 127–8, 141
  from international markets 30, 33, 58, 64, 66, 80, 133, 181
education 2–3, 39–43, 55–6, 67, 74–5, 77–82
  and equality of opportunity 46–8
  and inequality 122–8, 141, 166–71
  impact on voting patterns 158–60
  levels of public investment in different countries 50–1, 71, 112, 130–1
endogenous growth theory 15, 28–30, 39–40, 43, 60, 68, 83, 114, 119, 147
equality of opportunity 46–8, 141, 171–3

European Central Bank 8, 81
European Commission 3, 41, 43, 47, 49, 56–7, 75, 80–1, 110
European Council 38, 41, 75
European Union (EU) 6, 25, 41, 53, 56, 69, 75, 99, 101, 112, 160, 181
  and "Europe 2020" strategy 3, 79–82
  and competition policy 58–9
  and freedom of movement 139, 179
  and Maastricht Treaty 65
  Structural and Investment Funds 49

Facebook 92–5, 106
Farage, Nigel 9, 162
Fielding, Helen 48
"flat-world" thinking 49, 72, 76, 79, 130, 137, 173, 182
flexicurity 56–7, 113
Foa, Roberto 157
Ford, Robert 158–9
foundational economy 175–6, 186, 188
Friedman, Thomas 49, 76, 130–1, 182

Gates, Bill 19, 61
geography, see regional inequality
Giddens, Anthony 17, 20, 43
globalization 6–7, 21, 36, 78, 82, 108–9, 118, 129, 173, 179
global financial crisis 11, 71, 76–84, 89–91, 99, 101, 138, 167, 183–4
  impacts on voting patterns 9, 145, 147, 151, 154
"Goldilocks zone" 182
Goldin, Claudia 123
Goodwin, Matthew 158–9
Google 65, 92–5, 97, 108, 116
Goos, Maarten 101
"Great Moderation" 88
green industries 3, 132, 185–8
Greenspan, Alan 70–1, 74, 123, 182
Grillo, Beppe 9
growth regimes 10, 15, 22–6, 36, 63, 88–90, 145–51, 158, 161–5, 189
Guterres, António 38, 41

Hall, Peter 23–4
Hartz reforms (Germany) 57

Haskel, Jonathan   99, 104
Hearson, Martin   138
helicopter money   184
Hewlett-Packard   31
housing   90–91, 111, 120–1, 126, 147,
    149, 151, 172, 179, 188
human capital   5, 8, 17, 29, 36, 43, 67, 75,
    91, 138, 171

immigration   3, 65–6, 129–30, 137–41,
    178–80
  hostility towards   9, 132, 153, 158, 160,
    164
increasing returns   30–1, 33, 39, 60, 63,
    66, 119, 136
India   67, 76, 80, 84, 87, 130–1, 181
inequality   103, 110, 171–3, 176–7,
    183–5, 188
  as a result of neoliberalism   5, 9, 11,
    35, 163
  as a result of the knowledge
    economy   6–7, 12, 18, 42–3, 45,
    48, 110, 113, 126–8, 169–71
  reduced by social investment   8, 11,
    43, 49, 74–5, 122–5, 167–8
inflation   6, 69–70, 82–3, 176, 182,
    184–5
Inglehart, Ronald   163
intangible assets   46, 99, 148
Intel   17, 31
intellectual property rights
  importance to knowledge-driven
    growth   18, 29–30, 54, 63, 78,
    132–3
  inhibiting competition   46–7, 98–9,
    111–2, 116, 128, 141, 167, 169–70,
    175, 178, 187
  located in tax havens   134
interest rates   30, 69–70, 82–3, 88, 97,
    99, 120, 182–3
International Monetary Fund (IMF)   81,
    96, 109, 111, 187
international trade   3, 30, 49, 65–7, 75,
    129–30, 178–9
  and protectionism   33, 132–5, 153,
    161, 180–1
Iversen, Torben   136

job polarization   103–05, 110, 187
Johnson, Boris   8–9, 153, 162

Katz, Lawrence   123
knowledge economy
  definition of   4–6, 16
  knowledge-driven growth in contrast to
    neoliberalism   19–22
  origins of the concept   16–19
knowledge work   5, 16–19, 36, 42–3, 49,
    66–9, 87, 92, 96, 147–9, 187–8
  abundance of   3, 43–5, 47, 51, 55–6,
    100–2, 129–30
  geographical concentration of
    119–22, 135–7, 173–5, 182
  impact of pandemic on   7–8, 167
  shortfall in   9, 103–9, 112, 115–7, 123,
    131–2, 141, 172, 185
  spillovers generated by   29–30, 42, 83,
    91, 135
Kok, Wim   41, 75
  Kok report   75–6
Krugman, Paul   27, 31

labour market liberalization   3, 54–7, 72,
    75, 113, 122, 141, 148, 158, 176–7
labour share of national income   110–3,
    116–7, 128, 168–71
Le Pen, Marine   155, 159–60, 162–4
Leadbeater, Charles   18, 47–8, 59, 68
"left behind" communities   1–2, 21, 79,
    149–50, 153, 173–6
  voting patterns of   160–2
Lehman Brothers   73
liberal values   35–6, 155, 157, 162–4
  conducive to knowledge-driven
    growth   37, 68, 131–2, 139,
    141
Lisbon Strategy   41–3, 49, 53, 69, 75–6,
    79
Lloyd, Caroline   105
Lonergan, Eric   171
lower-skilled work   43, 45, 76, 100,
    103–05, 114, 123–4, 148–9,
    169–70
  impact of migration on   139–40,
    178–80

voting patterns   145–6, 148–50, 157–60, 189

Maastricht Treaty   65
macroeconomic stability   6, 30, 68–71, 75, 83–4, 135, 182–5
Macron, Emmanuel   3, 83, 152, 155, 159
Mandelson, Peter   40, 44, 48, 59, 77
Manning, Alan   101
market concentration   11, 58–9, 94–8, 128, 140, 150, 177–8, 180
market-driven growth, *see* neoliberalism
May, Theresa   153
Mayhew, Ken   105
McCain, John   81, 156, 160
Mélenchon, Jean-Luc   155, 159, 162
meritocracy   46
Merkel, Angela   3
Microsoft   17, 19, 31, 59–65, 92, 95, 97–8, 108
Miliband, Ed   83
Minitel network   47
Mitterrand, François   34
mixed economy   6, 24–5, 89, 141
monopoly rents   98, 134, 169–71, 180
Morris, Sir Derek 15
Mounk, Yascha   157
Mulgan, Geoff   46

neoliberalism   19–20, 29, 74, 81–2, 148, 163–4
   era of   7, 24, 34–6, 42, 48, 52, 89–90, 141
   in contrast to knowledge-driven growth   11, 20–22, 36–7, 81
Netscape   60–2
network effects   32–3
   and city regions   32, 120–2, 137, 173–5
   and the digital economy   60–1, 63–4, 66, 88, 93–5, 97, 106, 112, 116, 133–5, 141, 178, 180–1
"No Child Left Behind" Act   74
Norris, Pippa 157, 163

Obama, Barack   3, 77–9, 81, 90, 156, 160, 178

opportunity hoarding   172
Organisation for Economic Co–operation and Development (OECD)   3, 6, 41, 57–8, 96–8, 101–02, 111–12, 118–19, 147, 166, 187
Osborne, George   153

pandemic (Covid–19)   4, 120–21, 147, 183
   economic recovery from   8, 166, 184–5, 187
   impacts on foundational economy   175–6
   impacts on remote working   7, 122, 149, 167, 174
Piketty, Thomas   111
policy learning   22–3
policy paradigms   24–6, 36, 41, 76, 146, 189
populism   9–10, 162, 164
Powell, Jonathan   40
Prodi, Romano   41
productivity   16, 66, 69, 120, 133, 135, 139–40, 168–9, 173, 177–8, 188–9
   contribution of competition to   52, 58, 91, 98
   contribution to economic growth   27–30, 45, 79
   contribution to higher wages   42–3, 78, 166
   decoupling of wages from   102, 109–11, 116, 141, 147, 172, 180
   productivity growth in knowledge economy era   17–8, 24, 75–6, 88–9, 101–2, 122, 149
   too yippity about   70, 90

Quah, Danny   48
quantitative easing   120, 183

Reagan, Ronald   19, 34, 70, 81
regional inequality   5, 7, 20, 30–32, 35, 48–50, 109, 118–22, 136, 140, 149–51, 179–82
   catch up and convergence   28
   solutions to   173–6, 188

Reich, Robert   21, 40, 44, 46, 48, 67, 71, 123, 137
Reinhart, Carmen   81
remote working, *see* telecommuting
research and development (R&D)   2–3, 8, 19, 41, 79, 98–9
  geographically immobile   137
  government support for   30–1, 34, 49, 71, 74–5, 77, 80–1, 166, 183, 185
  private investment in   28–9, 53–4, 69, 83, 92, 95–6, 126, 182
Resolution Foundation   147
Restrepo, Pascual   110, 113
risk aversion   121, 125, 149, 177, 188
Roche, Barbara   66
Rogoff, Kenneth   81
Romer, Paul   28–30, 34, 40, 44, 63, 98, 114, 177
rule of law   67–8, 132, 162

Salvini, Matteo   9
Sanders, Bernie   1–2, 9, 154–6, 162, 164
Schröder, Gerhard   6, 41, 54–5
Schwartz, Herman   98
secular stagnation   90
Shklar, Judith   157
Silicon Valley   30–1, 50
skill–biased technological change   74–5, 122–5, 169–71,
social investment   2, 6–8, 103
  as means of achieving social justice and social inclusion   43, 46–8, 74–5, 78, 80, 82–3, 115, 122–8, 167–71
  as means of empowering workers   56, 113
  as means of attracting foreign investment   44, 66–7
  as means of increasing productivity/ output   41–2, 75, 77, 80, 183, 185
  as means of reducing regional inequality   49–50, 173–4
differences between countries   8, 41, 50–51, 69–72, 112

social mobility   7, 48, 78, 82, 105, 118, 127–8, 167–8
software industry   4, 19, 31–2, 43, 45–7, 59–65, 91–2, 107–8
Solomons, Anna   101
Solow, Robert   16, 27–8, 40
Soskice, David   136
Stability and Growth Pact (EU)   69, 71, 81
start-ups   33, 53–4, 56, 58–9, 94–7, 108, 171, 177
Stiglitz, Joseph   31, 39–40, 56, 63, 68, 177
Summers, Larry   39–40, 59, 64, 66, 70–1, 78, 90
superstar effects   43, 45, 47–8, 103, 126–8, 141, 147, 150, 171
Syriza   1

taxation   19–21, 69–71, 74–5, 134, 139, 146, 167–8, 171, 175–6, 180
  and austerity   80–84, 101
  anti-tax movements   163–4
  lowering taxes to attract knowledge industries   3, 51, 53–4, 66, 69, 135–6
  potential for raising taxes   126, 137–8, 170, 177, 181–2, 184
telecommuting   5, 49–50, 121–2, 149, 173–4
Thatcher, Margaret   19, 25, 81
Third Way   6, 20, 41
trade unions   2, 20, 25, 36, 38, 55, 113, 141, 158, 179
  future role for   170, 186
Trump, Donald   2, 9, 153, 156, 160–3

virtual office, *see* telecommuting

Warsh, David   28
Westlake, Stian   99, 104
workfarist welfare regimes   56–7, 177

young people   79, 83, 124–5, 147–8, 150, 168
  voting patterns of   154–7, 162